Library Evaluation

Library Evaluation

Sonu Panwar

RANDOM

RANDOM PUBLICATIONS
NEW DELHI (INDIA)

Library Evaluation

ISBN 978-93-5111-947-0

Published in 2016 in India by

RANDOM PUBLICATIONS

4376-A/4B, Gali Murari Lal, Ansari Road
New Delhi-110 002
Phone : +9111-43580356, 011-23289044, 011-43142548
e-mail: sales@randompublications.com,
info@randompublications.com, randomexports@gmail.com

Reprint 2021

Type Setting by : Friends Media, Delhi-110089
Printed at : Replika Press Pvt. Ltd.

Preface

Library evolution is ideally suited for screening projects to improve the properties of your protein of interest. This technology enables the specific determination of modified nucleotides. The desired mutants are represented in the library.

The evolution of library reference work has been greatly influenced by the advent of new technologies, such as computing, electronic mass storage and networking technologies. From online commercial database searching entering the library world in mid-1970s, to synchronous Web-based chat reference appearing at the turn of this century, reference services have migrated from the solely print-resources-oriented services limited in a certain physical space, to a diversified service portfolio that could reach more people with more resources and less restriction of time and space.

Advances in both telecommunication and computer technologies have facilitated the designing of new software thereby making the delivery of information quicker, convenient and efficient than ever before. It is fact that users feel increasingly comfortable with computers. The communication technology land line and satellite communication have made the world a 'global village '. In such a challenging situation academic libraries have to welcome not only e-mail, LAN and similar services but also Intranet and Internet services in their libraries.

Information and communications technology has had a fundamental impact on library collection development policies. Academic libraries had traditionally applied an ownership or just-in-case approach to collection development.

The premise was that users would need the material and make use of it. Having the material available in the library would also provide immediate access to it than having to borrow it from a third party. The cost of maintaining collections and increased demands for more information had forced academic libraries to reconsider the ownership model and adopt another model. Unparalleled price increases and shrinking budgets had ushered in a new model called access or just in time where the focus is to give the user the information that they need when they want it.

This book will help the readers not only to better understand libraries place in the past, but also to understand its position, potential, and challenges in present.

– Author

Contents

1

Online Databases in Library Evaluation

EVALUATION OF ONLINE DATABASES

Whether or not to add online services to the library's collection or services usually is considered or evaluated extensively. Evaluation of online databases may occur at the time of initial selection of a database or service provider, when two or more databases are being compared for subject coverage or search efficiency and, less frequently, as part of a collection or service evaluation. Selection decisions are made by considering many of the same elements which enter into subsequent evaluations. The evaluation of whether or not to add an online service to the library centers around its use for subject searching but libraries also consider the database as additions to the collections. The substitution of online for a print portion of the collection has already been discussed.

Vendor Selection

Many directories, abstract/index services, and business or financial files are made available through three major vendors, BRS, DIALOG and SDC. A library may select one or more of these services, and, in so doing, it must acquire hundreds of supporting reference tools. In fact, in selecting a vendor package, many files are often added to the collections which would not have been if considered on a file-far-file basis. In addition, specific 'files are available from government agencies or professional organisations. The primary consideration in most selection or evaluation decisions is subject. For a monograph or serial the selector asks whether the title is in a subject collected by the library, and the type of treatment of that subject-*i.e.,* basic or research.

The selector of a database vendor has a more complex problem, because, as Nichol points out, each vendor has some unique and some duplicate databases. However, an overriding concern is still how well the blend of databases offered match the library's collection development policy. Williams, Nichol, Lancaster, and Stern summarise the other evaluative criteria used. Cost and means of searching are the primary considerations.

This results in the following questions being applied to the potential vendor's products:

- How simple or complex is the system to use?
  - — How much training is needed?
  - — Is training readily available?
  - — Can users search themselves or must librarians perform the searches?
- What are the comparative costs for:
  - — Online time?
  - — Communications?
  - — Printing?
  - — Royalties?
- What restrictions on access exist?
  - — Must the library subscribe to some print equivalents?
  - — Can it charge for the products?
  - — Is use restricted to searches from one portion of the searchers' organisation only?
- How does treatment of important individual databases compare?

These same criteria apply no matter whether one is considering choice of vendors, if broad coverage is to be obtained, or whether or not to obtain a given database direct from a producer when only one or two subjects are being considered. No one consideration dominates and different libraries make different choices based on their clients' subject needs, library staff skills and interest, budget and organisational structure. The criteria for comparing treatment of a subject area or the same database by different vendors follows.

Selection/Evaluation of Individual Databases

There is ample literature which can help make the choice between individual databases. Most of this has been written from the point of view of the searcher, who is evaluating how well similar databases meet specific user needs. These reports can also be valuable in vendor selection when specific subject areas are more important than others, or when a decision of whether to obtain coverage from a vendor or direct from the producer is being made.

First, there are the directories which were listed earlier in the section on 'Bibliographic Databases.' These titles typically give subject coverage, date coverage, frequency of updating, availability of tapes, producer, and vendor. Next, there are review articles in the trade literature such as *RQ, Database, Online,* and *Online Review.* And, finally, many journal articles have appeared comparing specific databases or subject coverage by two or more databases, or vendor coverage of the same database.

The following list is by no means comprehensive, but is indicative of the scope of published evaluations. Notes are added where the scope is not clear from the title. Methods of evaluation in these articles varied. The 'Georefi Geoarchive' article evaluated recall and precision for twelve subject searches and also compared timeliness and document type coverage.

The 'ERIC and LISA,, article compared precision and recall also. The authors, who were comparing results with known items from manual searches, were surprised at the low recall percentages for the online searches. The 'IRL/ BIOSIS' article compared journal coverage overlap, indexing practices and currency, but not recall and precision. Those articles which covered one or more databases in a subject area used the following evaluative criteria: subject coverage, file size, document type, date coverage, quality, and depth of indexing, proportion of unique results obtained, proportion overlap, currency, and cost for different vendors.

Donati used a different approach in the decision analysis article, selecting business databases in relation to crucial questions. The first decision point is whether or not information on a principle, practice or problem is involved, or whether information about a specific product or industry is needed. Further, key questions within each category are then analysed in relation to ABI, F & S Index, PROMPT, and other business databases. It is apparent from reading these articles that there is no standard set of evaluative criteria which have been developed for evaluation of bibliographic databases. They, like the spelling of the words *database* and *online,* vary. What weight is given to each factor? How does a library reach a decision as to which vendor to select or which databases to search when the problem is so complex? Evaluation of specific systems overlaps with comparison of individual databases within each system. The decision process itself is not reported in the literature.Finding out what happens in practice would involve analysis of how libraries who have recently decided to provide online search services made the following decisions:

- Should we provide online services?
- Which databases should be provided?
- From whom should we obtain the database(s)? The criteria for vendor selection would then apply.

In actuality these decisions may not proceed in the order and each one may be made by a different group within the library's administrative structure. Some libraries select a vendor with primary consideration being given to subject coverage or comparison treatment of individual databases, whereas in other libraries considerations of cost and staffing impact may prevail.

Is there a preponderance of anyone consideration over another? What factors cause different libraries to weight criteria differently? Factors which are certainly important are what group(s) is making the decision, where the money will be coming from, what library unit will be administratively responsible for service, prior experience of staff with databases, and the uses which will be made of the system. Articles in the premier issue of the journal *Science &*

Technology Librariei featured articles on planning to initiate online search services and described the issues which the authors' institutions addressed in the planning process. The articles did not, however, describe how the different factors were weighed in the decision process. At this point, it should be emphasised again that for the most part these decisions are not made as collection development decisions but primarily as service decisions.

Further, declines in library budgets may force libraries to evaluate whether such service should be continued, just as we now evaluate whether to cut monographs or serials, and, if serials—which ones. Databases have been treated as separate entities and are usually budgeted separately, but with their introduction to the collections, some libraries may come to evaluate them in relation to the acquisitions budget and the resource sharing budget.

At present, though, few libraries would probably extend the concept as far as did *Online Libraries and Microcomputers* when it suggested that: "With the proliferation of full-text databases and information sources which are only available online, it makes a great deal of common sense to fund equipment from the acquisitions budget." In this case the equipment being referred to are the computer terminals, modems and printers required to use online tools.

It would not be very different from the situation where a microform dealer offers a reader or reader-printer with large microform purchases. The money in this situation doubtless comes from the acquisitions rather than the equipment budget. At present, database acquisition and maintenance are not usually part of an acquisitions budget, although purchase of print reference tools is. Fees for bibliographic utility use primarily come from the cataloging budget, although the utility may be used for resource sharing. In reality, many libraries have budgets with rigid categories of salary, acquisitions and supplies/ equipment. Practically, it is difficult to shift the budget line from which something is taken once precedent has been established.

BENEFITS OF WEB-ENABLED DATABASES

Web-enabled databases have certain advantages over other means of sharing/publishing information over internet. These advantages are common to bibliographic databases also where libraries can put their OPACs and other databases on web. According to L.J.Haravu ; Kristin Aantelman and; Chong Ho Yu , the benefits of web-enabled databases are as follows:

- Global/wide ac cess to data with a sin gle user in ter face
- Format in dependent ac cess of data (text, graph ics, au dio, video, etc.)
- Up-to-minute up dated ac cess of data in real time
- Dynamic updation of data from many locations
- Cost-effective way of data sharing
- Instant feedback from users
- Seamless links from resource to resource

- Unlimited download/printing
- Environmental friendly.

Besides, Ortiz-Repiso and Norm Medeiros have written excellent papers on differences between traditional v/s innovative means (web OPACs) of library catalogs, while B. Ramesh Babu, *et al* have presented an overview of web OPACS with their advantages in libraries.

DATABASE TOOLS

In the early days of database development, it was the flat-file system to store data in a single file by using field separators and record separators. Later, such flat-file systems were facilitated by an index in which a single index file stored keywords and pointers to the records that were stored in main file. This made retrieval more efficient, still flat-file systems were seriously inefficient. It showed data-redundancy, poor data control, and did not supported complex data types (audio, video, graphics, etc.) .

After 1960s, two database models were developed in quick succession to solve the limitations of flat-file systems. These database models were Hierarchical Database Model and Network Database Model. The Hierarchical Database composes of a root segment, parent segments and child segments. This model depicts a set of one-to-many relationships between a parent and its children. However, this model has number of limitations. It does not include ad hoc querying capability and, a multi-parent relationship is difficult to implement, as in a many-to-many relationship. The Network Database Model attempted to deal with many of the hierarchical model's limitations. The network database structure easily accommodates the multiple child, although, its structural complexities often limit its effectiveness and efficiency.

Both of these database models are obsolete now mainly because of their incompatibility with web environment and have been replaced by RDBMS. RDBMS is the current database implementation standard being used for publishing information on the web. It includes the following features which make it suitable for web environment:

- Provide extremely useful tools for database administration;
- Adhere to powerful query language SQL (structured query language) developed by Microsoft Corporation;
- Compliant with ODBC/JDBC and other database interface tools;
- Work in client/server mode;
- Offer distributed database and distributed processing options; and
- Have referential integrity controls to ensure data consistency and, thus, suitable for web environment.

It is easier to design applications in RDBMS due to the following features:

- Requires less programming skill
- Availability of third party tools, and
- Inbuilt web interface.

These all features of RDBMS have made them ideal for library applications to setup bibliographic database solutions and publishing them over the web. In the early days of library systems development, vendors have designed library applications software by using pre-relational database technology. Still some library systems suppliers are continuing to maintain and develop such products.

These proprietary library applications software have their own advantages and disadvantages. However, in the library management systems marketplace, there is a growing trend towards the use of RDBMS. Some of the common RDBMS which can be used to design in-house databases in libraries are *MS Access, SQL Server, Oracle, Informix, Sybase, File Maker Pro, SAS,* etc. However, the selection of suitable RDBMS for library applications depends on the particular library requirements, kind of applications (bibliographic/full-text/ numeric), the application level (database level/data warehouse level), magnitude of data (number of records/length of fields), nature of data analysis (basic statistics, i.e., sum, average, mean/advance statistics) and, comprehensiveness and inter-operability.

Other points to be considered while selecting database tools for library applications are easiness, user-friendliness, flexibility and low cost. In most of the cases in libraries where bibliographic databases are dealt with, commonly available consumer database products such as *MS Access*, and *File Maker Pro* are sufficient. These products can support up to 1GB of data and provide cheaper solutions. However, these database tools are suitable for small databases and not useful for large databases, hence provide limitations in web environment.

There are specific database solutions for large databases available from *MS SQL Server, DB2, Oracle, Informix, Sybase,* etc. These database tools support up to several terra byte of data; permit thousands of simultaneous users; work in client/server mode; show natural affinity towards web environment and, thus, suitable for large bibliographic, web-enabled databases in libraries. However, to design full-text databases in libraries where large files are to be stored and retrieved, these tools do not offer good solutions as most of these tools support 200-255-400 characters field length. Although, many of these tools allow unlimited entries in memo field, the data inside a memo field are not searchable and thus, offer limited utility.

In this respect, *MS SQL Server* has extended the searchable field length up to 8063 characters and thus, provide solutions for moderate full-text databases. As a common trend , a number of libraries have been using open source software available either free or on nominal prices. These database management systems include the most common *mySQL, mSQL* and, recently updated *PostgreSQL*. These database tools are easy to work and run on various platforms such as UNIX, Lynux, NT, etc. Besides, there are some library specific text retrieval database tools for management of full-text large files, generally known as 'Free Form Databases', provide powerful search engine. Although, in some ways they are at the opposite end of the RDBMS, little database structure imposed on the designer and, thus, provide an easy and readymade database structure. However, they provide some limitations in achieving integration in the modules other than searching such as cataloguing, classification, management module, etc. These software are *BRS/Search, Basis Plus, Status,* etc.

WEB TECHNOLOGY

World Wide Web or WWW or web, sometimes wrongly mentioned as synonymous to internet, is a sub-set of it and is a most promising mode of publishing/sharing of data/information. Now, the web has emerged as the dominant protocol over internet due to its special features like easy interfacing of diverse platforms/technologies; provision to incorporate text, graphics, audio and video, etc.; permitting to access data/information in a non-linear way and; jumping from one document/resource to another through hyperlinks.

The superiority of www over other modes of online sharing viz. e-mail, FTP, Telnet, Gopher, etc., has been well explained by Paul Scully . In fact, web has provided a single user interface to facilitate the user interaction with the databases or systems resources. The web uses unique URL (universal resource locator) address which facilitates the access of information seamlessly across the diverse platforms in a client-server mode. The actual data represented in a structured way reside in a powerful computers called server, while the latter is equipped with server tools/software to populate the information over web.

The client/user equipped with web browser such as Microsoft Internet Explorer (MSIE) and Netscape Navigator, etc., which interact with the server through common communications protocol TCP/IP over high speed network/ internet. In fact, the client/user sends its query to the server while the latter processes the request and gets the response/results from the database and sends it back to the client/user over the web.

COMPONENTS OF WEB-BASED SYSTEMS

Web Browser

It is a software that helps users to interact with the server for sending queries and getting results over the web. MSIE and Netscape are the most popular web browsers, both of these are available free.

Web Server

Web server is the software that helps in sharing the system resources/ files over the internet through web browsers. The latter communicate with a web server via the standard Hyper-Text Transfer Protocol (HTTP). In fact, web servers receive queries from the client, process it, get data from databases and send it back to the client over web. The popular web servers are Apache,

Microsoft IIS, iPlanet from Sun-Netscape alliance, and newly developed *Zeus* from Zeus Technology Ltd. Although web servers are increasingly found as components within full-featured server operating systems, there are some basic selection points that should be highlighted. These points are scalability and performance; high availability and reliability; interoperability and open standards; system administration and; security . In fact, there are not much choice in the web server segments as many of them come along with database tools, show natural affinity with the database tools from same vendor, and some other work better with certain platform/operating systems. According to the widely followed Netcraft web survey, approximately 60 percent of web servers run Apache, with Microsoft's IIS and the Netscape/iPlanet web server as its major competitors. However, Gartner studies have given Netscape/iPlanet a larger share of public web sites, followed by Apache and Microsoft/IIS. Apache is being used for the public sites of companies such as Merck, American Express, Texaco, Chrysler, and others.

However, it is easier to find both Microsoft/IIS and Netscape/iPlanet as the servers for large corporate public web sites when using the lookup facility offered by Netcraft. Also, for intranets, most counts credit Microsoft/IIS and Netscape/iPlanet as the leaders, followed by Apache, IBM's Lotus Domino Go server, and others. Among hot e-commerce sites, E*Trade runs the Netscape/ iPlanet server, eBay runs Windows/IIS, and Amazon runs Apache (the Apache-based Stronghold Secure Server), according to the Netcraft web survey .

WEB AUTHORING TOOLS

Basic web server software does nothing except it sends HTML data in response to a browser request. However, certain other web-authoring and scripting tools are required to extend the functionality of web server to extract the data from databases. These web-authoring tools (*HTML* and its derivatives; and other Markup languages, etc.) and scripting tools (*Perl, C++, Java Script, JScript, VBScript,* etc.) are required to write web pages and scripts to interact with back-end databases. In early days of web-based applications, *CGI* (common gateway interface) programs were used extensively to extend the server functionality by allowing web users to interact with the web server to request specific data from the databases. Although, writing *CGI* program is difficult and requires programming skill, however, it works with high reliability.

Now a days, a number visual editors are available to generate the web pages and write scripts automatically. The common editors are *Microsoft Front Page, Visual Interdev, Netscape Composer, Web Builder,* etc. Besides, other technologies have been introduced to communicate with the back-end databases. These technologies are Microsoft *Active Server Pages (ASP*) and *Java Server Pages (JSP)* from Sun Micro Systems. Both the technologies have combined the HTML codes with the scripts in a single page and thus, making it easier to interact with back-end databases. During last few years, object-oriented and component based solutions were added to further make it easier to interact with the back-end databases. These solutions include:

- Microsoft COM/DCOM,
- ActiveX Data Objects (ADO);
- OMA and CORBA (Common Objects Request Broker Architecture) from Object Management Group;
- Sun's EJB (Enterprise Java Beans),
- Java Applets (for client) and
- Java Servlets (for server), etc.

Besides, some database connectivity tools such as ODBC and JDBC have also emerged as in-built features of operating systems, etc.

FREE WIZARDS AND THIRD PARTY TOOLS

Writing HTML codes and scripts for database interaction is the most difficult part, requires programming skill, systems logic and manipulation planning, especially for non-computer professionals. However, a number of free wizards and third party tools are available on internet which can generate hundred of lines of codes automatically with a single click, thus, making it easier for non-skilled users to set up web-enabled database solutions in libraries. Some of the free wizards are Rule Zero, Power ASP, Active Server Pages Tools & Components, etc. Besides, *Microsoft FrontPage* also provides database wizard to generate *ASP* pages/*VBScripts* automatically to interact with back-end databases, while *Visual InterDev* provides a visual interface to develop a web-enabled web site with minimum efforts.

COLLECTION OF LIBRARY EVALUATION

Some readers may be surprised to find this article in an issue on collection evaluation. Are online databases indeed a part of the collection, or are they a type of reference service? In actuality, they are both. Databases have become an important part of libraries' reference collections and may in some cases serve as a substitute for the addition of print materials to these collections.

Online databases, both bibliographic and numeric, have been reported to be part of library collections. The literature will be analysed from this point of view. An online database is a machine-readable file of organised information with which the user interacts by means of a terminal connected to the computer housing the file. The terminal may be wired directly to the computer or it may communicate with it via a telecommunications network. The important feature of the online mode is that the user interacts with the information in the computer, sending and receiving messages in an almost instantaneous time frame. This chapter deals only with those databases which can be accessed directly by a user from his/her own library and does not deal with many available in information analysis centers to which the user cannot be directly linked online. Many information analysis centers receive, analyse and prepare online files. These are, for the most part, accessed only by center personnel or others in the information center's host institution or agency. For the most part dial-up access to the information analysis centre is not available for libraries.

Instead, the library usually submits a search to the centre, which then performs the search and sends back an answer. The emphasis of this chapter is on online access by a library to a database the library staff did not prepare, but which has been made available outside the preparing agency for direct access. It is only recently that databases have begun to be considered a part of a library's collections. No wonder. They only became available in libraries in the 1970s. The first articles on machine-readable bibliographic databases began appearing in the *Annual Review of Information Science and Technology* early in the decade.

The first stage on 'Use of Machine-Readable Databases' appeared in the 1974 volume. As online database availability was increasing, library funds for acquisitions were decreasing. This decrease forced libraries to move from the concept of comprehensive collections of all that their users could possibly want to collections of most heavily used items with a dependence on access to others' collections for lesser used items. Online bibliographic databases provided quick and improved access to others' collections and to information about publications which a library might or might not have in its own collection.

The means of access itself, rather than the materials became a component of any individual library's collections. The collection development literature is slowly beginning to acknowledge this change. Although some standard collection development texts such as Gardner now have a section on computer-based materials, Bonk and Magrill does not. Even though databases or tapes may be mentioned as items to consider in the sections on selection, they are nowhere to be found in the sections on collection evaluation. George Bonn's classic *Library Trends* article on 'Evaluation of the Collection' which appeared in 1971 makes no mention of database evaluation.

It was too early. This chapter will focus on developments since, 1974. The ALA *Guidelines for Collection Development* lists datatapes as one form of material collected but the section on collection evaluation gives no specific guidance on their evaluation or the evaluation of any other of the special forms such as newspapers, manuscripts or audiovisual materials. Online files are not mentioned. So, although some sources view databases as part of the collection, few standard sources evaluate them as such.

The new ANSI standard on library statistics does list databases as a part of collection resources and groups them with currently received periodicals in a category titled 'currently renewed resources.' The number of databases to which the library provides access for its users is to be reported. In addition, the standard specifies that database transactions should be reported as a subset of reference transactions. Databases are viewed in the literature and in the standard as a part of the collections and as a reference service. The nature of databases and their role in libraries are still evolving. A quick scan of the bibliography for this article will indicate that we have not even decided how to spell database yet. Is it one word or two? Earlier usage was primarily *data base,* but the current trend seems to be one word. This author will use *database,* as does the journal of that name which began publication in 1978. The fact is that in a very short ten-year period databases have found their way into library services and collections.

CONTEXT OF EVALUATION

Digital libraries are complex social, institutional and technical systems. No evaluation can possibly address all of these aspects together. Thus, different approaches have been used for different evaluation goals.

Context includes selection of a goal, framework, viewpoint or level(s), basic approach or perspective of evaluation. There are different types of approaches of digital library evaluation on the basis of different aspects.

No single approach can exhaustively evaluate the all aspects of any digital library. Here we try to incorporate most of the approaches as possible.

The approaches are:

- *System-centered approach*: Most prevalent. Involves study of some aspect of performance. Includes assessing effectiveness and/or efficiency of some feature or some specific design or some technological component. Applied in a number of studies with results that may inform specific choices in design or operations.
- *Human-centered approach*: Also widely applied. Involves study of behaviour in respect to given information needs, such as information seeking, browsing, searching including performance appraisal of given tasks, either predetermined or observed in natural settings. Used in a number of studies that illuminated human behaviour, requirements, needs, or difficulties encountered. Provides implications for design, but indirectly rather than directly.
- *Usability-centered approach*: Involves assessment of different features, particularly in respect to portals, by users. It is a bridge between systems- and human-centered approaches. Used in several studies with mixed, or self-evident results.
- *Ethnographic approach*: Involves study of life-ways, culture and customs in a digital library environment. Also involves study of impact of a digital library on a given community. Applied successfully in a few studies, with illuminating results, particularly as to impact.
- *Anthropological approach*: Involves study of different stakeholders or communities and their cultures in relation to a given digital library.

Applied in one study with interesting results illuminating barriers between stakeholder communities.

- *Sociological approach*: Involves assessment of situated action or user communities in social setting of a digital library. Applied in one study with disappointing results.
- *Economic approach*: Involves study of costs, cost benefits, economic values and impacts. Strangely, it was applied at the outset of digital library history (*e.g.,* project PEAK) but now the approach is not really present at all.

CRITERIA FOR EVALUATION

Criteria reflecting performance as related to selected objectives. They include:

- What parameters of performance were concentrate on?
- What dimension or characteristic were evaluate?

  Criteria refer to chosen standard(s) to judge things by. Criteria are then used to develop measures. The importance of criteria follows from this truism: there can be no evaluation without explicitly or implicitly having some criterion or criteria first.Since, 1950's evaluation of IR systems uses relevance as the basic criterion for evaluation. Libraries use a variety of (more or less) standardised criteria for evaluation of components, such as a collection, or services, such as reference. Digital library efforts have not as yet developed anything similar as to evaluation criteria. A summary of most often used criteria follows.

USABILITY

Usability has been used widely in digital library evaluation, but there is no uniform definition of what does it cover in digital library context. Usability is a very general criterion that covers a lot of ground and includes many specific criteria – it is a meta term This was pretty much the umbrella under which usability was used in digital library evaluation. Here is a list of specific usability criteria applied in various studies:

- Content (of a portal or site):
  - Accessibly, availability
  - Clarity (as presented)
  - Complexity (organisation, structure)
  - Informativeness
  - Understanding, effort to understand
  - Adequacy
  - Coverage, overlap,
  - Quality, accuracy
  - Validity, reliability
  - Authority

- *Process*: Carrying out tasks such as search, navigate, browse, find, evaluate or obtain a resource, etc.
  - learnability to carry out
  - Effort/time to carry out
  - Convenience, ease of use
  - Lostness (confusion)
  - Support for carrying out
  - Completion (achievement of task)
  - Interpretation difficulty
  - Sureness in results
  - Error rate
- Format:
  - Attractiveness
  - Sustaining efforts
  - Consistency
  - Representation of labels (how well are concepts Represented?)
  - communicativeness of messages
- Overall assessment:
  - Satisfaction
  - Success
  - Relevance, usefulness of results
  - Impact, value
  - Quality of experience
  - Barriers, irritability
  - Preferences
  - Learning

SYSTEMS FEATURES

As digital libraries are systems, many traditional systems evaluation criteria were used.

Some pertain to performance of technology others to performance of given processes or algorithms using technology.

- Technology performance:
  - Response time
  - Processing time,
  - Speed
  - Capacity
  - Load
- Process/algorithm performance:
  - Relevance (of obtained results)
  - Clustering
  - Similarity
  - Functionality

  - Flexibility
  - Comparison with human performance
  - Error rate
  - Optimisation
  - Logical decisions
  - Path length
  - Click throughs
  - Retrieval time
- Overall system:
  - Maintainability
  - Scalability
  - Interoperability
  - Sharability

USAGE

A number of studies concentrated on use of a digital library, considering this as evaluation.

Usage in itself is a criterion involving studies of:

- Usage patterns
- Use of materials
- Usage statistics
- Who uses what, when
- For what reasons/decisions

ETHNOGRAPHIC AND OTHER CRITERIA

Several ethnographic and anthropological studies used criteria derived from those fields. Among others, these involve determination of conceptions and misconceptions in and between different groups, their practices and environments, their culture, their language and frames of reference, priorities, learning, impacts and similar aspects that provide comparative evaluation in a broader context of a digital library..

ICDL: EVALUATION METHOD

The range of methods used in digital library evaluations is wide. It would be hard to find a scholarly evaluation method that was not used. It involves: What measures and measuring instruments were used? What samples were used? What procedures were used for data collection? What procedures were used for data analysis? In the present study involves mainly limited user study and systematic study of web site of ICDL with respect to Intel Pentium PCs with MS Windows having 14", 17" and 19" monitors.

Actually methodology includes:

- Surveys, including direct questionnaires and online surveys
- Structured interviews

- Focus groups
- Observations
- Task accomplishment
- Think aloud
- Case studies
- Transaction log analyses
- Experimentation
- Records analysis
- Usage analysis
- Documents, meeting, communication analysis (anthropology)
- Economic analysis

CURATED DATABASES

The term 'curated' comes from the Latin curare–to care for. Of course, all valuable data sets are cared for in some way or other, but the term curated database is normally re- served for those databases whose content has been collected by a great deal of human effort through the consultation, verification, and aggregation of existing sources, and the interpretation of new raw data.

Many curated databases act as publications and are currently replacing the traditional reference works found in libraries such as dictionaries, encyclopedias, gazetteers, etc.

Some notable examples of curated databases include:

- UniProt, which forms the standard reference for protein sequence data in molecular biology. It currently consists of over 300,000 entries. This database has a large team of dedicated curators and is typically regarded as a 'gold standard' of protein databases.
- The CIA World Factbook, which is probably the most widely used source of demographic data. It was first published as a book around 1990 and was there- after released annually. For the past 8 years or more the Factbook has also been published on-line. Recently, the interval between releases of the on-line version has been reduced to two weeks.
- The IUPHAR receptor database, which describes the molecules that transmit information across the cell membranes. This database is typical of a very large number of small curated biological databases. For ex- ample, unlike UniProt and the World Factbook, it is not backed by a large organisation: most of the cu- ration effort is supplied by volunteers, and only two people are involved with its direct maintenance.

Wikipedia and other wikis are also curated in that they are the product of direct human effort, and they provide some of the features we believe are desirable for curated databases. Wikis differ from most curated databases in that there is little or no structure imposed on the entries. Curated databases—whether or not they are supported by relational database technology—are usually designed to be machine readable and thus amenable to data extraction tools, such as query languages that are common for databases. Socially, curated databases differ from wikis in that the curation process is usually more heavily orchestrated in the latter.

How ever, there is much to be gained by trying to combine the best of wiki and database technology and some of the research we describe in later parts is an attempt to do just that. The examples above form only the tip of the iceberg. The number of publicly available curated databases is exploding thanks to today's web technology, which makes it relatively easy to publish new databases on-line. Molecular biology alone, for instance, boasts over 1000 on-line databases, many of which are curated.

Measured by the work that goes into producing them, the cost of curated databases is huge. For example, there are over 150 people listed as working full-time on UniProt. As publications, curated databases provide academic kudos: the 'authors' of databases such as UniProt and OMIM are known primarily for providing comprehensive reference works. Given their importance, good tools to support the creation, maintenance, and evolution of curated databases are required. In this respect, curated databases have some characteristics that may challenge some of our precepts of how a database functions:

SOURCE

The majority of curated data is data that is copied and edited from existing sources, perhaps other curated databases or printed articles. Often, the closest one may get to 'source' data is an opinion of the curator that has been added as an annotation. All the other data has been painstakingly extracted from other databases. Since, the value of curated databases lies in their quality and organisation, knowing the origin of the curated data—its provenance—is particularly important. Manually recording provenance is both tedious and error-prone, thus automatic provenance recording support is desirable.

ANNOTATION

In addition to the core data, curated data-bases also contain annotations that carry additional pieces of information such as provenance, the conjectured function of a gene, etc. For the purpose of easy construction of such annotations, it becomes necessary to propagate annotations made on a user's view of the database back to the actual core data, a non-trivial problem as we shall see.

UPDATE

A common practice is to maintain a working database that is updated by a community of curators and periodically to 'publish' versions of the database by distributing copies of the working database or by converting it to an appropriate format for web publishing.

Given the role of curated databases as publications, it becomes important to be able to cite particular versions of the database, and to be able to retrieve a particular cited version when looking up a reference. In other words, one must make sure that the previous versions of the database are digitally preserved.

Since, human data entry is slow, curated databases do not grow or change rapidly, and specialised archiving techniques can be used to reduce the amount of storage necessary to record the complete history of the database. Archiving techniques should also support temporal queries, which are particularly important for databases like the World Factbook.

For example, one might want to query previous versions to retrieve useful information such as the Internet penetration of Liechtenstein over the past five years, and perhaps correlate it with economic data in this or another archived database.

SCHEMA AND STRUCTURE

Many curated databases are constructed 'on the cheap', starting life with a simple, structured design that allows basic description of the database 'entries' which are usually stored in a text file. Almost inevitably, the structure of the entries evolves over time. UniProt, for example, has always been distributed electronically in a specialised data format, but the format has been evolved to include new fields. As they evolve, curated databases may increase their dependence on database technology, but the design is seldom fully normalised; the fields themselves may contain structured text, and there is often some redundancy.

In other words: database technology is used more to support persistence, concurrent access, and indexing rather than the data model. In order for database technology to succeed in also providing the data model for future curated databases, it is important to gain an understanding of the processes by which the structure of curated databases evolves. There are economic and social factors that are equally important to the long-term usefulness of curated databases. It is therefore worth taking a brief look at these factors because they may also suggest some interesting long-term challenges for database technology.

SUSTAINABILITY

During the nineteenth and twentieth century, thanks to the development of public, university and other institutional libraries, the function of libraries changed from one of ownership of data to one of distribution. A secondary but useful effect of this is that much more was preserved. Nearly all of our knowledge has been preserved by copying it: by an oral tradition, by copying manuscripts, by the printing press, and now by a plethora of digital media and computer networks such as the Internet. Concentrating it in archival institutions such as the libraries of Alexandria, Baghdad, Cotton, and Louvain, which were all destroyed in various ways, was probably counterproductive. Today—by archiving at remote sites—we have reasonable methods for protecting our data from physical destruction, but this is no guarantee against the economic collapse of the organisation that maintains the data. There has been a proliferation of data centers over the past years—many dedicated to the storage of scientific and economic data—but one wonders whether, by analogy with early libraries, we are endangering our data by placing it in such centers.

These depend on continued public funding and there are signs that such centers are no more sustainable than early libraries. A move towards massive systematic distribution of electronic publications is the LOCKSS project in which a large number of university libraries each keep a repository of a set of publications, and a peer-to-peer synchronisation process ensures that the repositories are consistent and cannot be corrupted either by bit-rot or deliberate interference. We have likened curated databases to publications, so could one build a LOCKSS system for databases? In addition to the requirements for files, such a system would have to work on incremental updates and would also have to work well with archiving.

OPEN ACCESS

Another transition that was in part due to the proliferation of university libraries was that, in the second half of the twentieth century, academics and other scholars stopped having to pay to get their research into print and disseminated. Unlike textbooks, research articles are, unfortunately, not a highly saleable commodity.

The fact that we no longer must pay for their distribution is largely due to libraries who purchase our papers on behalf of the communities that they serve. This economic model of distribution is still very much in use for electronic publications, but it is showing signs of collapse.

Although there are costs associated with the production of an electronic journal, they are mostly initial costs and should be small compared with paper distribution. The idea of open access is that the initial costs should be paid for by the person responsible for a publication. After this it should be freely available. Curated databases are unlike research papers in that they are constantly updated.

So while many scientific curated databases are open access, it is not clear that this is the right economic model for sup- porting them. It is almost impossible to obtain indefinite funding to support the development of a database, and un- less there is institutional support for a curated database, it is likely to lead a hand-to-mouth existence. Of course, many curated databases—

encyclopaedias, dictionaries and other reference works—have evolved from paper publications that were sold, and they continue to charge for their use. But charging policies vary and are generally ill-defined: we give you small amounts of data for free, but you have to pay for the whole database; or, we give you the old data for free but you have to pay for the current stuff. For scientific data, if we draw an analogy between a curated database and a textbook or reference work, it is not unreasonable to expect the user of the database to pay for access, but how does one charge? Could a system of micro-payments be designed for these databases? The problem is complicated by the fact that curated databases copy one another and if one database charges for access to some piece of data, it might be required that some of payment goes to the sources of that data.

If such a scheme were to be developed, a satisfactory model of provenance is essential. These are just two areas of curated databases in which the right model of data and data communication could be enormously valuable. Open access impinges on copyright and intellectual property issues, which are hugely problematic areas even before databases are considered Organisation.

PROPAGATION OF ANNOTATIONS

In UniProt the fields are classified into core data and annotation. Core data includes information like the protein sequence itself, which is extracted from other databases. An- notation is additional information, like the conjectured function of a gene, that has been entered manually or is machine generated by classification and sequence matching programmes. In UniProt, the process of annotation is carefully controlled and annotations are placed only in designated annotation fields.

By contrast, the *Distributed Annotation Server* (DAS) is a client-server system that conveys annotations that are external to the underlying database between user interfaces. A an arbitrary user may annotate something such as a segment of sequence data that appears in his or her interface the data, and the annotation will appear to another user using a different interface. Each user interface can combine information from a number of annotation servers, each of which acts as an external database for annotations.

Annotation Models

As a mild leap of faith, we liken DAS to the process of an- notating a view of some data and asking that the annotation be carried backwards to the source data as well as forwards to some other view. Since, we are typically annotating a small piece of data, such as a base data value, this requires us to identify where, in the source, that piece came from–its where-provenance. The importance of being able to connect elements of the output of a query with those in the input was first recognised in in the context of data integration.

The process of annotation immediately complicates traditional notions of query equivalence and hence, query optimisation.

Consider the two SQL queries:

- Q1: SELECT R.A, R.B FROM R,S WHERE R.A=S.A AND R.B=50
- Q2: SELECT S.A, 50 AS B FROM R,S WHERE R.A = S.A AND R.B=50

These queries are normally regarded as equivalent, and the simple rewrite of R.B to 50 as B in the select clause is a typical low-level optimisation. If one regards the queries as copying base values from the input to the output, however, the queries behave differently: A-values in the output of Q1 are copied from R, while A-values in the output of Q2 are copied from S. Moreover, B-values in the output of Q2 are apparently created by Q2 itself. It is initially annoying that we need to break the principle of substitution of equals for equals for the purpose of annotation propagation; it calls for a different model of both the underlying data and query evaluation.

The model that is developed in and implicitly used in is to add unique colors to components of the input. These colours may be used to represent annotations or to identify components for provenance tracking. We then formalise how queries operate on colored tables. In the following example there are instances of R and S in which each base value has been annotated with a distinct colour, b1, b2,...,. The output of the two queries Q1 and Q2 shows how these colours are propagated.

A	B
10^{b1}	49^{b2}
12^{b3}	50^{b4}

R

A	B
11^{b5}	49^{b6}
12^{b7}	50^{b8}

S

A	B
12^{b3}	50^{b4}

Q_1

A	B
12^{b7}	$50^{\perp}$

Q_2

One can consider an alternative representation of these annotated databases in which colours are first-class values by pairing each column with another column of colours. An immediate question is whether the transfer of colours that is implicit in our queries can be represented by another query on the alternative representation that explicitly manipulates colours.

The problem is that in operations such as union and set-theoretic projection, two base values can be 'merged' and the annotation is then a set of colours. For conjunctive queries, it is established in that there is indeed an explicit query that can be used to express the annotation transfer.

The authors also examine the extension of SQL with explicit statements to 'steer' annotations through queries. In addition, they propose the 'DEFAULT ALL' propagation scheme in which any two base values that are explicitly found to be equal in a selection or that are implicitly identified in a union or natural join have their annotations merged. Finally, the authors also investigate the efficiency of computing annotation propagation. Although most work on annotation has considered annotations only on single base values or whole rows, provides a system for attaching annotations to sets of base values occurring in the same tuple.

The authors point out that an annotation on a base value should be regarded as a curator's opinion of the validity of the value and that this is better modelled as an annotation on the relationship between the base value and the key for the tuple containing that value. In addition, they introduce a query language—a 'colour algebra'—for querying annotations. Again an explicit relational representation of such block-coloured databases is introduced and the colour algebra is shown to express exactly all queries that the positive relational algebra can express over the explicit relational representation of block-coloured databases. This result was later extended in to full relational algebra.

Reverse Propagation of Annotations

We noted earlier that there is a need to propagate an- notations from a user's view of the database back to the source data: if an annotation is attached to some base value in the output of a query, to what base value in the input should it be attached? Given the rules proposed in for propagating input colours to the output of a query, one can in principle answer this question by reversing the propagation rules. In the case that the query contains a union or a projection, however, a given colour on an output base value could be produced by more than one possible placing of that colour on an input value.

Moreover in the case of a join, a colour placed on an output base value can only come from a single base value in the source, but that colour when carried forward may 'spread' to other base values. A source annotation that does not have any such side-effects, *i.e.,* that produces precisely the view annotation, is called side-effect free. In the problem of finding a side-effect free annotation is shown to have NP-hard query complexity for queries containing both a projection and join and was later strengthened to DP-hardness in. In all other cases of positive queries, there is a polynomial time solution.

The problem of finding side-effect free annotation placements is related to the view deletion problem: find a minimal set of tuples in the source to cause the deletion of a tuple in the output. It is yet to be seen whether any of these complexity results form a practical barrier to building general systems for the reverse propagation of annotation. In fact shows that these problems become tractable for classes of key-preserving queries. We should note, however, that these results are for the default propagation rules for relational algebra. There appear to be no results for reversing the more complex forms of annotation suggested in.

UPDATES IN CURATED DATABASES

We have discussed annotation for queries and its relation- ship to where—provenance in some detail, but let us return to the larger picture of curated databases. In systems such as DAS, annotations are external to the core database and are superimposed on it. In UniProt, however, an annotation is simply a part of the database that has been entered or modified by a curator. Curated databases are created by copying or abstracting data from other sources and later correcting it.

This is a process that is entirely familiar to anyone who has constructed bibliographies for papers such as this one. When doing so, one typically tries to find a bibtex entry on the web, copies and pastes it into one's own bibliography, and then corrects it in accordance with one's own preferences. If this entry were an entry in a scientific database, where-provenance information would include both the source for the entry and a record of what update was made and who made it. A whimsical account of duration is given in.

It is important to reiterate that curated databases are constructed by updates to an existing structure; they are not views. So while UniProt contains some parts—such as the taxonomic lineage and the citations—that have probably been imported automatically into the database, many of the fields are entered by people making individual updates, and it is this activity that gives value to the data-base. The source of these updates is sometimes information extracted by the curator from a paper; it is also sometimes simply copied from another, possibly curated, database. It is quite common for this copying to be done by the common copy and paste commands that work in most desktop environments. When data is copied between applications or systems, its annotation, context, and especially where- provenance information is lost.

A Copy-paste Model of Curation

In an attempt to model this process exploits a model in which curated databases are semi-structured trees, and the fundamental operation is to copy a data element—as sub-tree—from one tree to another. This provides a simple model of provenance in which it is possible to ask questions such as when some data value was first created, by what process did that value arrive in a database, when was a sub-tree last modified, etc.

The cost of storing such provenance information appears to be prohibitive if done naively because some trail of information needs to be kept of each node in the tree. However this can be mitigated by two observations: first that provenance information is hereditary: unless a node in the tree has been modified, its provenance is that of its parent node. Second, one can collect a sequence of basic operations into a transaction, and there is a description of the effects of the transaction that is shorter than recording the log of basic operations.

The latter is potentially useful for databases that are published periodically. The major unsolved challenge here is the practical goal of building provenance recording into the tools that a curator normally uses. This is a hard problem involving not only data management, query language design and efficiency issues but also usability and organisational problems. While addressed the problem of recording and storing provenance, the task of formulating queries against the resulting provenance store was left to users. Can we design a query language that provides good high-level support for writing sophisticated queries against curated databases involving provenance, the raw data, and perhaps previous versions? This is challenging, since, reasoning about copy-paste operations on trees is non-trivial. On the organisational side, how can we convince both database, operating system, and other application vendors and independent database curators to adopt common standards for provenance? This is a significant long-term challenge requiring both technical and social development.

In practice, updates to a curated database are performed through the update expressions of SQL. This includes both manual copy-paste operations and bulk loading of data into one database from another. Just as where-provenance has been studied for query languages we may ask how update languages manipulate where-provenance. Figure shows three SQL programmes. Although they all have the same 'result', the way they carry provenance is different.

The first SQL programme is a query and is copying as a provenance-preserving transformation. The second and third programme are SQL updates and are not copying as provenance-preserving transformations: they preserve the colour of a tuple or table while changing one of its components. Updates in this language satisfy a weaker semantic provenance condition than queries, called kind-preservation: if a value appears in the output with a given colour, then the corresponding value in the input must have the same type; furthermore, if the value is an atom, then the corresponding value in the input must be the same atom.

Thus a kind preserving transformation can drop or add fields in tuples, or insert and delete elements of sets, while preserving their provenance. The update language with implicit provenance is shown to be complete with regard to the update language in which colours can be explicitly manipulated under the kind preserving, bounded inventing, and no colour-equality test conditions. It is still not known how these results for the complex object update language transfer to SQL updates on flat relations.

When measured by the transformations between input and output domains that they express, update languages such as the update fragment of SQL do not add anything to query languages; in contrast, provenance mappings provide an alternative method of characterising update languages that highlights differences with queries. But kind- preservation is a very weak condition.

It allows one to empty out a tuple and insert completely different fields into it while preserving provenance. Whether this is a useful knowledge is debatable and reminiscent of Theseus' paradox: suppose we build a ship, and then replace each part of it over its lifetime; is it the same ship? There appear to be other possible models of provenance for update languages, for example one could associate provenance with some form of key preservation. In addition, there has yet to be any work on provenance in update languages for XML and other forms of semi-structured data. Although it appears straightforward to extend the approach of to where-provenance for XQuery-style queries, update languages for XML are still in development. Most of them abandon a key design principle of XQuery by permitting unrestricted side-effecting operations inside queries. Their semantics is sufficiently complex that designing provenance-tracking techniques for them is probably premature.

Why-Provenance and Updates

We have argued earlier in the chapter that updates are essential in curated databases. If where-provenance makes sense for updates, what about why-provenance? A curated database is built through a long sequence of updates. It is likely that only a very small number of those updates had any effect on the data of interest, and that a satisfactory answer is to provide the subsequence of relevant updates and their sources. But what does 'relevant' mean here, and is it sensible to use the same approach as in why-provenance for queries? Our experience with where-provenance suggests that simply translating sequences of updates to 'equivalent' queries may be unsatisfactory from the point of view of provenance.

Provenance and Workflow

No discussion of provenance would be complete without mention of the large amount of work on workflow provenance. Many scientific data sets are derived from raw data by a complex analysis process involving several programmes—a workflow. Scientists need to record the enactment of the workflow for two reasons: first to record precisely how the data set was described and to avoid recomputation; second because it is sometimes cheaper not to keep the derived data, but to recompute it when needed.

The recording of a workflow enactment is also called provenance. Workflow provenance is sufficiently important that there is a workshop largely devoted to this topic; and workflow systems such as Taverna and Kepler have been developed that record this form of provenance.

To date there has been little interaction between workflow and data provenance research. In the workflow setting, the solution to recording interactions with databases is simply to record the state of the database itself and the query. Note that this solution presupposes some form of archiving. Quite recently, the importance of combining the two views of provenance has been recognised.

In there is a proposal for a stream-based model of workflow equipped with a notion of provenance for elements of a stream. In a more sophisticated model is developed based on Petri nets in which the tokens are complex objects and the transitions can perform certain elementary operations on these objects. While this is a rather low-level description of workflows, it may well lead to a general notion of provenance that embraces both data and workflow provenance. Reconciling these two notions is one of the most immediate and interesting challenges of provenance research.

BIBLIOGRAPHIC DATABASES

It is primarily in the area of reference that bibliographic databases have gained a secure footing as part of the collection. Bibliographic databases contain those elements of bibliographic description used to describe books, journals, documents, and other publications or portions thereof. In the 1980 Supplement to Sheehy a section on 'Data Bases' appeared for the first time which acknowledged that "the use of computer-readable data bases...is now considered to be a normal part of library reference work.

Their presence in Sheehy, however, was short lived, not because the use of databases became abnormal, but because, as the Second Supplement published in 1982 states, "rapid changes and developments in the field of data base computer searching... ' had made it 'impractical either to update or augment that earlier list. So Section F of the 1980 Supplement became in 1982 a listing of recent directories of database services. Walford's *Guide to Reference Material* lists magnetic or machine-readable files with the print version. There are numerous directories of the burgeoning number of databases. Schmittroth's *Encyclopedia of Information Systems and Services,* Cuadra Associates' *Directory of Online Databases,* Williams's *Computer-Readable Databases,* and Aslib's *Online Bibliographic Databases* are amongst the most prominent and up-to-date.

The fifth edition of the *Encyclopedia of Information Systems and Services* had 25 per cent more entries than the fourth edition, which had been published one year earlier. Cuadra Associates publishes a quarterly supplement to its directory. In the Summer 1980 issue of *RQ* Danuta Nitecki's 'Online Services' column was introduced. The column deals with automation as it affects public services. A year later, in Summer 1981, *RQ* began reviews of databases for generalists. Here, editor Helen Josephine referred to the databases as "online *reference* tools, definitely a part of the collection and used to answer questions as the print tools have been. The reviews are for generalists—*i.e.,* reference librarians rather than searchers-and they keep generalists aware of the content and scope of each database.

Comparisons between access for the print and online versions of a file are made. The databases discussed thus far are primarily online bibliographic files which are the online equivalent of print abstract and indexing services, and this probably explains their ready acceptance into reference services. There are, however, in actuality several categories of online databases and all of which have found slightly different placement and use within the library's collections.

The bibliographic databases are three major types: online union catalogs of library holdings, such as OCLC and RUN, henceforth referred to as bibliographic utilities; online equivalents of print abstracting indexing services such as COMPENDEX, CA Search or INFORM. These seem to have developed no distinctive designation, but are by far the greatest in number and are usually referred to as simply databases or bibliographic databases; and full-text databases of newspapers, journals, directories or court cases such as New York Times Information Bank or *Haroard Business Review* online, LEXIS, or WESTLA W which contain the full text of the publication online.

The numeric databases are files of primarily statistical information-either numeric or brief textual-from which a patron extracts specific pieces of data. Patrons may extract data for further manipulation or, in some cases, may revise data in the numeric file. Because these databases are constructed in different ways and are used differently in libraries the evaluative criteria applied vary.

This chapter will not discuss evaluation of their extended subject searching capabilities, but it will discuss evaluation from the point of view of selection for the reference collection or evaluation once added to that collection. Also not considered will be discussions of a library's own online catalog or circulation system, although these are certainly bibliographic databases. The scope of this chapter is bibliographic, numeric and full-text databases which are not the library's own and which the library decides to access as a means of developing its collections and/or services. This review will probably raise as many questions as it provides insights, for the concept of online files as a part of collections is still forming.

It is a credit to libraries that they have managed to embrace online databases, have incorporated them into the day-to-day operations of normally slow-moving institutions, and still have had time to report their progress in doing so. Much, however, remains unreported, and many readers will doubtless know of online uses or evaluations of them which exist. This chapter is a survey of trends as reported in the literature and no attempt was made to survey existing practice to supplement that reported.

Ready Reference

All three types of databases are extensively used in ready reference. James Sweetland's 1979 article, "Using Online Systems in Reference Work, was the first of a rash of similar articles which appeared in the period 1981 through 1983. The reasons advanced for their uses in reference varied. Sweetland needed to establish high-level information service in a new library with limited staff and physical size.

He specifically selected OCLC, Lockheed and the New York Times Information Bank for searching. In other cases, the introduction of online searching into reference activities was more of a spin-off from the fact that the library was already providing search service as reported by Miko, Cochrane, Droessler, and Friend. Librarians who already knew how to perform subject searches on files such as DIALOG, BRS (Bibliographic Retrieval Services), or SDC (Systems Development Corporation) found themselves itching to use their terminals when faced with verification problems at the reference area. And so some terminals moved from back rooms into the reference desk.

Evaluations reported here are primarily compilations of information on the type of searching performed and the cost. Searches performed at the reference desk are primarily for verification of incomplete citations, but other uses-such as providing addresses of authors or publishers, preparing lists of recent works by an author, determining subject headings to use in a catalog search, and determining which library(ies) own a specific title-were reported by these authors and by Durkin and Dolan, who surveyed BRS users in 1979. Online searching is faster than manual searching and is therefore very helpful to staff who, even if their numbers remain constant, face increasing service demands. Online searching provides a wide range of search tools in one place, and may provide access that is not available in print tools.

For example, there are usually more access points than the print file and access points may be searched simultaneously. Online indexes are not at the bindery or temporarily not located for other reasons. With online indexes, the computer system may be down, or a file may be temporarily unavailable while it is being updated, but the online version usually is more current than the print version. Access to the database of a major vendor may provide a tool that would not normally have been purchased for the print collection. Costs that have been reported are not comparable or especially meaningful, since, no one includes the same elements for computing cost for either online or manual searching. Comparison of uses or costs between libraries would suffer from the usual problems of reference service measurement.

What actually constituted a 'search' had not yet been defined when the Association of Reserch Libraries (ARL) compiled a SPEC Kit on 'Online Bibliographic Search Services' in 1981. Should a ready-reference online search constitute a hash mark—as part of other reference statistics—or should reference librarians keep separate track of the number of queries which were answered with online assistance? How can we evaluate the quality and not simply the number of searches? What elements must be included when calculating costs? Thus far, no reports of evaluations of ready-reference searching have appeared as part of collection or services evaluations.

Print vs. *Online Migration*

The added advantages of online reference tools as compared to their print counterparts which were just described has led to what has been termed the print *v.* online migration. Marydee Ojala makes an interesting point when she states that a significant difference between print and online reference tools is that: "With the printed tool, the money has already been spent, and the time involved in becoming acquainted with the peculiarities of the book is not measured in dollars. With online indexes the opposite is true.,, One public librarian went so far as to state that, "instead of buying books, we do online searches on demand.

It's much more cost effective to provide materials that people actually need, on demand, rather than buying materials that mayor may not meet an actual information need.,, This is, doubtless, an extreme statement, but as libraries discovered the advantages of accessing online reference materials, it became inevitable that at least some of these libraries would question whether it was necessary to subscribe to both the print and online services.

The fact that this consideration exists supports the point that online services are indeed part of the collections. And it is at this point that collection development staff may become involved in the evaluation process. Those articles in the literature indicate that although libraries may be considering cancellation of print titles, few are taking action. A notable exception to this general trend is an article by Pfaffenberger and Echt on the "Substitution of SciSearch and Social SciSearch for Their Print Versions in an Academic Library." The authors selected *Science Citation Index* (SCI) and *Social Sciences Citation Index* (SSCI) for study because of their high print subscription costs. SCI and SSCI were removed from the reference area and replaced by a sign which told patrons that they could have a free search instead of doing the search themselves.

It was found that it was less expensive to provide the online services for SCI, but that it was not economical to substitute online for SSCI. The primary difference was that there was heavier use of the SSCI and use was primarily by subject, rather than by citation as with SCI.

Most other papers, while they report a perceived migration do not indeed show significant numbers. Childs and Carmel, in a survey of the use of print *v.* online *Index Medicus* in twenty British Regional Health Authority Libraries, found *increased* or changed use of the print tool when online became available.

Lancaster and Goldhor in a 1979- 80 survey of 200 academic and special libraries in the United States found that subscriptions to abstract/indexing services were declining, but felt that this was only partly due to availability of online equivalents. Much more important, they stated, was the fact that "subscription costs are increasing while the relative purchasing power of many library budgets is declining.,, This analysis was confirmed in a more recent paper by Miller and Kobelski who surveyed 193 New York State special libraries. They report that 40 per cent of the responding libraries had cancelled some index/abstract journal subscriptions since, beginning online searching, but that 50 per cent of the responding libraries had also *added* subscriptions.

Only twenty-two of the ninety-one libraries who returned the survey stated that online availability was an important factor in the cancellation decisions. Other major factors considered were cost, volume of usage and whether or not the tool was of primary importance to the library's mission.

Online availability is only one factor amongst those weighed in a collection development decision to cancel a subscription. Lancaster and Goldhor found some evidence to suggest that availability of a tool online might be influencing libraries which never had a subscription before to opt for the online service. An obvious difficulty with selecting an online service is that you cannot be assured that it, or all portions of it, will always be online. If it is a tool of interest primarily for current information this is not a major consideration, but if it is of interest also for current and retrospective information this *is* a consideration.

Bibliographic Utilities in Reference Work

As stated earlier the means of access to other collections when used in lieu of a completely comprehensive collection of one's own can be considered to be part of a library's collection. The major bibliographic utilities, Online Computer Library Center (OCLC), Research Libraries Information Network (RLIN), University of Toronto Libraries Automation System (UTLAS) and Washington Library Network (WLN), do not have print equivalents and are used in this way.

For the most part, these tools found application in reference because they were already in the library, and staff found them useful for more than shared cataloging or interlibrary loan. However, Sweetland, and Droessler and Rholes made conscious decisions to use OCLC and RLIN respectively at the reference desk even though they were not in previous use at the library.

The primary use made of the online abstracting indexing services was for bibliographic verification, and this is also true of the reference use of bibliographic utilities. Baker and Kluegel report extensive use of OCLC in reference amongst ARL members. Farmer evaluated RLIN as a reference tool and has trained librarians in California and Nevada in its use as such. Miller summarises the uses of both OCLC and RLIN, and, in addition, he evaluates the specific reference capabilities of each. RLIN is preferred for reference use because the search capabilities exceed those of OCLC.

RLIN has truncation, subject search and combined index searching, whereas OCLC's primary advantage is retrieval by predetermined truncated search keys and by year(s) of publication. Jacobs *et al.* came to much the same conclusion, and also they evaluated WLN. WLN, like RLIN, has subject and keyword access and combined index searching is possible. This probably arises from the fact that it was the first among these bibliographic utilities and it was designed primarily as a cataloging database, with later additions of interlibrary loan, acquisitions, and serials union list subsystems. RLIN, which came later, was designed to support not only cataloging, but also shared access to collections and cooperative collection development, and WLN was also designed from the start to support multiple functions.

Online bibliographic databases-especially abstracting-indexing services and the bibliographic utilities-have been incorporated rapidly into reference work and their acquisition may be viewed as part of the building of the library's collections. Their use as part of the collections has not been extensively evaluated, but widespread reference use attests to their ease of use, cost-effectiveness over print resources in some cases, and the improved access which they provide over manual tools.

CONCEPTUALISING SPATIAL DATABASES

Much like maps, spatial databases store representations of phenomena in the real world. Geographic information systems use spatial databases, aka GIS databases. Spatial databases comprise a system, or hierarchy, of data models. The representations of the data and its potential applications across a network area drive its definition. The data model closest to the level of the end user is referred to as a conceptual data model.

To design an effective database, the developer must know how the spatial data will be used and what the intended product will be. The definition at this level will identify what possible applications the spatial data will have, such as flood zone analysis, voting district redistribution, or library user analysis. The "commonly used conceptual data model is the entity-relationship (ER) model; it uses primitives like entity type to describe independently existing entities, relationship type to define relationships between entities, and attributes to describe characteristic values of entities and relationships". A conceptual database schema is the definition for the entire hierarchy of data models. A central assumption for the design of a spatial database schema is that spatial phenomena in a real-world setting exist in Euclidean space.

Complex relationships exist between all the phenomena in the real world. These relationships have a variety of characteristics that give them specific spatial and temporal attributes. The real-world phenomena depicted can also be classified thematically. The thematic classification of data in layers can depend on the purposes for the data depicted.

The data can thus relate to items such as economic zones, library service areas, hydrographic areas, or physical features. Kainz suggests that "the representations of spatial phenomena are stored in a scale-less and seamless manner. Scale less means that all coordinates are world coordinates given in units that are normally used to reference features in the real world. From there, calculations can be easily performed and any (useful) scale can be chosen for visualisation". As in print maps, the accuracy of the data being recorded or captured is significant in the composition of a spatial database. Information derived from direct observation of phenomena should have the geographic coordinates defined. The accuracy of spatial database attributes is also affected if the data was derived from a secondary source of cartographic information such as a map. The scale of the data from the map would shape the feature coordinates in the database.

An advantage of digital spatial databases is that a database does not depict boundaries between spatial phenomena, such as in map sheet boundaries or other partitions of the geographic space, other than imposed by the spatial features themselves. Spatial databases are real-world models in "that they are scale-less, potentially three-dimensional, dynamic, and seamless. It is easy to query a database, and to combine data from different layers. Spatiotemporal databases consider not only the spatial and thematic but also the temporal extent of the features they represent". (The number of spatial, temporal, and spatiotemporal data models that have been developed is too large to address in this volume). However, the basic elements of a spatial database schema provide a structure in which to design a system for spatial querying and retrieval of information.

STANDARDS FOR CREATING BIBLIOGRAPHIC DATABASES

The concept of "standard" in the field of library and information science is interpreted as codes of cataloguing rules, classification schemes, subject headings and various other documents contained recommendations for good library practice, all of which are subject to varying interpretation. But, for another professionals, standards are extremely precise technical specifications for communication between software and machines in an automated information-processing environment. For example, Operating Systems, TCP/IP etc. Standards are documented agreements containing technical specifications or other precise criteria to be used consistently as rules, guidelines, or definitions of characteristics, to ensure that materials, products, processes and services are fit for their purpose Field of bibliographic standards are not limited to the rules only but spread up to the authority files such as person names, corporate names, subject headings, classification schemes, series names, institution names, software and standardization form and format etc.

In beginning, during the initiation of automation to library professionals, there was not much focus on bibliographic standards and were creating databases in any formats. That affected to the automation of their libraries, which forced them to think over the issue. Now, gradually, the libraries and information centres are realizing the importance of bibliographic standards. Centres like Information and Library Network (INFLIBNET), Ahmedabad is playing important role in bringing all libraries together to work on a single platform of standards with linking under one huge national network i.e. UGC-

Infonet. INFLIBNET Centre is an Inter-University Centre of University Grants Commission (UGC), working on Academic library system in India. In 1990, UGC launched it as a programme for five years on pilot basis. On June 1996, the programme was recognized as a full-fledged Centre. UGC-Infonet is a project of UGC being implemented by INFLIBNET Centre in collaboration with ERNET (Education and Research Network), New Delhi. It is an Intra-Network of Indian universities and colleges across the country based on the Open IP platform, employing state-of-the-art technologies like IP or TV, enabling online response to queries. The network facilitates Intranet and Internet access to its users on high data rates.

STANDARDS FOR BIBLIOGRAPHIC DATABASE

Well-known simple definition of database is a set of records and record is a set of fields, where, field is a combination of different pieces of information. Bibliographic database is a database of resources available at libraries in print format. With the revolution of information technology in the field of libraries, bibliographic catalogue has come up into the form of bibliographic database. For making compatible with these changes, there, many library institutions have come up with different standards and formats such as CCF, AUSMARC, CANMARC, UKMARC, USMARC, UNIMARC, MARC21, AACR2, ISBD, LCSH, MeSH etc. Some of the Internationally recognized standards and formats being used by many libraries of different countries for creating databases. As per the INFLIBNET's guidelines following standards are recommended for use:

Standardized Bibliographic Formats

During the inception of the Programme, The Task Group on "Union Catalogue, Data Capturing and Standardization" was constituted by UGC. The Task Group was assisted by a Sub-Committee on implementation of Common Communication Format (CCF) for data capturing and data exchange. Later on, the Sub-Committee formalized some fields based on CCF and named it as "Guidelines for Data Capturing: a user manual". During the initial stage of automation, Micro CDS/ISIS software (developed by Unesco) were suggested to use for creating bibliographic databases based on the format recommended by the Centre.

Simultaneously, other DBMS such as DBase, FoxPro, FoxBase etc. were also being used by different libraries for creating the databases. In addition, the Centre had also the library house keeping software called "ILMS – Integrated Library Management System" developed on COBOL language on Unix platform, and was distributed freely to the member libraries of the Centre. Later in February 2000, Centre developed another library house keeping software called "SOUL – Software for University Libraries" on Power Builder language on Windows platform by using the client-server architecture to keep in mind the shortcomings being faced in ILMS software. The software is developed based on the format formalized by Sub-Committee of the Task Force. Later, early 2001, The Ministry of Human Resource Development (MHRD), Govt. of India visualizes building up a national database of library holdings in the country based on the MARC21 format. Further, after approval the committee directed INFLIBNET Centre to implement the MARC21 format in all libraries of the country. In this regards, the Centre formed the MARC21 Core Group during December 2001, which formalized the fields for implementing it with the SOUL library house keeping software. The main reason for preferring MARC21 over CCF and other formats was that most of the countries in the world use MARC and it is comprehensive having number of fields. Also there is constant development taking place in MARC21 and is updated regularly whereas CCF has become stagnant.

STANDARD FOR RENDERING INFORMATION/ BIBLIOGRAPHIC DESCRIPTIONS

AACR2R, ISBD and CCC are standards for bibliographic descriptions. But, INFLIBNET Centre suggests their participating libraries to follow the Anglo American Cataloging Rules-II (AACRII) Revised version for rendering bibliographic information.

STANDARDIZED SUBJECT HEADINGS

Different subject headings list are available, developed by different institutions such as LCSH, Sear's List of Subject Headings, MeSH, Thesaurus etc. But INFLIBNET suggests to its member library to use LCSH (for generalized subject headings) and Engineering Index, MeSH and thesaurus (for specialized Subject Headings).

STANDARD FOR CLASSIFICATION SCHEMES

There are various classification schemes have been developed by different organizations for classifying the books on different subjects. Functionally, most of the libraries are using the Dewey Decimal Classification (DDC) for assigning the Classification Number to the documents. But, under INFLIBNET umbrella, all the libraries are free to use any classification scheme for classifying the document, as it is very difficult for any library to reclassify the entire collection based on any new scheme. As per the library practice any classification scheme can be used as MARC21 has capability to adopt any kind of classification schemes.

ISO–2709 INFORMATION EXCHANGE FORMAT

This standard specifies the requirements for generalized interchange format that will accommodate data describing all forms of material. It describes a generalized structure designed specifically for exchange of data between processing systems and not necessarily for use as a processing format within systems. The format may be used for the interchange of records using various communication media. INFLIBNET Centre recommends to follow this Exchange Format for contributing records to the Centre. The exchange format has implemented too with the in-house developed software SOUL for exchanging records.

Physical Structure

General Structure of the Record:

Leader

Each record begins with a leader of fixed length of 24 character positions and is the first instance of the ISO 2709 format of a record. It contains:

- Record length (5 characters): The length of the record includes the leader, directory, data fields and record separator.
- Record Status Code (1 character): Always '0' for output files, ignored on input files.
- Implementation Codes (4 characters): These codes are defined for each specific implementation of the ISO 2709 format. Second character position represents Bibliographic level codes (i.e. s- serials, m- single volume monographs, c- multivolume monographs, a-component part) and rest of the character positioned not used. Here, Bibliographic level is defined here as per the INFLIBNET's use. For the MARC21 based records, it follows the description defined for bibliographic level in MARC21 bibliographic format.
- Indicator length (1 character): This is always '0', because here at INFLIBNET database indicator is not being used. But the value is '2', when we export records from SOUL to MARC21 in ISO 2709 format.
- Subfield identifier length (1 character): '2' The subfield identifier length. This shows the number of characters being used for the subfield identifier.
- Base address of data (5 characters): A decimal number indicating the number of control characters (length of leader plus directory and field separator) which precede the variable data fields. This number, when added to the starting address of the record, gives the address of the first character of the variable fields.
- For user systems (3 characters): These character positions are not used. Always '000' in output files.
- Length of "Length of Datafield" field (1 character): '4' the length of "Length of Datafield" in the directory. (Use of 4 characters permits datafields as long as 9,999 characters)

- Length of "Starting character" position (1 character): '5' the length is "Starting character position" in the directory.
- Rest (2 characters): These character positions are not used. Always sets on '00'.

Directory

A directory entry in this bibliographic record is made up of a tag, length-of-field, and field starting position. It is of variable length and consists of a series of fixed fields, referred to as "entries". One directory entry is associated with each datafield present in the record. Each directory entry is 12 characters in length and is divided into three parts:

- Tag: A three numeric ASCII character code identifying the datafield, which corresponds to the directory entry. In software, names of the fields are being used in alphabetical name, but during the export in ISO 2709 format and display on screen, it converts in three-numeric digit ASCII character code.
- Length of datafield: A four digit number showing how many characters are occupied by the datafield, including datafield separator but excluding the record separator code if the datafield is the last field in the record.
- Starting character position: A five-digit number giving the position of the first character of the datafield relative to the base address of data, i.e. the first character of the first of the datafields.

Datafields

A datafield consists of subfield and datafield separator:

- Subflield : A subfield consists of a subfield identifier followed by a data string, which is terminated by either another subfield identifier or a field separator. A subfield identifier consists of a subfield identifier flag i.e. cap (^) sign followed by one another character, that can be alphabet a to z (small or capital) and numeric 1 to 9, INFLIBNET Centre uses here small alphabets. For MARC21 based records "$" graphical sign is used as a subfield identifier.
- Datafield Separator : The datafield separator i.e. hash (#) sign constitutes the final character of every datafield. ASCII value 30 (character 1/14 of ISO 646) is being used as a field separator in MARC21 based data.

A datafield, which has a single subfield, will be organised as follows:

Record Terminator / Separator

The record terminator is the final character of the record i.e. hash (#) sign. It follows the field separator of the final datafield of the record. ASCII 29 (character 1/13 of ISO 646) is being used as record separator in MARC21 based data.

OTHER STANDARDS RELATED TO BIBLIOGRAPHIC DATABASE

Z39.50 Retrieval protocol

Z39.50 refers to the International Standard, ISO 23950: "Information Retrieval (Z39.50): Application Service Definition and Protocol Specification", and to ANSI/NISO Z39.50. The standard specifies a client/serverbased protocol for searching and retrieving information from remote databases.

OAI (Open Archive Initiative)

The Open Archive Initiative (OAI) for metadata harvesting is a new protocol dedicated to solving problems of digital library interoperability by defining simple protocols, most recently for the exchange of metadata. Although, Z39.50 Information Retrieval Protocol is also one of the harvesting protocols. Some digital library systems are using for retrieving and searching the records for example Maxwell System. It is crucial to explain, discuss, and disambiguate the concepts and terminology used among OAI implementers to harvesting approach to interoperability. The harvesting protocol defined by the OAI is a request / response protocol with 6 request types, viz. *Identity, ListMetadataFormats, ListSets, GetRecords ListRecord, and ListIdentifiers.* It has defined in such a way to support a common set of principles and a technical framework to achieve interoperability. Although, both the standards are not being used with the INFLIBNET database right now, but being explored to implement it in near future.

PURPOSE OF THE BIBLIOGRAPHIC STANDARDS

Mostly, purpose of using these standards for creating bibliographic databases or suggesting using it at libraries of India, has following reasons behind it:

- Pursuing Universal Bibliographic Control
- Exchange of information among union databases for the purpose of global resource sharing
- Cooperation at the local level, transferring data from one system to another

IMPORTANCE OF THE BIBLIOGRAPHIC STANDARDS

Following bibliographic standards for creating the databases produces following importance:

- It makes uniformity in records
- It provides better resource sharing between different resource centres

- It helps in exchanging of records and facilitates it without data loss
- It helps in creating national / International bibliographic union database
- It helps to adopt any system and provides platform interoperability

USE OF BIBLIOGRAPHIC DATABASES IN COLLECTION EVALUATION

There are two areas where online bibliographic databases have played a role in collection evaluation. These are in comparison of collections in coordinated collection development and in evaluation of periodical collections.

Bibliographic Utilities in Coordinated Collection Development

The ALA "Guide to Coordinated and Cooperative Collection Development,, states that these functions presume easy bibliographic access not only to cataloged items, but also to automated order and in-process files when available. Online access is easy, especially when compared to no access, use of many microfiche or book catalogs, or making guesses based on known collection development policies.

It is well known that online catalogs have revolutionised resource sharing. They are used by selectors considering retrospective purchases to determine whether a title of suspected little future use is held by an institution with which one has a cooperative arrangement or from which one can borrow readily. But moving from sharing of existing collections to a coordination of future collecting is a quantum leap.

Pat Battin ably expressed the situation when she stated: "When one's resources are not equal to the demand, dependencies replace resources in the sharing equation."

Before resources can be coordinated, existing strengths and collecting policies must be analysed. An essential component of this process, as Reed-Scott states, is agreement on the methodology or methodologies for evaluating their collections. A major product of Research Libraries Group's Cooperative Collection Management Development prog-ramme is its RLG Collection Development Manual, which describes how member libraries should report existing collection strength and current collecting intensity.

Member libraries have completed the conspectus in many subject areas and have accepted collection responsibility for the group in defined subject areas based on analysis of the results. The conspectus results are now online on RLIN. Why online? The information is easier to search this way and there is access by subject words and phrases, institutions, Library of Congress classification number, primary collecting responsibility, and collection level.

The multiple access characteristic and currency of information facilitate its use for comparing and analysing collections. Gwinn and Mosher describe the development of the conspectus and its use in regional and specialised national planning. The conspectus is a powerful collection evaluation tool and

Association of Research Libraries has evaluated the adoption of the RLG Conspectus On-Line for use by a larger, less cohesive group of research libraries.

The Association of Research Libraries has recommended that it be adopted with modifications to enable national cooperation in collection development to become an ongoing reality. If this happens, collection evaluation results will be online on a grand scale. Although collection strengths cannot be compared online, OCLC participants can conduct analyses of their tapes between any two or more institutions. Interpretation of the results of overlap studies is not clear-cut and they do not seem to have been widely applied in coordinated collection development.

Serials Evaluation

In 1978 Barbara Rice surveyed the use of bibliographic databases in collection development activities and found that they were being used in the selection process for verification, but little was being made of them in collection evaluation. While that paper was being written, BRS and DIALOG both announced the availability of a collection development service which lists the total number of times journals are cited in the subscriber's searches for a six-month or one-year period. Lancaster/however, echoes Line's criticism of the use of citation counts to evaluate periodical holdings, and states that, "no measure of journal use other than one derived from a local-use study is of any significant, practical value to libraries."

On the other hand, use studies are viewed with considerable suspicion by many and the controversy has by no means been resolved.

Recently, ALA published its "Guide to Collection Evaluation through Use and User Studies," and citation studies are listed as one possible type of user study. The guidelines conclude with a warning that no technique alone is sufficient for evaluation and that anyone type has distinct advantages and disadvantages.

All use studies are cumbersome; and online citation methods, especially the collection development services, offer a quick way to compile a list of titles which patrons may well have requested from the library.

Since, Bourne and Robinson's early article describing the use of references from online selective-dissemination services to test document delivery, there have been a number of articles describing the use of citation counts from online bibliographic databases to identify titles for addition to the collection and for collection evaluation.

Hafner, Rice/Seba and Forest, Danilowicz and Szarski, and Trubkin all used lists which they generated from retrospective search or selective dissemination services. Garfield maintains the validity of this technique and has used it to produce his *Journal Citation Reports* for both *Science Citation Index* and *Social*

Sciences Citation Index. Sprules pointed out that the technique may be valid for a special, discipline-oriented library, but that it did not work for a large multidisciplinary collection. Part of the problem with all use studies is that each type measures a different use, and opponents and proponents are at odds because we really have not defined what 'use' is.

When Rice compared lists of chemistry titles generated by BRS's collection development service with those generated by *Journal Citation Reports,* an in-house use study, faculty choice, and the "List of 1000 Journals Most Frequently Cited in Chemical Abstracts," she concluded that no list can match the unique purposes of anyone collection. The BRS collection development service seemed most useful for identifying titles which should be added to the collection. However, the BRS and DIALOG services were not popular and are no longer available. Collection development staff and serials librarians obviously did not regard them as valid selection tools.

FULL-TEXT DATABASES

Bibliographic databases were initially described as falling into three major types: bibliographic utilities, online equivalents of print abstract-index services and full-text databases. Full-text databases have been on the scene since, 1977, and in the last two years access to them has begun to change dramatically. The major and obvious difference between full-text and other bibliographic databases is that the full document is available for search and for retrieval. Let's first consider the effect on search strategy.

In the other bibliographic databases, documents are described by information extracted from the document and information added by a cataloger or indexer such as subject headings, index terms or an abstract.

The searcher retrieves a reference to the document by searching any combination of the extracted information. In full-text searching, a user can search any term in the document in natural language. There is no need to translate hi s query into controlled vocabulary terms, which usually forces a more general search. On the other hand, the user must know all possible synonyms or ways of expressing the subject for which he searches and must deal with more false drops resulting from the fact that most terms have more than one meaning or context in which they may occur.

Perez summarises the advantages and disadvantages of controlled vocabulary and free text searching in newspapers and other general publications. Newspapers are examples of a type of publication which are available in two different ways online-either as files which are the equivalent of abstract/index files or in full text. *The New York Times* is an example of this. New York Times Information Bank (NYTIB) became available online in 1973.

It consisted of bibliographic citations and abstracts for *The New York Times* and other major newspapers. Searching was by descriptor terms, and, in this form it found quick acceptance in libraries within traditional reference—much more quickly than the other bibliographic databases. In 1975, just two years after the first commercially available NYTIB installation began operating, Bachelder reported that 50 per cent of NYTIB terminals in public, college or university libraries were at the reference desk.

Why libraries were so quick to place this database in the reference collection is not clear to this writer, although Bachelder maintains that the reason is "obvious: the Information Bank is an excellent reference tool.,, The problems associated with making effective use of the NYTIB in reference were ably described by Rieche.

In 1980, search capability was enhanced by providing free-text access to the abstracts, and in July 1981 the *New York Times Online* was introduced, offering full-text access to the paper from 1 June 1980. In April 1983 *The New York Times* stopped offering the NYTIB, but made it available through Mead Data Corporation. Mead incorporated the Information Bank and the *New York Times Online* into its NEXIS service which, since, 1979, had offered the *Washington Post,* AP, UPI, and PR wire services online in full text. Other full-text systems for online newspaper searching are INFOGLOBE and VU/TEXT. In addition, many newspapers are available in the index form or index plus free-text searching of summaries. All of these are thoroughly described by Nina Ross. Stephen Smith reviewed the changes which had occurred in online news retrieval in 1983.

Many of the newspaper files exist in combination with other files which contain information that users need on a very timely basis, primarily business, financial or legal information. Mead Data Corporation, which produces NEXIS, is also the producer of LEXIS, one of the major full-text legal databases which are commercially available.

The other, WESTLA W, is a product of West Publishing Company. The two have been competing for users of Computer Assisted Legal Research Systems (CALR) since, their introduction in the early 1970s. Larson and Williams review the literature on the evaluation of LEXIS, WESTLA W, and the other CALR systems, JURIS, AUTO-CITE and FLITE. They identify the following interrelated evaluation criteria: time saved, cost effectiveness, efficiency, quality of results, manual *v.* computer effectiveness, user friendliness and operation by end-users compared to trained specialists.

The new evaluative criterion appearing here-not found in those listed when evaluating vendors of bibliographic databases or comparing databases-is end-user searching compared to trained specialist operation.

The legal systems were developed by or in close cooperation with lawyers and bar associations to search the text of cases or to trace the history of cases and certain compilations of law, such as the *United States Code.* Their first widespread use was in law schools, during the time period 1977-80 as reported by Neth, Mersky and Christensen, and Munro *et al.* Neth reports that the terminal at Case Western was installed in the law school and used by students and faculty members. Mersky and Christensen, describing experience in Texas law schools, imply that the terminals are in libraries when they show that acquisition of LEXIS or WESTLA W depends on the size of the library budget; and they confirm this by reporting that, in most instances, training is coordinated through the law school library or in others by a full-time member of the teaching faculty. In any event, the persons being trained are students, and one would predict that CALR should soon be in great use in law firms.

Myers in 1978 surveyed the impact of LEXIS on large law libraries. Of the respondents, 86 percent had a terminal, and for most subscribers the terminal was in the library or an adjacent office. Many of the librarians had had LEXIS training. However, most of them were not doing many searches, the majority reporting zero to four per week. Unfortunately, the number of searches done by lawyers was not reported. More recent studies could not be found, but, on the basis of that report, it is safe to say that legal databases do not yet seem to have become as much a part of law library collections as have bibliographic databases.

Will this continue in the future? In 1980, Greguras *et al.* described the changing information needs of the legal profession. Probably in response to expanded needs for information beyond the purely legal, Mead and West are now brokering access to DIALOG, BRS, SDC, Legi-Tech and a wide variety of specialised databases to LEXIS and WESTLA W subscribers. Will lawyers learn the idiosyncracies of DIALOG, BRS or SDC databases, or, needing assistance with these, will the lawyers see that librarians are competent searchers and leave the searching of bibliographic as well as full-text legal databases to librarians? Although there is little evidence that full-text legal databases have found their way into library collections, other databases have.

Just as the bibliographic and full-text legal databases came of age in the 1970s, the 'News and Trends' section of *Online Libraries and* M *icrocomputers* predicted that the 1980s may be the age of the online full-text books, periodicals, directories, texts and encyclopedias. Perusal of the BRS and DIALOG database catalogs shows a variety of full-text files.

Notes are added to the following titles if the database is not the online equivalent of the same print title:

- American Chemical Society Primary Journal Database (BRS). Full text of 18 primary ACS journals.
- Kirk-Othmer Encyclopedia of Chemical Technology (BRS).
- American Men and Women of Science (BRS, DIALOG).
- Mental Measurements Yearbook (BRS).
- CHEMLA W (DIALOG). Full text of U.S. Federal regulations, as published in the *U.S. Code* and updated in the *Federal Register,* for

manufacture, use, storage, transportation, and disposal of chemical substances.

- CHRONOLOG NEWSLETTER (DIALOG).
- Critical Care Medicine Library (BRS). Full text of twenty-five prominent medical textbooks in emergency and critical care medicine.

At present, use is expensive, but future development of optical disk technology may change this. The age of the electronic journal, predicted for some years is still not with us, although it is certainly closer. More and more full-text databases are available. An advertisement in the April 1984 *American Libraries* announced that full text of many of the articles in *Magazine Index* and *Trade and Industry Index* would soon be available online. As more directories and journals become available online, libraries will be questioning whether or not to subscribe to one or both and the print *v.* online migration may become more extensive than earlier reported. But in this case the choice is not print or online for a secondary service such as an abstract/index tool, but print or online for the full entity, *i.e., American Men and Women of Science,* or *The New York Times,* or a court opinion. Access is usually faster and greater, but costs are higher.

COLLECTION OF NUMERIC DATABASES

A numeric database is a computer-readable collection of data which are predominantly numeric in nature: Numeric databases were developed before bibliographic databases and have been described by Luedke, *et al.* Initially access to these data was through the information analysis centers, professional organisations, or government bodies that produced them. More recently, the development of software packages for access and further analysis have made feasible the use of numeric databases by other than the producers.

Fried *et al.* describe an online numeric database as a system-a combination of numeric database and search system which retrieves data and presents it online to the user. Fried was the first in what was to be a series of online columns on numeric databases. Only two such columns appeared. Economic and financial data are the most accessible commercially. This is probably because there is a fairly large audience for this type of information and thus commercial vendors have a market for it.

Major vendors are Data Resources Inc., Wharton Econometric Forecasting Associates, Chase Econometric Associates, and A.P. Sharp, Inc. Information is available either online through a time-sharing system or via direct access to the producer's computers. Although some special libraries doubtless access these systems, there is little use reported.

A 1977 survey by Wisdom and Houghton in Great Britain showed that the files were being used primarily by financial analysts, economists or managers. Only a handful of librarians were using data files other than Predicasts. In 1976,

Predicasts and Lockheed began the first combined online bibliographic and numeric data retrieval and analysis system, Predicasts Terminal System (PTS). In addition to the Predicasts literature, the system gave access to economic, social and industrial numeric data. It was this venture that doubtless introduced many libraries to numeric databases for the first time.

A 1983 DIALOG catalog listed twelve numeric databases, all in the area of business and economics. The first listing of online non-bibliographic databases in *Online Review* in 1977 contained 127 entries, and in six months that number had increased to 246. Online non bibliographic databases do not seem to have found their way into libraries to any large extent, with the exception of those available through DIALOG. The major reporting of library use or involvement is in the area of social science data, involving tapes, rather than online use. The Winter 1982 issue of *Library Trends* was titled "Data Libraries for the Social Sciences.,, Rowe described the need for incorporation of knowledge about machine-readable data files (MRDF) into the reference process but stated that MRDF are normally housed at data libraries in academic departments, research institutes or computer centres.

She went on to say that a few libraries have incorporated MRDF into their collections and a few others have acquired codebooks or documentation, but not the tapes. Most libraries, she continued, have done nothing. Those libraries which have are described elsewhere in the *Library Trends* issue and by Ferguson in a *Drexel Library Quarterly* issue devoted to "Machine-Readable Social Science Data.', Jones described complete integration into collection and services and Ruus described a data library operated jointly by the library and computing centre. The difficulties attendant in housing the tapes and documentation separately from the computer may be overcome if these files become available online. The Summer-Fall 1982 issue of the *Drexel Library Quarterly* was devoted to numeric databases.

Bartkus described the use of scientific numeric databases in reference and information services at duPont. There, scientific numeric databases have been selected and used by either the engineering or information services department, whereas access to commercial and business databases has been coordinated through the information services department. Bartkus predicted that numeric databases will tend to be searched by the individual, rather than an intermediary, because other databases will be available to the individual to manipulate the data extracted, and because the individual uses it directly in his work.

Access to the databases has been centered in the organisation of the searcher-user, rather than the library. Bartkus went on to outline several possible roles for the library in the acquisition and use of numeric databases; a clearinghouse coordination or specialist services function. Wherever they are selected and evaluated, the criteria described by Ewbank may be applied. The evaluation process for numeric databases has multiple steps, as does selection of a bibliographic database, since, both the database and the system used to access it must be evaluated. The evaluation revolves primarily around the content of the database, the system used to access it, and factors relating to management of the database.

Factors to consider relating to content evaluation are scope completeness, source coverage, the process by which data are selected and evaluated, redundancy, references, consistency amongst units measured. Factors to consider in relation to database management relate to production and maintenance of the file. Is there adequate technical and institutional support? periodic update and revision? adequate documentation? A key element of evaluation which must be performed in the case of numeric data is that of the access system.

As Wisdom and Houghton point out the searcher of a bibliographic database is looking to see whether or not information on a subject exists, whereas the searcher of the numeric database knows what is available and searches to find it. He/she needs a good access system and ways to extract and further manipulate the data.

Ewbank recommends evaluation of system documentation, indexing system, availability, report formats, and protection from user changes. Although his criteria were developed primarily for scientific data, Autrey applies identical criteria for social science numeric databases and then goes on to raise several issues specific to social science files, namely, user training, privacy and confidentiality of computer records of organisations' internal data and those from personal questionnaires and interviews.

Scientists are usually conversant with computers and have used them in their work for a generation now, whereas social scientists have only come to use them more recently. More training or more user friendly systems are presently necessary in order for social scientists to use numeric databases online. In a 1983 review of 'Online Searching in the Reference Room' Bonta specified three different areas of expertise involved in searching online databases: knowledge of the database being searched, knowledge of the search system, and knowledge of the subject itself. Greater knowledge of the subject matter has been suggested to be more crucial for searching numeric databases, and perhaps for that reason they have not found their way into libraries.

However, even in those institutions where persons with advanced degrees are employed as searchers, the user's need to incorporate the information obtained directly into a work product or to manipulate the data further make intermediary searching a hindrance rather than a help. Rumble has summarised the basic reasons why only a fraction of the existing numeric databases in science are actually available online. These are the high cost of data entry, difficulties in database building, lack of obvious economic benefits, a small number of well-articulated demands, and lack of encouragement from major online vendors.

END-USER SEARCHING

Just as end users search numeric and full-text databases, especially legal and newspaper files, the time for end users to search bibliographic databases may have arrived. BRS introduced its AFTER DARK service in January 1983 and DIALOG its KNOWLEDGE INDEX service in November 1982. Special evening rates and simplified search strategies are offered to encourage individual users, many of whom have all that is necessary to access these files.

A search software package using one language to search the different major vendors-SCI-MATE-has also recently been developed in combination with a data management package by Institute for Scientific Information. In February of 1984, Menlo Corporation announced a software package for use with DIALOG databases which is menu driven and guides users through searches and database selection. The software is available with several microcomputers. Other end-user software packages are available. Will patrons prefer to do the searches themselves or will they still turn to librarians as intermediaries?

The conditions seem similar to those which have caused users of numeric databases to do the searches themselves, *i.e.,* knowledge of subject content, an easy access system and a tool for further manipulation of the information. Some libraries have already subscribed to BRS AFTER DARK for patron use.

KNOWLEDGE INDEX offers document delivery in connection with the service, an attractive feature for the user who would like to avoid the frustrations of dealing with a library and would prefer to have the document delivered to his home or office. On the full-text systems, of course, the document can be printed online, in some cases in advance of when the information is available in print. Some independent dealers are beginning to offer selective database coverage, either through one of the major vendors or independently. For example, EXEC INFO service offers a combination of full text- *Harvard Business Review* and *Academic American Encyclopedia-and* bibliographic abstract-index-Management Contents and ABII Inform-through BRS for a flat monthly rate. VU/TEXT offers a wide package including full-text news-papers, the Pennsylvania Legislative Database, PTS Prompt, ABI/Inform, and current stock market quotes.

These developments are summarised by Smith. Although Stabler argued at the 1984 National Online Meeting that librarians will continue as intermediaries for the bibliographic databases, her arguments are based on 1983 technology where only a limited number of files are available through the simplified search routines of BRS/AFTER DARK or KNOWLEDGE INDEX systems and the fact that, since, the access system has been simplified to encourage end users, search results are not as comprehensive or specific as those performed by librarians. This could change, depending on the success of these new services, users' direct access to more full-text files, and development of simplified search software.

ONLINE BIBLIOGRAPHIC DATABASE SERVICES

The online bibliogtapic database services are different. Local holdings generally are not an issue, but what is important is the for-pay access these services provide for a myriad of databases. Mainframe computers are used also for maintenance of, access to, and searching of such online bibliographic database services as DIALOG, ORBIT, BRS, WilsOnline, and others. Such data bases are searched by users from all over the world, typically gaining access via some form of telecommunication device and a local terminal or computer.

Some pros and cons need to be indicated here, and can be elaborated upon later. Even though these databases are online, they are not online in real time the way OCLC and the others are. The individual databases serviced by DIALOG, for example, are updated monthly, quarterly, or even more slowly than that. OCLC is updated instantaneously. When a library enters a holding to the database, it is immediately made available to all 6,000 users. For want of a better definition, this notion of instant updating and record availability is a way of understanding "real time".

A second major deficiency of DIALOG, ORBIT and BRS is that the various databases to which they provide access, all have different search rules (protocols is the fancy word for rules). This means that someone who knows how to speedily and effectively search ERIC may not have any idea how to search Predicasts. On the other hand WilsOnline, being a service offered by a single company for all of its databases-a couple of exceptions notwithstanding-does not require a different set of protocols for each of its databases. This is an important issue and points to a major direction for the future, that is, the normalisation of databases. Lets continue with technology review.

Minicomputers are smaller, but still quite powerful computing devices which have been quite effectively used in local library or regional automation efforts. They have been especially effective in such applications as online circulation control systems for individual libraries (as with many college and university libraries, plus some public libraries), and libraries in combination (*e.g.* public libraries with many service outlets; regional public library systems consisting in many individual public libraries; and consortia, *i.e.* several libraries in combination, sharing a single minicomputer.)

For almost twenty years the MINICOMPUTER has been successfully used to maintain control of all of the books (and other library materials) held by all of the libraries participating in the system. It indicates where they are located (*i.e.* on the shelf, in circulation, or any other status), who has them, reserves or holds them for use by library patrons when they are not immediately accessible; it maintains a complete record of all of the registered library users which includes their name, address and other appropriate information so that the user can be notified if he or she has overdue books, a reserved book is available, or for other information pertaining to library service; it also keeps track of the amount of money owed by individuals who returned their books late. Individual suppliers of these minicomputer based systems have addressed such applications as online acquisitions; online catalogs [confusingly referred to as PACs (Public Access Catalogs)]; serials acquisitions, cataloging and check-in; film control and booking; and special collection control (an important application for libraries which have special collections such as videos which may circulate only for one or two days at a time).

More and more libraries are using these minicomputer-based systems for full public access catalogue use and complete circulation control. Note well that the precondition for such applications to run on the minicomputer is the creation of a machine readable database of the library's holdings. The conversion of library holdings to machine readable form has been the biggest obstacle to the complete and successful automation of libraries. Invariably the conversion of the data to a form manipulable by the computer is the most problematic, difficult, and expensive part of automation.

MARC

Things would be a hell of a lot worse if there were no standardised format, the MARC format. Because of MARC everyone can use and share the same data for conversion purposes. Of equal importance is that a competitive market exists of automation purveyors, all of whose systems are predicated on MARC-based databases. All of the software for these minicomputer systems is written to operate on MARC records. There is no way to adequately explain within the time constraints how incredibly important this standardisation of cataloging data, the MARC format, is. Let's move on to the most exciting and fun machines to use.

MICROCOMPUTERS are used primarily in single library and single function applications. There are a variety of microcomputers available and in use by U.S., libraries. Microcomputers are being used in such administrative applications as fund accounting, word processing, and data base management. The kinds of microcomputers used to perform these functions typically are based on the Intel chips, that is, the 8088, and the 80286 - 80486 chips which are on the IBM PC, XT, AT, and compatibles; and the Macintosh, which is based on the Motorola 60000 series of chips. From smart toys and hobbyists' enthusiasms, micros have evolved to become devices with as much as 16 to 64 million bytes of random access memory, and which store over 600 million bytes of data on a single hard disc drive. Devices of such monstrous capacity (and smaller ones, too) can support sophisticated local area networks of PCs and/or terminals. Microcomputers are being used to perform such library functions as acquisitions, cataloging, serials control, and circulation control. In the last couple of years they have been used, too, as public access catalogs and sophisticated database storage and searching devices. Typically, most micro based systems do not accept, process or output cataloging data in conformity with library standards, that is, the MARC record. However, there are exceptions, and definitely more are coming along.

What has made the big difference in capacity for micros is the storage medium, CD-ROM. CD-ROM stands for Compact Disk - Read Only Memory. The CD-ROM platter is capable of storing over 16,000 pages of information, and is approximately 511 wide. The combination of the PC, a CD-ROM reading device, and a CD-ROM disk with a database on it, have made possible unprecedented extensions of automation, and more specifically have made possible the distribution of databases on to PCs which heretofore could only be stored on mainframe computers with massive disk storage.

With all of the equipment required to use a CD-ROM now costing less than $2,000, a library now has the hardware for storing and accessing the entire U.S. MARC format database. The compaction of data, the relative inexpense of the CD-ROM storage medium, and the reduction in unit cost for data processing as represented by the PC have made it possible to provide the most sophisticated applications to operate wholly self -sufficiently in the most remote and tiny locations. The only requirement is a stable power source compatible with the equipment.

CD-ROM is the extremely powerful solution to the tremendous costs of remote site online telecommunication charges to a host computer. With CD-ROM the database sits out there in Timbuktu. With terminals online, we have to pay the phone company for providing the connection between the terminal where we are and the computer at some remote site. Many public libraries have several databases that are on CD-ROM at their disposal: Books In Print Plus and Ulrich's from R.R. Bowker, Dissertation Abstracts, WilsOnline, InfoTrac, etc In addition to such bibliographic databases, companies such as the Library Corporation of America make the MARC database available on CD-ROM as well as software to search it and prepare catalogue cards and labels from the MARC records. This particular product is called Bibliophile and it has been very successful in as a source or medium for inexpensively capturing Library of Congress cataloging data. Bibliophile also provides for the printing of catalogue cards and labels from the Library of Congress catalogue record. No more typing catalogue cards and labels. Through Bibliophile a database of MARC records could be created for the books cataloged. Library Corporation will take the records created locally from its Bibliophile product and create a CD-ROM catalogue of the library's holdings. Public and other libraries all over the country have availed themselves of this service.

MICROGRAPHICS

The two major areas of micrographics employed in libraries today are the traditional photographic micro reduction of hard copy documents, and computer based micro reduction. With photoreduction, the hard copy document is photo-reduced to microfilm, 16×, 24×, reductions all the way down to 75× and 150× in some ultrafiche reductions. Computer micro-reduction is usually 42× or 48×, that is, a reduction to 1/42nd or 1/48th of the size of the original document, had there been one. Both microfilm and microfiche have been used for storage and/or preservation of: deteriorating materials, infrequently used materials, and those items which suffer from vandalism, misuse, or for some other reason need this protection. The other reason is simply to save space. In addition microform is an alternate and cheaper means of subscription to some materials, *i.e.* many libraries with limited budgets in an inflationary economy find it acceptable to acquire given serials in microform rather than hard copy. The disadvantage is that the serials cannot be received on a timely basis.

COMPUTER-OUTPUT-MICROFORM (COM)

Computer-Output-Microform (COM) is a medium used by libraries since the 1960's which successfully utilises both the data processing and microform technologies. Instead of photoreducing hard copy documents, the information displayed on COM is converted into machine readable copy from hard copy format or directly keyed into machine readable form, thus manipulable by the computer to suit the given library application. The machine readable data, instead of being displayed (*i.e.* printed) in hard copy form by the printer, is input to the COM device. The COM device, also called a "camera" because of its camera-like function, converts the machine readable data into its visual analog format, *i.e.* it displays it on a cathode-ray-tube (CRT) screen in a human readable (not digital) form. The CRT display is then projected through a lens onto reel microform at extremely high speeds. In this manner either 16mm microfilm or microfiche are created. (Note that the microfiche are created as a single roll of film and cut into the individual sheets later.)

There are a large number of libraries in the U.S.A., which have COM catalogs, but since the inception of CD-ROM, their number is diminishing. It is an extremely compact medium, a given sheet of microfiche can contain the equivalent of 224 pages of computer printout. It is relatively inexpensive, as the largest costs are associated with the data processing effort required for organising the machine readable data into the desirable manner of display, *i.e.* the way the catalogue is to look. The costs for the COM master and the copies from which it is made tend to be modest, assuming the catalogue is not too large. Many libraries have found that COM catalogs are a viable intermediate step between the card catalogs which still exist, and. the online catalogs which require far more expensive equipment to use, host computers with online terminals. Libraries also are choosing CD-ROM catalogs as final options which are replacing the COM catalogue, and eliminating online catalogs as a goal. The cost of online catalogs and the problems of telecommunications have provided the basis for the success of the CD-ROM catalogs in competition with online catalogs. Note that they are not a panacea.

CD-ROM catalogs are always out of date, and the frequency of updating is a function of the size of your pocket book. Getting back to COM, it generally has functioned as an inexpensive storage medium and it has eliminated bulky and comparatively expensive paper listings. It is used best as a disposable product, and is not thought of as an archival medium. For example, many libraries use COM microfiche for current on-order information. Since libraries tend to order, receive and cancel (orders for) books on a frequent basis, a COM listing of the status of the orders must be fairly frequent if it is to be of value. Hence the disposability of the COM on-order file and its regularly being supplanted by a more current edition. It is also the case that libraries use COM as a substitute for any necessary computer generated report that involves a large amount of paper.

Finally COM does not enjoy a great future; as the cost of computing storage and processing continue to drop, the viability of online interactive systems increases, thereby eliminating a major reason for utilising COM. The other major reason COM will further erode as a remote display medium is the aforementioned CD-ROM. Major COM catalogue manufacturers now offer CD-ROM catalogs to customers with increasing success in selling the medium. All of the costs associated with CD-ROM are far greater. As noted the CD-ROM requires a PC and the CD-ROM player. With COM all that is required for display is a $150 – $200 reader. The preparation of the COM masters and duplicates are appreciably cheaper as well. Typically the master costs from $10 – $25, and each duplicate fiche is about $.25 depending on the supplier.

MORE ABOUT CD-ROM

This leads to a discussion of the CD-ROM medium. The more comprehensive term is laser recording and display media. By the use of the laser technology the information is encoded on to a silver platter of varying size and varying storage capacity. There are Optical Disks and CD-ROMs, the two laser media prevalent today.

Optical Disks are relatively new as regards library usage. Experimentation is proceeding with this medium as a storage device capable of holding much more information than is found in microform; two gigabytes (*i.e.* 2 billion bytes or more than 65,000 pages) stored on a single optical disk; they are capable of producing appreciably clearer images on playback or display; and lastly, they are capable of combining on a single optical disk both digital and analog (*i.e.* pictorial) information. The Library of Congress and other major research libraries are studying this closely as another means of preserving deteriorating books. Since optical disks, as noted, include digital information much work is being done to find applications which will combine the computer's indexing, searching and control capability with the laser disk's capacity for accessing pictorial information through digital data encoded on the disk as well. Note that the optical disk is read or examined by a laser device and displayed on a television monitor or some other form of cathode-ray-tube display device such as a computer monitor. One company has taken huge medical databases and placed them on optical disks, and reduced the storage device costs of the databases by many factors. Some optical disks are known as WORM disks, *i.e.* WO for Write Once, RM for Read Many times. These applications are usually tied to devices significantly more powerful than microcomputers.

CD-ROM: This disk, to which reference has been made several times, especially in the microcomputer discussion, has become a, hot item in United States library discussions, and its impact is just beginning to be felt. CD stands for Compact Disk, and ROM means Read Only Memory. Each disk can hold about 500 million bytes of information, which means that over 16,000 pages of data can be stored on a single platter. The extraordinary impact of CD-ROM is that it provides the distribution of massive databases, including sophisticated retrieval capability, while at the same time requiring none of' the prohibitive telecommunications costs normally associated with the distribution of databases to remote sites. All that is required for access to a database, such as the Library of' Congress MARC database, is a PC compatible microcomputer with a CD-ROM reader and control card, and the CD-ROM platters with LC' MARC, which is several million records large at this point.

In the past libraries would incur major phone line charges to call the computer upon which resided the database to be searched. Plus the library had to pay towards the cost of storing that database on the computer online. As noted here and earlier, tremendous cost savings are thus realised, and the CD-ROM is sitting there waiting to be used whenever one chooses to use it. Several libraries have chosen the Bibliophile product over membership in OCLC because it is so much cheaper for them to catalogue with Bibliophile.

Many U.S., library systems or consortia, rather than face tremendous telecommunications charges, are putting their public catalogs on CD-ROM, rather than connecting terminals via dedicated phone lines to the circulation system computer. This application strikes one as particularly valuable when one thinks of regional or distributed networks where resources may be scarce and access to sophisticated telecommunications technology may be either limited or prohibitively expensive. If CD-ROM would be the primary distribution medium, there would always be a built-in delay for the time required to create and duplicate the platters from the machine readable data (four to eight weeks).

Most recently, with the help of consultants or specialised in-house staff, libraries are creating Local Area Networks (LANs) which connect several micros and/or terminals to a host microcomputer which has the CD-ROM product. In this way, many people can simultaneously (almost) have access to the single CD-ROM station. This is a high tech way to make the lean dollars of the 90's stretch even further while still providing cutting-edge service.

Perhaps one last point should be made about CD-ROM and its advantages over COM. COM is a much cheaper medium, but one cannot utilise the indexing and searching capability that the computer and CD-ROM provide in combination. Boolean searches on keywords, subject terms, names, parts of names, etc. all are possible with CD-ROM based systems. So the extra cost of CD-ROM versus COM pays for appreciably greater search and retrieval. capability, a capacity far exceeding that of the traditional card or book catalogue. Without further belaboring the CD-ROM technology's virtues, one will now discuss telecommunications, the big giant to which the little CD-ROM seems to be providing an alternative.

Telecommunications is an area of great specialisation and, as a major technology, has its own discipline to be mastered. No attempt will be made to indicate just how complex this area of technology is, nor even to explain the various telecommunications processes. It will suffice to indicate the kinds of roles telecommunications may play in a distributed information network.

The use of telecommunications in the contexts discussed here means the use of phone lines as the means by which a user at a remote site communicates with the central site computer or anyone at another remote site. (Much less frequently, other means for transmitting messages such as satellite, microwave dish, or radio frequency transmitters may be used.)

If there is a phone line specifically established for such communication, and if it is used solely and exclusively for that purpose, then it is called a dedicated line. If a phone line can be used for a variety of calling purposes, one of which is calling the computer from a remote site, then the remote terminal. has dial-up capability. For both dedicated and dial-up lines to be used, special equipment is required on the terminal and on the computer that will permit the data to be converted into a form that can travel between the computer and the terminal, and then converted back so that it can be displayed on the terminal or processed by the computer-depending on the direction the data is headed.

The telecommunications equipment is expensive, but even worse, the telephone charges themselves are extremely dear. And worst of all, the weakest link of all online systems is the phone line. WLS has non-stop transaction processing equipment, that virtually never goes down. But, our library users are connected to this computer via phone lines which go up and down far too frequently. It is pathetic how much we are at the mercy of Ma Bell.

The library has a telecommunications bill of over $10,000 per month. It would have been double that price if we had been unable to take advantage of a special federal tariff. What is painful to realise is that there is nothing in the actual usage of the lines that has any bearing on the doubling or halving of the charges. It is simply a matter of our escaping the local billing policies and coming under the jurisdiction of the federal tariff. The telecommunications equipment was approximately 1/4 of the price of the total system, that is $350,000 of a $1.4 million dollar purchase price. The system currently supports 220 terminals at 45 sites, those being all WLS member libraries, plus the Bedford Hills

Women's Correction Facility. These astronomical costs are why U.S., libraries are turning to CD-ROM and other non-phone line alternatives for distributing data. The interesting trend that seems to be emerging is that online terminals are used and will continue to be used where the data must be accessible in real time and must be maintained and current to the moment. Online circulation systems which keep track of who has which books and which books are in or out, are examples of the justification of online communication with the computer. Online catalogs are harder to justify. For example, if a library's database consists of 500,000 volumes, if it adds twelve thousand volumes per year, and its CD-ROM catalogue is updated quarterly, then the most someone will be denied access to will be 1 per cent of the library's holdings. And there are alternate ways of making that three to six months of information available so that it is not entirely inaccessible to the library user. In this way the library is spared the substantial telecommunications bill for online public access catalogs, while the users will still have access to most of the titles held by the library. The discussion of technologies would not be complete without briefly touching upon Video and Cable communications.

VIDEO AND CABLE COMMUNICATION

Video and Cable communication are technologies being used by libraries in a variety of ways:

- Video and cable communication are being used simply as entertainment and educational media within libraries much the same way they are used in the home. Libraries have extended this function by either videotaping, broadcasting or otherwise making available information of value to the local community not otherwise accessible to that community.
- Public libraries have been especially exploiting the home videocassette market by buying and circulating to their clientele entertainment and educational videocassettes.
- The potential for this medium as an information dissemination tool is great. It is not yet being used very effectively in this manner. Libraries have focused on theatrical videos as a boost to circulation. It is hoped that they will find a way to promote the growing wealth of information and programming available on video that goes beyond the box office hits.

WLS uses cable communication as an educational, political and entertainment medium. Guests have ranged from the WLS Board President, to the County Executive an Assemblyman and other politicians, to Arthur Ashe, Roger Kahn, Alan Arkin, Paul Schrader, the President-Elect of NYLA, your speaker tomorrow, and many others. It is shown regularly by the County's several cable companies. Two-way cable communication has been used by some libraries to enhance reference service. Libraries have placed TVs in public areas, both for cable and video playback viewing. Libraries have also served as Cable Studio or broadcasting facilities This is an extraordinarily powerful information medium that as public library people, we must exploit more fully. We are in the information business, and we must work with all information media.

THE FUTURE

There are a few things that have to be said, now that we have gotten this far:

- First, I don't believe that I will ever read a mystery in bed that is in any form but a book. I do not believe that people will wish to read fiction, poetry, or serious literary or philosophical works in a medium other than the printed page.
- Second, microforms are the worst form of displaying materials in the library. No one in their right mind, all things being equal, could possibly prefer to view or read anything on microform if the same information is available on a printed page or a CRT display, either of which are incomparably better than the microform picture. It is interesting hoe little the microform display has improved over the last several decades.

As artifacts and as media for protracted use, and not to mention, pleasure, books have a secure place in libraries, and for sure, in my home. Much more can be said in addressing the future in libraries, but I'll make a few more points and turn the floor over to you for questions and comment.

- The database services will reach more and more, and smaller and smaller public libraries, via the CD-ROM medium. Even with the growing sales of the WilsOnline product, there has been no decrease in the number of subscriptions to the parallel print products. Regarding Bowker's products, it would be interesting to know If libraries discontinued their BIP subscriptions once they subscribed to the BIP+ CD-ROM product. In any case, over the next 15 years, libraries will add more and more micro-based products. CD-ROM (and whatever more compact medium succeeds it) will become increasingly prevalent. Depending on the phone lines and the future of telecommunications, it is likely that public libraries will eventually have most of their bibliographic control processes accessible via online terminals. The extent to which these services will be available online to the public will be mostly a function of cost. I would safely predict that there will be a blend of CD-ROM and online services available to the public at the local library. The CD-ROM data is the best backup for the online database, even if it is a bit pricier than COM.
- Cataloging and technical services will fall into even greater disrepute because of the impossibility of having quality databases without

attendant costs. The basest canard is the attack on the catalogers for doing what they are supposed to do.

OCLC suffers from irreversible bibliographic chaos because there is little quality control over what goes in, and all-too-little quality control over what comes out. What catalogers called authority work, and what lay people expect simply as consistency in headings, has been deteriorating at an accelerating pace since the 1960s. It costs a great deal of money for a library to ensure that all works of an author can be presented to the user, or that all editions of a work are related properly, or that all materials on a subject are brought together. With OCLC as the chief cataloging resource for US libraries, with the decreasing numbers of catalogers, and with the increasing determination of library people to have everything online NOW, less and less will be related by human enterprise, and more and more will be lost to the unsuspecting user.

Machine searching power will compensate somewhat, by permitting searches with wild cards or question marks. But how can the computer possibly know that Donald Westlake and Tucker Coe are the same author? To the extent that local systems will have authority files, *i.e.* files of names and topics, and all the appropriate references to and from those names; and to the extent that those files are linked to the catalogue files, the user will stand a better chance of getting all of Westlake's works displayed as the result of a single search. The sorry story is that libraries will find it increasingly difficult to pay for catalogers to review and revise names and headings for a local database. In addition there still is a long way to go before local systems will be able to readily import the name and topic data for their internal authority files, and there still is much much more to be done to develop local system software which will integrate and refresh all of the locally resident bibliographic records to reflect correct names and topics.

The most positive note is that the unit cost of data processing technology has been decreasing dramatically each year. Computers and related technologies are there for us to use, to enjoy and to deliver essential information and recreational services to our clientele, the citizens of our community. It is essential that the public library continue to be the bulwark of our democracy that provides barrier-free access to its resources, be they print, machine-based, or human. We will continue to need all three if we are to continue to maintain a high standard of service over the next decade.

2

Information Technology in Library Evolution

HISTORICAL BACKGROUND OF TECHNOLOGY

The period middle of the 19th century and 20th century needs a special mention because the period marks the age of revolution with new modes of communication technology. Instead of 'paper' man made use of terminals, computers printers and other types of data communication devices. 'The use of paper', has been completely superseded by the Super Highway Technology.

In this electronic age, academicians have come very close to non-book materials. During 1990s, we had more justification for this feeling than any other generation. In the history of mankind so many technologies have emerged and all of a sudden compelling us to change ways of thinking. People have started recognizing the importance of Information Technology as an effective tool in satisfying the human needs. In efficient governance and in developing human resources, efforts are being directed towards improving the utilization of the scarce academic resources, thereby integrating the society globally. Telecommunication and computerization are being increasingly seen today as means to improve efficiency of operation.

The quality of ' library service ' has vastly improved with the introduction of communication technology.

Telecommunication plays an important role while designing an effective functioning of the on-line libraries. Digital technology, improved antennae systems and use of microcomputers have been instrumental in achieving a communication revolution. The recent trends in telecommunications are the use of and Internet technology and E-mail technologies. They accommodate a wide variety of multimedia communication services that are very popular in most developed countries and are now gaining importance in developing countries like India as well.

Advances in both telecommunication and computer technologies have facilitated the designing of new software thereby making the delivery of information quicker, convenient and efficient than ever before. It is fact that users feel increasingly comfortable with computers. The communication technology land line and satellite communication have made the world a 'global village '. In such a challenging situation academic libraries have to welcome not only e-mail, LAN and similar services but also Intranet and Internet services in their libraries.

OVERVIEW OF INTERNET

A world- wide communication system that links millions of computers has been developed. Such a network is called the Information Super Highway or Cyber Space most popularly known as the Internet. The Internet permits two way speech which allows millions of people to communicate by either sending messages through their computers or receiving messages from other computers all over the world.Internet in normal usage is a network of computers. In other words we can say that it is a network of networks. Internet made a humble beginning way back in the 1970s in the United States under the Department of Defence-Sponsoring a collection of computer network known as ARPANET. It connected about 64 computers providing admissions to researchers and commercial sectors. Within a span of thirty years, the system has considerably advanced in research and technology. It connects millions of people and shares information in different fields like agriculture, defence, transport, economics, sports, medicine, education and libraries. Although its popularity is spread over the developed countries, Internet has been only a recent development in India.

INDIAN EXPERIENCE

Just a few years ago that the public sector organization VSNL introduced Internet to the Indian community. At present approximately 4,00,000 commercial users have access through VSNL whereas from education and research communities 5,00,000 users have access through ERNET. So, around 10,00,000 Indian people are directly connected to the NET which is a small fraction of the total population of India. VSNL has been channelising the information particularly from the four International Gateways at Mumbai, Delhi, Calcutta, and Chennai.

To give more access to E-mail and Internet, VSNL has installed new Gateways at Ahmedabad, Kanpur, Ernakulam, Jullandar, Bangalore and Hyderabad.

INFRASTRUCTURE NEEDED

To have admission to the Internet, specific equipment is required. Primarily the computer forms the backbone of the network. A personal Computer, a commonly used machine that is easily available can perform the task. Telephone lines form an important part with information passing through these lines and this facility can be availed of through additional payment to the telephone department. A device which is necessary to use the Internet is called Modem. The Modem sends/passes the information across phone from one computer to another computer. Now a days computer has become part of the Internet.

One has to subscribe to an *Internet Service Provider* (ISP) which gives the user admission to the Internet. In India, the VSNL is the service provider that is connected to the webs of many popular countries including USA. VSNL has its main internet admission node in Mumbai. It also has various other remote admission nodes at Pune, Calcutta, Delhi, Bangalore and Chennai that link to the US Web through the main node in Mumbai.

INTERNET APPLICATION IN LIBRARY MANAGEMENT

For instance, when the Librarian in Sri Sathya Sai Institute of Higher Learning wishes admission to the Internet, the modem connected to the Library's computer establishes the link to the VSNL which automatically connects the Librarian to the main Web through the Internet admission node in Mumbai. The VSNL offers admission to the Internet for a reasonable fee. Once it gets connected to the service, a list of areas that he/she can use appears on his/her computer screen in the Central Library. For instance, topics like Sciences, Social Sciences, Humanities and Engineering subjects also will appear on the screen.

Using the mouse the Library staff can click on any item of their interest and information on the particular subject will automatically appear on the screen. Penguin India, Foundation Books, Allied Publishers, Springer, Kluwer and other publishers are tied up in the web to help book lovers while placing orders for books and subscribing journals through on-line.Internet application – Technical section: A subscriber/teacher/library staff can use the on-line catalogues for selecting recent editions of books. The Librarian can send an order via Internet whether to Penguin India or Informatics or any other related publisher and avail discounts too. It also provides instant information for library executives regarding the subscription of journals; sending reminders for missing issues and informing payment clearances.

Internet application – Reference section

The Academic library especially at the University level associates with outstanding scholars who expect ready made information like SDI. To satisfy them every librarian should maintain close contact with professional and non-professional bodies like INSDOC and INFLIBNET –INFONET etc., The staff should refer various types of information sources available on Internet. They may be commercial databases, open access databases, licensed databases and full text articles of journals.

ADVANTAGES IN BRIEF

Internet can be convenient and efficient in the context of desktop automation; Internet is purely a paperless tool in the communication chain;Internet as network medium disposes of transmission delays imposed by geographical distance.Internet does not cost much;Internet can shrink social as well as geographical distance;Internet can support and sustain academic interests of the research community.

INFORMATION COMMUNICATIONS TECHNOLOGY – CREATING NETWORKS WITH GROWING REACH

It involves rapid advances in two technologies – digital storage and processing of information and satellite and optical fibre transmission of information– are creating new and faster ways of storing, handling, distributing and accessing information. These innovations enable the processing and storage of enormous amount of information, along with rapid distribution information through communication networks. For example in 2001 more information can be sent over a single cable in a second than in 1997 was sent over the entire internet in a month.

Linking computing devices and allowing them to communicate with each other creates networked information systems based on a common protocol. Individuals, households and institutions are linked in processing and executing a huge number of instructions in imperceptible time spans. This radically alters access to information and the structure of communication extending the networked reach to all corners of the world.

TECHNOLOGICAL TRANSFORMATIONS

Today's technological transformations are intertwined with another transformation, globalization and together they are creating a new paradigm – the network age. These transformations expand opportunities and increase the social and economic rewards of creating and using technology. They are also altering how and by whom technology is created and owned, and how it is made accessible and used. Technology is not inherently good or bad the outcome depends on how it is used.

SOME INITIATIVES IN IT SECTOR

The Department of Information Technology has setup Community Centre (CICs) at 487 blocks in the seven North Eastern States 9 Arunachal Pradesh, Assam, manipur, Meghalaya, Mizoram, Nagaland, Tripura) and Sikkim to provide connectivity at the block level and thus promote application of Information Technology for accelerating socio economic development of the region.

INFORMATION TECHNOLOGY ACT

The Government of India has created the necessary legal and administrative framework through the enactment of the Information Technology Act, 2000. While on the one hand it seeks to create the public key infrastructure for electronic authentication through digital signatures.

DIGITAL LIBRARY

Digital Libraries are a form of information Technology in which social impact matters as much as technological advancements. Future knowledge networks will rely on scalable semantics, to automatically indexing the community collections so that users can effectively search of billion repositories.

NATIONAL INFORMATION CENTRE (NIC)

It provides informatics services for decision support to government offices/ bodies at national, state, district and block levels. It offers network services. NIC also provides video conferencing facilities.

INFORMATION TECHNOLOGY USE IN LIBRARY MANAGEMENT SYSTEM

The IT revolution has also embraud the library system. A massive and rapid computerization process throughout the levels of the library system has made IT an integral part of the library management scene in many countries all over the world. The incorporation of IT into the day-to-day activity of libraries has a strong impact on virtually every aspect of their management processes. Although there is no agreed definition of IT, the term "IT" includes three main components – *management information system* (MIS) or *decision support system* (DSS), hardware, and human factors. A management information system is the set of structure and procedures that govern the collection, processing, analysis, presentation and use of information within an organization.

IMPACT OF ICTS IN LIBRARIES

Technology is changing the nature of libraries and librarians, and it continues to exert a major influence on the strategic direction of libraries in society. Today the library services are transitioning from local traditional collections to global resources provided on demand via the most advanced networking technologies.

DIGITAL DATA STORAGE IN LIBRARIES

Digital data storage media for storing digital data are constantly being developed, improved or superseded, and any discussion of them here can only be taken as description of the current situation i. e., optical discs, magnetic media, other media for digital data storage. The concept of the "digital library" evolved out of potential for digitization of all forms of media: print, image, sound, complex data sets, and computer simulations of non-time-bound sequences, otherwise not demonstrable events, etc., and retrieving them in context of multiple networked information systems.

The digital library often serves as a multidimensional catalogue or index to bring together the resource discovery information of every resource that was topically, creatively, or by reason of other connections generatively related. A digital library does not only consist of digitized and digitally born information resources, but also of electronic metadata on non-digital objects. Digital Data: Considerable attention is now being paid to the possibility of converting the intellectual content of items in library collection into digital data by electronic means and storing it on magnetic tapes or discs. Both textual and pictorial information can be converted. For example by using optical character recognition devices which convert texts into their digital code equivalent, or by using scanners to convert text or, more usually, pictures into an analogue form.

Text can also be input by keyboarding. In addition to information already in another format being converted to digital format, much information is now originated in digital form and may appear only in that form in the library. Digital data have considerable advantages. They can be rapidly duplicated and speedily transmitted without deterioration through electronic communications networks to whatever the user is working. Storage: It is a mainly technical requirement, although new media may complicate storage decisions and costing. Today's large digital repositories use multiple level of mass storage media and mechanical robots to locate and mount the media.

Phases of Digitization: Undoubtedly, digital media will have to co-exit with print media. Different kinds of collection could be digitized at different times depending on the priorities of the library. To start with, any one type of collection, for example, important out of print publications could be made available in digital form. Feedback of its usage can be sengut and analyzed. In the next phase, another type of data could be converted into digital form. Digitization Process: Digitization is a process of converting paper documents to electronic format. Scanning process does the conversion.

Digital information can be transmitted and received anywhere in the world where the infrastructure to send and received is in place. Due to the implementation of the IT, the librarian need to be well aware of the technical issues, potential problems involved, trained manpower available, the hardware required, document management systems, *optical character recognization* (OCR) technology for implementing digitization of the collection and services. As been know the concept of digital library is growing very fast globally. It is a welcome trained that various institutions and professional societies are involved to provide opportunities for the library and librarians to upgrade and enhance the professional knowledge about digital library. Various important aspects like digital libraries issues, architecture, electronic publishing, collection building, storage, organization, transmission of digital information, creation and use of hypertext and hypermedia system, networks and their implications, manpower development etc. We are in the early stage of a transmition from a print-based to a digital society.

The latest technologies offer cheap computer processing power, cheap mass storage, inexpensive and ubiquitous access to high speed networks and retrieval devices give us the ability to create, to manipulate, to storage and especially to transfer large quantities of information in digital form at low costs. Digital information can be stored on any medium that is able to represent binary digits 0 and 1.

Conversion from the conventional storage to digitized format required discrete analysis as the primary function, based on user electronic storage and retrieval system. Some of the common digitized storage media that are presently used world over are the Hyper books, CD-ROM, Multimedia. New media are constantly being developed. Some that are still in experimental stages or have been only very recently introduced are digital videotape, digital audiotape and digital paper.

LIBRARIES AND INFORMATION UNITS

We are living to-day in a world of change and the changes we see all around us due to availability of information quicker than before, faster communication through E-mail, voice mail and video conferencing and the great influence of the Internet and web pages. The use of computer-based system in the libraries and information units is now commonplace all over the world. Computers are used to assist in a variety of functions such as maintaining and providing access to the catalogue of items in the collection, managing the issuing and returning of items from the collection, the acquisition of new items for the collection, controlling the serial publications and allowing the retrieval of information from the databases relating to bibliographic data financial or numeric data or the full text of documents.

DIGITAL INITIATIVES AT J.N.N. COLLEGE OF ENGINEERING LIBRARY

It is experienced that Bar-coding has revolutioned the library activities globally. A Laser Barcode printer was purchased and Bar-coding software was also installed. The Bar-coding labels for each book were generated.

BAR-CODING OF BOOKS

Printing barcode labels and pasting in three places of each book, *viz.*, Title page, Secrete page and due date slip were entrusted with a contractor. This generating of Bar-coding labels and pasting the labels for all 53,500 volumes were completed within five months. Retrieving of information through barcode labels using barcode scanner was tested. The computer displayed the Accession Number and the relevant bibliographic information was retrieved from the book database. The bibliographic information includes Accession Number, Author, Title, Call Number, Publisher and Keywords.

BAR-CODED IDENTITY CARDS

The work of bar-coding of identity cards for all users J.N.N. College of Engineering. College was entrusted to the Frontier Information Technology, Secundarbad. The identity card contains the attributes: Class, Dept, Eligibility, Valid up to, Blood group, Residential address, residence phone number. A stamp size photo of each member was scanned and printed on each card. Both Librarian and Principal are signed on this ID card. The identity cards looked good rather than the old traditional plastic card. Each user used to carry this card and produce the same in the issue counter along with the books and get it issued. Now user feels happy in handling this bar-coded identity card. They also feel proud in producing the same card wherever he visits either inside the college or outside the campus.

NETWORKING AND MANPOWER TRAINING

J. N. N. College of Engineering, Library is a member of the DELNET. The users of the library access the resources listed in this network through the net connectivity. The library staff had their sufficient training at Frontier Information Technology, Secundarbad on various divisions of the library such as Acquisition, Cataloguing, Circulation and Periodicals control. They received special training with regard to preparation of Bar-coded identity card. Various processes include:

- Scanning of the User's Photo.
- Printing the photo in the special art paper using the colour printer.
- Composing various fields, *viz.*, name class, branch, valid up to, eligibility, blood group, residential address, residence phone.
- Laminating the above paper using laminating machine.
- Books issue through scanner.
- Books return through scanner.

Our Library staffs were sent to nearest libraries to have practical exposure towards developing of barcoded identity cards. J.N.N. College of Engineering Library staff underwent hands on training nearest libraries studied the system form all perspectives. The hands on training assisted the Library staff to develop the barcode identity cards. For this purpose the following equipments have been identified.

- Digital camera.
- Colour printer.
- Scanner.

J. N. N. College of Engineering Library staff has also studied various operations in DRTC Library, Bangalore.

DIGITAL ASSETS

- Floppies: Certain Books are accompanying floppies; such floppies are assigned the concerned Book Accession Numbers. These floppies are arranged serially and kept in the floppy boxes. J.N.N. College of Engineering Library has 200 floppies. Users lend and read these floppies in OPAC systems.

- CDs: Some new books contain CDs also. Such CDs are assigned the Concerned accession Number and kept in CD container. There are about 1,400 CDs available in Library. Users refer these CDs through OPAC system.
- Software used in J.N.N. College of Engineering: There was one software, which was developed by one programmer of computer science Dept. It had some limitations. Now, 'LIBRIS SOFTWARE' has been purchased and installed. This software put into use.
- LAN: Local Area Network was established by connecting all 6 systems in Library with a Main Server. Each system was connected Ethernet and Win proxy Card through Co-Axial cables.
- UPS: An UPS was purchased and connected with all 6 terminals in the Library.
- Computers: There are 7 computers available in the Library. PC's Configuration: -
  - Pentium III/650 MHZ and above, 512 KB internal and external
  - Cache memory 815 E-Intel
  - Chipset motherboard 128 MB SD RAM.
  - Minimum 17.1 GB/HDD IDE Drive.
  - 1.44 MB FDD, 32 Bit Graphic Card 52*CD Drive, 17 inch Colour
  - Monitor with electronic turner and energy saving windows
  - Keyboard, Logitech Mouse, ATX Cabinet with preloaded and O.S.Windows 95/98.
- Printers: There are one Dot Matrix and one Laser Printer available in the Library.
- Bar-Code Printer: One Bar-Code Printer is also printing in barcode labels in Laser Printer was purchased along with 2,500 Book Barcode sheets and 5000 ID Barcode Label Sticker Sheets.
- Book Database: A book database was created with 53,500 records. Bibliographic information about each Access No. Title, Author, Call Number, Keywords, Publisher, Price, etc.
- Periodical Database: A periodical database was created entering all current journal's bibliographic information. The data entry for receipt of periodicals is being entered into computer. Reminders for non-receipt of periodicals is taken as print out and sent to the periodical suppliers.

ADVANTAGES

Computerization of Library operations saves much time of the Library Staff and users. Students and Staff members feel happy to handle Bar-coded Membership Card. Bar-coding facilities stock verification of books and journals.

DRAWBACKS

Since we implement computerization, our library staff does dual job entering all operations manually and through computer. Staff finds this as a job. In the beginning it may be do their, jobs through computer only. During power failure time, staff face problems to operate computer. These problems can be solved using UPS. An UPS* was purchased and connected to all systems in the library. This UPS solves power problem up to some extent.

HOW TO IMPLEMENT IN FUTURE

Our library staff will prepare bar-coded identity cards for fresh students in future using the barcode equipments. Similarly barcode labels will be generated and pasted in three places of each new book purchased in future. Stock verification will be done online using the barcode scanner in future.

PURCHASING CD CABINET

To preserve CDs it is proposed to purchase a CD Cabinet. All CDs will be serially arranged and kept in proper order. Whenever a user requires particular CD, Library Staff can provide the same for reference purpose.

ROLE OF OPEN SOURCE IN HIGHER EDUCATION

WHAT IS OPEN SOURCE

Traditionally, a programme is defined as a set of instructions which tells a computer what to do. For example, the Windows operating system by Microsoft is a programme, or a set of instructions, which tells the user's computer how to send information to the disk drive, how to take information from the user, and how to communicate with pieces of hardware such as the modem or the network card. However, these programmes are compiled, which means that they are translated into the binary code which the computer understands. The lines of instructions, which are translated into the binary code, are called the source code of the programme. If a user or a programmer has access to the source code behind the programme, then the user is able to alter the programme, changing the way that it works.

For most proprietary, or closed source, programmes, the source code is not available for users or programmers to alter. This means that if a user encounters a bug in the closed source programme, they will not be able to fix it themselves, but must rely on the software vendor to fix the error. As many frustrated users know, this can often take a very long time. Open source software, by contrast, is software for which the source code is freely available. The web server Apache, for example, is a programme which runs as many as two-thirds of the web servers on the Internet. Apache is open source, which means that anyone can access the source code for Apache and make changes in how the programme works.

OPEN SOURCE PLAIN AND SIMPLE

Open source software (OSS) refers to software programmes that are distributed with the source codehence open source. The open source license allows users the freedom to run the programme for any purpose, to study and modify the programme, and to freely redistribute copies of the original or modified programme.

Open source is a way of building software

Open source software is often constructed using the same time-tested methodologies and practices used to construct proprietary software. However there are a number of interesting differences that result from the difference in rights conferred by the license:

- The software evolves more rapidly and organically. Many individuals and teams working in parallel produce advances beyond the capacity of a single team. The improvements are managed into releases by a core team much like the proprietary alternative.
- Users' needs are rapidly met as the OSS model harnesses their collective expertise and contribution. Improvements to the software are often contributed by users who have fixed a problem or added new features.
- New versions are released very often and rely on the community of users and developers to test it, resulting in superior quality software tested on more platforms, and in more environments than most commercial software.
- The development "team" is often largely volunteers, distributed, many in numbers, and diverse. Often, paid members of the development team will manage the project and organize the work of the volunteers.
- Security is enhanced because the code is exposed to the world. In proprietary packages, shortcuts and poor programming are more easily overlooked because only a select few see the code. Like peer reviewed papers, open source code is subject to much greater scrutiny and thus produces a higher calibre result.

Open Source is a Way of doing Business

Open source is often thought of as free software. In fact, one of the benefits is that anyone can use, modify, and redistribute the software without a license fee. While the code is free, the benefits have much more to do with the freedoms than the cost. On the surface it may appear that free software is in opposition to the 'business' of software and, while the open source model challenges the traditional models, open source represents great opportunity for customers and businesses alike. Without the restrictions of a proprietary software license, any institution or company with the skills can use the software to solve their own needs or offer products and services of value to others. Businesses based on open source software typically add value by:

- Offering services such as implementation, training, and support;
- Packaging and integrating open source software to make its installation and use easier for a wider market;
- Creating complementary, add-on, or enhanced software for sale. Open source affords institutions, as consumers of software, unparalleled control over the use of software to meet business demands and control over where they deploy their budget dollars. Taking into consideration its core competencies and available resources, an institution may use its own people and resources, hire external resources, or partner to share costs. The principles of open source software-freedom to run the programme for any purpose, to study and modify the programme, and to freely redistribute copies and modifications-are simple, yet have powerful and far reaching implications.

COMPARISON TO PROPRIETARY SOFTWARE

One of the great misconceptions about open source is that it is an alternative to commercial software. Rather, open source software is an alternative to proprietary software, but often acquired through or supported by a company-in other words commercial. Fundamentally, the difference between open source and proprietary software has to do with control. Where the open source license imparts freedoms to use, modify, and redistribute the software, the proprietary license restricts use, modification, distribution, and more. Vendors of proprietary software restrict access to and use of the source code because the source is knowledge-and knowledge is power.The open source license corrects the balance of power between producers and consumers of software. Access to the source code is about freedom and choice. After all, most of us aren't software engineers-we can't start adding features and fixing bugs just because we have access. Yet access to the source code is important to all of us because access is control. Open source clearly offers advantages for the consumer, but it also represents a significant competitive advantage to companies that adopt compatible strategies. IBM, HP, Sun Microsystems, Apple Computer, Red Hat, Novell, and many other companies attribute significant revenue from strategies built on commercialization of open source software. Mainstream press coverage of open source has been accelerating all over the world, but the press coverage in higher education has been nothing short of explosive in recent months. Vendors of proprietary software have been carefully crafting their powerful and influential messages about open source. Some attempt to categorize open source as something applicable to research and experimentation. Others cast open source as comparable to open standards. Still others warn about considering open source software for mission critical applications. Each of these messages uses generalizations that distort the truth. Let's examine some of the important attributes and how open source and proprietary approaches compare:

ATTRIBUTE OPEN SOURCE PROPRIETARY

License Licensed to provide freedom to use for any purpose, modify, and redistribute.Licensed to restrict use to "acceptable uses", protect against modification and redistribution.Control Balanced. Consumers and providers of commercial offerings have equal access. Vendor is in control. Often large up-front investments in the software, training, and other implementation costs create a lock-in situation that strips the consumer of control. Innovation Rapid and diverse. Leverages a very large community of users and developers working in parallel. Limited to vendor investments. Typically caters to the features sought by the largest audience. Low levels of innovation. Longevity/ Risk of abandonmentSoftware will always be available as long as it serves a useful purpose. The larger the adoption the safer the investment. No single point of failure. Dependent on the success of the vendor. Single point of failure.Security and reliability As the great tradition of peer review produces high quality academic and scientific works, open source projects produce software that is generally more secure and reliable. Like peer reviewed papers, open source software is subject to greater scrutiny and leverages a larger collective intelligence than proprietary software. *Total cost of ownership* (TCO) Acquisition cost Low or no initial license cost. License costs on the rise in education. Implementation and support costs OS community support and competition for commercial support keeps costs low.

Choice allows consumer to bear costs internally which may further decrease cost. Costs determined by and coupled to vendor. Lack of choice. Alternative service organizations often lead to higher costs. Costs of scale No additional license cost with additional users, servers, etc. License costs generally rise with increased use. Platform support Broader platform and server support increases leveraged investments in existing institutional infrastructure. Platform support limited to what the vendor offers. May not fit well with institutional infrastructure. As we can see from the comparison, open source promises some impressive advantages over proprietary software. While open source has a rich history in education, a recent convergence of powerful drivers and enablers are precipitating a strong movement towards open source in higher education.

ROLE OF OPEN SOURCE IN HIGHER EDUCATION

Open source is changing the nature of the software business in many settings, but the movement is particularly impressive in education. While open source has nearly a 20 year history of success producing leading software, it has mostly been in the infrastructure domain-the protocol implementations, servers, development frameworks, and utilities that enable the e-mail programmes, browsers, and other applications we all depend on. Open source has not been a significant model for producing application software-until recently. In the past few years colleges and universities have begun to produce enterprise open source applications like course management systems and electronic portfolios that compete directly with their proprietary counterparts. These e-learning applications are leading a movement in higher education from proprietary software towards open source. A snapshot of the current proprietary software environment in education reveals some compelling drivers.

- Tight budgets have focused attention on software acquisition costs, and total cost of ownership
- Growing resentment of vendor power, particularly in the wake of price increases and licensing changes that many institutions felt powerless to reject.
- Lack of innovation. Learning technology has not lived up to its potential to improve learning. and some enablers of a more effective model:
- Collaboration technology has made large-scale collaborative work across institutional, geographic, and cultural boundaries more effective.
- Software design patterns, development technologies, and standards have evolved in a way that facilitates modular, interoperable software components.
- Proven business models and education focused companies that embrace open source.
- Strong cultural appeal of open source in academia

We observe many of these drivers and enablers beyond the context of higher education. Perhaps the cultural appeal in academia represents the 'tipping point' for a powerful movement unique to colleges and universities. At the heart of the cultural fit between academia and open source are common philosophy and values. Creating and sharing knowledge for public good is a key part of the mission of colleges and universities, and a core part of the philosophy driving open source software. Colleges and universities are also home to some of the best software engineers in the world. Yet most institutions don't have a plentiful supply of available talent to meet evolving needs-individually. The open source model provides colleges and universities a way to leverage cultural values of collaboration and sharing to gather resources and work together for the common good. Unlike contexts outside of education, working together doesn't blur institutional brand or threaten a school's income. As a result, higher education not only boasts some of the best software engineers, but also has a plentiful supply of willing talent- a critical success factor for open source. A common challenge to developing software is understanding the needs of the users and turning that understanding into a suitable software design. While there are many different approaches and software methodologies, the open source model clearly has an advantage since the individuals most involved in teaching and learning are deeply involved in the development of the software for teaching and learning.

Another critical success factor for open source is the emergence of education-focused companies that embrace open source as the preferred model for business. Although colleges and universities are well suited to develop world class enterprise software, supporting that software for other institutions isn't an activity that helps fulfill their mission. A new ecology has emerged where commercial organizations, colleges, and universities play complimentary and collaborative roles. The Andrew W. Mellon foundation, the William and Flora Hewlett Foundation, and others have recognized the need and the potential and have made considerable financial resources available to seed open source projects and help create the new ecology. While there are literally thousands of active open source projects all over the world addressing most application domains, there are a number of notable projects particularly interesting for institutions of higher education.

LIBRARY APPLICATION IN ENCODING METHODOLOGY

An essential component of any library application is an encoding methodology that allows computers to process characters and symbols used to represent language information in written form. For years the encoding mechanism was not developed under a unified umbrella nor did it reach various languages equally. Without a standard unified character code, users have to use different software and terminals to display or enter data in different languages, especially when dealing with more than a few scripts. The international library community began developing large multilingual digital libraries in the 1990s. Language representation is a particular concern for major research libraries, whose collections may include materials in as many as 400 written languages. Standards for record structure and character sets were established long before either Unicode or the Internet was created. Hundreds of millions of bibliographic records exist around the world in variations of the MARC format, although in multiple character-set-encoding formats and multiple forms of transliteration. USMARC was implemented with the *American Library Association* (ALA) character set, which extends the English language keyboard to include diacritics from major Roman-script languages. The ALA character set is used by *Online Computer Library Center* (OCLC), the largest bibliographic utility in the world, and by most American library applications; languages not included in the ALA character set tend to be transliterated. The increasing interest in adapting USMARC and other forms of MARC to Unicode reflects the fact that other systems will have to accommodate the huge quantity of

MARC records that already exist in other character-set formats. The Library of Congress – which contributes its records in digital form to OCLC, to RLG and to other cooperatives in Europe and elsewhere – has done original-script cataloguing for the JACKPHY languages since the early 1980s. RLG pioneered the ability to encode the JACKPHY languages in their original-script form for bibliographic records, using available script specific standards. The Library of Congress, OCLC, RLG, and other bibliographic utilities around the world exchange records encoded in full-script form. Libraries took a long-term view of their data, capturing and representing non-Roman characters in their fullest form many years before search and display technologies were widely available. Full vernacular script in these records can be printed on catalogue cards, but until very recently scripts could only be displayed on computers with special equipment.

Even though JACKPHY records from OCLC, RLG, and other sources are loaded into the online catalogues of individual libraries, most applications only support searching the transliterated forms. Integrated library automation software that supports Unicode is becoming more widely available, thus allowing records in non-Roman scripts to be displayed on most terminals and computers. The Library of Congress has implemented a new integrated library system that incorporates Unicode, enabling them to display their JACKPHY records on public terminals in full form.

Previously, these records were viewable only through other systems outside the Library of Congress. The international library community is more and more concerned about multilingual, multi-script data exchange as new regions of the world come online. The European Union is promoting Unicode and is funding projects to support Unicode implementation in library automation. In the mid 1990s, Borgman conducted a study of six countries in Central and Eastern Europe each with its own national language and character set, found that a variety of coding systems were in use. More than half of the research libraries in the study used Latin2, one used Unicode, and the rest used a national or a system-specific format to encode data; none used the ALA character set.

ACADEMIC LIBRARY STRUCTURES

Organisational structure can be defined as "one of the interrelated components that define any organisation referring to the definition of individual jobs and their relationship to each other as depicted in organisational charts and job descriptions." It clarifies how information is distributed, and jobs are organised. For decades the hierarchical structure of management was regarded as the most efficient way of managing an organisation. This system worked well in and environment where the future was predictable and librarians were in the driving seat. Hierarchies were not designed to foster creativity and lead workers to self-fulfilment.

It is therefore very difficult to introduce fundamental change within hierarchical structures which are naturally resistant to change. In an effort to bring about reorganisation within organisations institutions try to either modify the existing hierarchical structure or replace it with something else. Deming as cited by Mullins states that management systems still prevalent today have had a destructive impact on people. According to Deming "people are born with intrinsic motivation, self-esteem, dignity, curiosity to learn... " Qualities such as these are undermined by a management style that reward top achievers and punish those that do worse. Managers that exhibit such management styles use disapproval as a negative control measure. This approach leads to a climate where staff performance is primarily directed at pleasing their superiors and that inevitably lead to average performance.

According to researcher managers have a natural tendency to maintain the status quo. They would instinctively fall back on models and practices that worked in the past. The volatile nature and unpredictability of information services is forcing managers to adopt new management styles. It is beginning to dawn on people that the bureaucratic way of management is becoming outdated and that change will be more effectively achieved through education, sharing, motivation, teamwork and coaching.

Moran states that unprecedented change has forced managers to re-evaluate structures. Customary practices designed to maintain organisational stability are being questioned. To cope with change, organisations have started flattening structures to induce more flexibility within those organisations. These new structures being adopted have decreased levels of hierarchy, increased flexibility and resulted in diminishing boundaries between departments.

Issues to Consider when Introducing New Structures

Management theorists are very reluctant to prescribe to a particular structural model but advise that structure should rather be designed to meet organisational needs and goals. Organisations should try and learn as much as possible from others who have implemented organisational change. They should never introduce a structure simply because it is being used elsewhere but always to meet specific organisational needs. Of cardinal importance is to determine how people within the organisation will adopt the new structure. Researcher shares the following points learnt from a process of restructuring:

Before implementing a process of restructuring it is important to have clear vision, goals and objectives with the focus on service delivery. It is useful to establish a core team to lead the restructuring process. It is vitally important that senior management support the process, e.g., a deputy vice-chancellor. It is important to involve the entire staff component, listen to their inputs and concerns since ownership by the staff is vital for successful change implementation. Staff development programmes should be part of the process to prepare staff for new functions or roles they may be involved in. After implementation it is important to critically analise the performance of the academic library within the new structure. Managers often do not adapt easily to the flatter less bureaucratic structures that are generally being adopted. Even staff members at lower levels experience this problem. Generally it is very difficult to introduce change that goes against prevailing organisational culture. Proper planning is needed to take the organisation from the existing structure to the new one.

Employee input in developing such a strategy is crucial. Research indicates that organisational transformation had been most successful in scenarios where employees had maximum input. Finally evaluation is necessary after change implementa-tion to determine its success. In reorganised libraries structures are always flatter resulting in manager's roles reverting from directing to coordinating. The prime purpose of reorganisation is to create a more effective organisation. Reorganisation results in academic libraries becoming learning organisations.

The learning organisation is characterised by staff empowerment, is team based, decentralised, practices participative management and information sharing. In the learning organisation the person closest to a problem has the responsibility and authority to deal with it. Tom Wilson as cited by Moran states that the academic library is in bad need of reconstruction. To Wilson academic libraries were essentially designed to manage physical artifacts. The rise of the Internet has completely transformed the way information is created, distributed and accessed.

The e-journal is a typical example. Johansen and Swigart as cited by Moran states "we had outlived the usefulness of models from the Industrial era but don't yet have robust organisational models for the information era". It is therefore of paramount importance that academic librarians continuously re-evaluate current structures and through an experimental process adopt new models. Moran states that for people who advocate restructuring there is good and bad news. The good news is that people understand that technological change will compel fundamental organisational change. The bad news is that there is a lack of urgency. Generally organisational change appears to be incremental rather than radical.

IMPACT OF ICT CHANGE ON ACADEMIC IBRARIES

The Internet has made information access and retrieval both simplistic and complex. Information retrieval systems are being designed to suit the needs of end users and therefore try to simplify the process. Simultaneously however the user is overwhelmed with so much information resources and choices that the process becomes complex. This creates a situation where the users need skills and knowledge in terms of search strategies and conceptualisation.

Herrington is of the opinion that information literacy instruction at the point of need can be very effective. Wood and Walther is of the opinion that unlike popular believe the Internet will not completely replace the skills of professional librarians but rather make them indispensable.

Changes in the Job Description of Academic Librarians

An overview of the core competencies required by academic library and information workers gives one an idea of how dramatically information and communications technology has changed the library profession.

Cheng identifies the following core competencies needed by the future librarian:

- Good communication skills.
- Should be more than just computer literate and should have a good understanding of ICT and its relation to information resources.
- Should have an in-depth understanding of organisational and user needs that is research based and should organise library resources to satisfy those needs.
- Competent in Web publishing techniques.
- Skilled in manipulating metadata to organise digital information.
- Skilled in training users in the use of e-resources.
- Skilled in filtering, evaluating and appraising Internet information.

Researchers identifies another quality required, an in-depth understanding of what information resources are available on the Internet, as well as insight in terms of its reliability and scope.

The Changing Nature of the Academic Library

ICT is busy transforming the nature of academic libraries. A variety of terms such as hybrid, digital and virtual library are used to refer to the academic library. A digital library can be defined as "a managed collection of information, with associated services, where the information is stored in digital formats and accessible over a network".

The virtual library has been defined as "remote access to the contents and services of libraries and other information resources, combining an on-site collection of current and heavily used materials in both print and electronic form, with an electronic network which provides access to, and delivery from, external worldwide library and commercial information and knowledge sources". Hybrid libraries are libraries that provide access to both electronic resources and paper-based resources. From the definitions it is clear that most of today's academic libraries fall in either the hybrid or virtual category. The library of the future is unlikely to be a physical entity as we know it but would probably be a Web portal providing access to information. The emphasis will be on access to information rather than physical ownership. Akeroyd supports this view and states that as a physical space entity the library, as we know it is unlikely to prevail in a digital environment. One reason for this is that because of Web access the digital library is accessible from anywhere.

Changes in the Information Seeking Behaviour of Users

Academic librarians have a good understanding of the tremendous value of printed and electronic resources available to students at academic libraries. Academic library users do not necessarily share this insight. New generation academic library users have a preference for Web resources rather than visiting the library. Research done on undergraduate engineering students in 2004 revealed that they would turn to the Internet as the primary resource for information for their projects. Moyo refers to a scenario where users were asked what they expect from an academic library service.

They responded as follows:

- All resources should be available in full text and be printable.
- The library service should be fast and easily accessible.
- 24/7 availability of a virtual reference service.
- Wish to do all library transactions online.
- Web resources that is easy to use and Web search engines that meet information needs.

What is clear is that new generation academic library users prefer the convenience of digital access above reliance on assistance from librarians. This preference for the Internet poses a serious challenge to the academic library which has to move from a paradigm of the library as a physical entity to a library where the users do not have to come to physically to make use of it's services. Electronic access to information resources does have many advantages, e.g.:

- Multiple access which implies more that one user can access a resource simultaneously.
- Lots of resources are available in full text.
- 24/7 access which means users can access resources remotely, e.g., from off campus or from dormitories.

One of the disadvantages of remote access from an academic library point of view is that users are not always aware of the fact that they are using library resources. One user stated: "No, I don't need to use the library, I use Internet resources". Despite the apparent preference for digital content the need for access to high quality digital content remains constant. Greater cooperation between library and faculty is necessary to develop ways to connect users and high quality digital materials.

IMPACT OF ICT ON COLLECTION MANAGEMENT

Collection development can be defined as the selection and acquisition of library materials based on current and potential user needs. Collection management goes beyond this. It is concerned with managing the utilisation, storage and accessibility of a collection. Collection development can thus be seen as a subdivision of collection management. Academic librarians find themselves in an era of unparalleled access to information. The latest edition of Uhlrich's has indicated the availability of more than 1,72,000 journal titles. Although this appears to be a most ideal situation it is not because the financial resources available in acquisitions departments have not necessarily increased. The sheer volume of information available also makes selection of the most suitable information a complex task. The impact of electronic resources has made collection management a very complex and challenging task. There are budgetary constraints, numerous formats, ever changing user needs. Collection management implies involvement in tasks such as analysis of needs, negotiation of contracts and evaluation of resources. There was a time when the size of an academic library collection determined its stature. At that time the library's resources were generally adequate to meet most of its users needs. Since then the academic library has exchanged the ownership model for an access model where physical location becomes completely irrelevant.

Access versus Ownership

Information and communications technology has had a fundamental impact on library collection development policies. Academic libraries had traditionally applied an ownership or just-in-case approach to collection development. The premise was that users would need the material and make use of it. Having the material available in the library would also provide immediate access to it than having to borrow it from a third party. The cost of maintaining collections and increased demands for more information had forced academic libraries to reconsider the ownership model and adopt another model. Unparalleled price increases and shrinking budgets had ushered in a new model called access or just in time where the focus is to give the user the information that they need when they want it.

Cost

Technically it is more cost effective to produce an e-resource, for example an electronic journal, because the first copy costs are reduced. There is also savings in terms of packaging, delivery and storage. In practice these savings have not lead to reductions in the cost of e-journals. It has been suggested that the academic library adopts a pay-as-you-use approach. This make sense according to research done in 1997 that indicated that 22 per cent of science articles published in 1984 were never cited for the next 10 years. In the social sciences this figure goes up to 48 per cent.

Storage Space

With the access model there is no need for storage space, *e.g.*, back copies. Moahi cites Cooper who states that the storage cost per single copy is between

$25 and $40. Calculations to determine JStor pricing lead to the conclusion that the cost per single volume was between $24 and $41. When costs for re-shelving and maintenance were included, the estimated cost rose to $45 per title per year for a core journal and $180 per title per year for a large research library.

Enhanced Access to Information

One of the benefits of ICT is enhanced access to library services and resources. The academic library can expose its users to a much larger collection than it can house physically because users can access information remotely. With online access it is possible to accurately measure utilisation of e-resources and that is invaluable in determining which resources to purchase. It is easier to search e-resources and access speed is greatly enhanced. Other advantages are that users can simultaneously access the same resource, and there are no incidences of lost copies or mutilated issues. Singh is of the opinion that a paradigm shift is taking place within the academic library as more academic librarians are doing collection management rather that collection development. The focus is rather on interpretation of information rather than selection. Librarians are becoming knowledge managers rather than collection managers.

Digital Preservation of Data

One of the major costs facing the academic library is the cost related to the conversion and preservation of information in digital format. The cost of this process amounts to $1 per page. This does not include the cost relating to the annotation for indexing purposes and the cost of conversion of audio-visual material. One of the problems with converting records into digital image is the fact that the technology used to store these pages as a digital photograph results in large files which have storage implications and place demands on band-with. Funding allocated to preservation of digital material is generally inadequate. This has to do with expectations that the costs of digital preservation over length of time might be very high. It is also difficult to forecast cost in terms of how long to retain digital material in an archive and computer architectures needed to access material. Preservation of digital materials poses many challenges. It is further complicated by the fact that computer technology changes at an unprecedented rate.

There are concerns that changing interfaces, standards, formats and operating systems will render it impossible to read today's computer discs at some point in future. The implication of this is that one needs migration strategies to move data to new operating systems and structures or have scenarios where computers can simulate data structures and operating systems of previous eras. This scenario will make digital preservation prohibitively expensive. A great deal of current research into digital preservation is based on overcoming the technical issues to ensure long-term preservation of digital content. The issue of digital preservation initially came to the fore as an impending crisis. Fears were expressed that large portions of our cultural heritage were in danger of disappearing forever. Examples were cited of Web sites available today that might be gone to-morrow.

Although digital materials are more fragile by nature than analog materials the risk varies within different categories of digital materials. Although it is true that a Web site currently available may disappear overnight, the same does not apply to electronic journals. This realisation has transferred the focus from the immediate rescue notion to an approach that sees digital preservation as part of a carefully planned digital access management process. One way academic libraries can deal with digital preservation is through cooperation. Through cooperation various institutions can share costs. Another advantage would be that it would reduce redundancy. Because of the fragile nature of digital materials libraries cannot put off decisions to preserve digital information *ad infinitum*. Time is of the essence.

Unlike a book that can be repaired or rebound, once a digital file becomes corrupt it may be impossible or prohibitively expensive to restore the data. Another problem facing the academic library is the long-term preservation of digital information. There are questions concerning the long-term stability of digital information stored on disks and tapes. There is the potential of these media deteriorating over a period of time. Another way digital preservation is approached is by letting the vendors do the preservation. These days there are also escrow repositories, e.g. Elsevier has agreed to provide the National Library of Netherlands with a copy of Science Direct which the National Library will maintain and make available should Elsevier be unable to do so.

ELECTRONIC RESOURCES

ICT has fundamentally changed academic library collections. Forever gone is the era when an academic library's physical collection determined its stature. In the modern networked technological era the emphasis has shifted from ownership of physical resources to access to electronic resources that are globally accessible.

Internet Information

There are huge amounts of unedited information on the Internet. There are countless Web sites and no single listing of them all. There is also the phenomenon of Web sites disappearing overnight that create problems in terms of access.

The Invisible Web

Academic library users make use of search engines such as Google and Altavista to find information on the Web. As a result they are only exposed to a small portion of the Web called the 'Publicly Indexable Web' These students are only exposed to Web pages accessible via hyperlinks. Search engines do not index Web pages that requires authentication or Web pages behind search forms. The Web consists of two components namely the 'Publicly Indexable Web' also referred to as the visible Web and the invisible Web. The invisible Web refers to all those information resources available yet not indexed by conventional search engines yet accessible via the Web.

Masses of information available via the invisible Web are found in subject databases. Most of the databases that academic libraries make available to their users resort under the invisible Web, e.g. EbscoHost and Eric. Conventional search engines can find databases such as EbscoHost but cannot access them. Search engines can only find content that was indexed by their software called spiders or crawlers. The problem is that they only index Web content available in formats such as HTML and PDF. Michael K. Bergman in year 2000 in a paper on the invisible Web for an Internet Search Company called Bright Planet suggests that the invisible Web is 500 times larger that the visible Web with approximately 550 billion documents.

The Issue of Quality of Resources Available on the Visible Web

The Internet had become a very important research tool for academic endeauvour. Slaouti as cited by Stapleton notes that the relevance and importance of the Web as a research tool should not be underestimated. There is a stark contrast in the way resources are published on the Web versus traditional publishing. In the traditional print environment publishing generally was done by a publisher hence a controlled environment that impacted on quality as well as the scope of the audience being reached. The open nature of the Web, the development of sophisticated search engines, browsers, Web creation and publishing software and easy access to networks via low cost connectivity has developed the Web into a tool that can be easily utilised by the masses for publishing purposes, people who were formally shut out of the publishing process. This has lead to a flood of Web publications of variable quality. During the 1990's library scholars recognised this dilemma and suggested criteria to evaluate Internet resources, *e.g.*, authority, purpose, coverage and objectivity and accessibility. These days a single search can yield hundreds of thousands of items. The unfiltered nature of Web resources has made evaluation of these resources essential. One often finds that unlike in traditional printed media, e-resources found on the Web often lack important criteria such as author or date. Web pages because of its non-linear textual nature has added new effects to the search process such as sound, videos and access to thousands of items by clicking a mouse. These new elements imply that new sets of skills are required on the part of the researcher.

Reference Works

According to Moyo reference statistics in academic libraries are plunging. At the same time electronic access of these resources are increasing. This tendency can be ascribed to the fact that users can access these resources remotely via the Internet. Internet connectivity and e-resources had become absolutely essential for the new reference service paradigm. One of the key elements of e-reference service success is that the service is available at the point of need. The tremendous growth in the use of online reference works has created a need within the academic library to develop services to support this type of service.

Academic libraries are turning to on-line real time reference tools also referred to as ORR to support students remotely. The Pen State University library has more than 300 databases that students may access. On-line real time reference support is used to assist students at the point of need. E-reference works share all the benefits of e-resources, e.g., 24/7 remote accessibility, concurrent access for multiple users and the potential for online updating to keep content up to date. Electronic communication had become the primary mode of communication in e-reference services. Online chat had become the method of choice. Some e-reference application providers have added *Voice over IP* (VOIP) to their products which enable voice dialogue with the library user.

E-reference services have many advantages, e.g.:

- Availability via the Internet.
- Service at the point of need.
- Easy for people who are unable to come to the academic library, e.g., the physically disabled.

Moyo cites Stormont who states that online real time reference support is very labour intensive. In order to cope academic libraries have adopted a distributed staffing model where the load of the service is shared among various libraries.

E-Journals

The e-journal can be defined as "a version of the traditional print or paper-based journal which is disseminated electronically in some form or other directly to the end user." Although e-journals had been in existence since 1976 it became prominent during the 1990's. Since it's inception in 1665 the printed journal remained the primary vehicle for communication among academics and researchers. The advent of the Internet transformed publishing radically as it made it possible to publish cheaply. Internet also made access universally available. Because of the Internet academics and researchers became more creative and productive.

Cost Factors

There had been major increases in the cost of journal subscriptions during the last two decades. According to researcher between 1986 and 1996 the average increase per journal subscription had been a whopping 147 per cent. This state of affairs had been laid at the door of the commercial publishers.

Moahi states that simultaneously there had been a significant increase in the number of science and engineering journals published. Because of ever decreasing budgets academic libraries are unable to purchase the titles they deem necessary. Falk cites McCabe of Georgia Institute of Technology stating that publishers offer libraries bundled packages of e-journals under the pretense that it is cheaper but these deals actually inflate prices.

Moahi is of the opinion that a consequence of these bundled deals is that academic libraries end up with titles they do not want or need. Despite the fact that publishers have substantial cost savings on first copy production of e-journals and also save on distribution costs, these savings are not passed onto their customers. Cost of e-journals tend to be similar or higher that their printed counterparts. What further complicate matters are the fact that provision has to be made for connectivity and desktops, which means additional costs. Aggregate publishers also tend to drop titles without prior consultation with academic librarians.

Academic Library's Response to Publishers

Despite general expectations that e-journals should be cheaper than printed versions publishers maintain the status quo by maximizing profits. Publisher's attitudes have forced academic institutions to take a tougher stance against them. Recently the Senate of the University of California instructed the library to sever all ties with Elsevier, *e.g.*, cancel subscriptions and cease submission of research papers if negotiations with them fail to obtain a reduction in the price of subscriptions. Harvard University has cancelled their Elsevier subscriptions of bundled journals. The Senate of North Carolina State University urged that excessive prices from publishers be resisted.

Four North Carolina universities had signed a deal for a bundle of 1300 journals in 2003 with the proviso that no titles are dropped. When these institutions wanted to renew subscription for 2004 the price was so exorbitant that they all cancelled the deal. Cornell University and the University of Missouri also cancelled subscription with Elsevier for the same reasons. Three North Carolina universities have drafted policies to only forward research to publishers whose journals are reasonably priced and widely accessible.

In the event of this not being possible they will include an "authorisation to publish' clause in contracts that empower the author to retain copyright to reproduce research for academic and research purposes. Kansas University includes a clause in their contracts that give them permission to use their research for teaching and research purposes and retain the right to make it available on public accessible Web sites.

Open Access Journals

The open access initiative is aimed at making scholarly research freely available via the Internet. Open access journals are journals available on the

Internet for academics, researchers and the general public. The open access journal philosophy received a tremendous stimulus with the birth of the *Public Library of Science* (PLoS). At its conception 30,000 scientists promised their support in terms of submitting research. The first open access journal to emerge was PLoS Biology in the year 2003 which was received with great enthusiasm. In the publishing arena the Biomed Central publishing house embarked on free access to peer-reviewed journals. Recently the *Directory of Open Access Journals* (DOAJ) made open access journals available covering different languages and subjects.

Open Access Archives

Many leading universities are setting up electronic archives as depositories for their research output and are granting access to it. There are plans in progress to use theses archives as a platform to provide open access journals. The *Massachusetts Institute of Technology* (MIT) has made software freely available for managing electronic archives. Currently there are approximately 140 universities that have established open access archives. The number of journals held in these archives have increased from 20,000 in 2001 to 1.3 million in 2003. Although this is still fairly insignificant compared to the 2 million peer reviewed journals printed annually it nevertheless sends out a clear warning signal to commercial publishers of what is to come. In Europe the Open Archives Forum was established. The goal of this forum is to establish electronic archives and make it globally available.

e-Books

There are various definitions for e-books but e-books are essentially published books and reference materials that were digitised and are distributed electronically. In the year 2000 e-books were heralded as the new publishing revolution. One market research company predicted that by 2005 there would be 1.9 million users. Forrester Research predicted that income generated from e-book sales would increase from $9 million in 2000 to $414 million in 2004.

Unfortunately e-book popularity never rose to expected heights. Despite the negativity surrounding e-books it had not demised completely. There are still some companies dealing with e-books that are profitable and experiencing growth. One of the first commercial e-book services, NetLibrary, was established by OCLC in 1998. The NetLibrary collection has since grown to over 400 000 titles. The shortcoming in the NetLibrary system is the fact that an e-book can only be used by one user at a time. Questia, another commercial e-book service went live in 2001. Their target market was students and they employed librarians to manage collection development. By 2003 Questia had more than 400 000 titles from more than 200 publishers.

Advantages of e-Books

E-books have numerous advantages. There are no printing, storage, warehousing and shipping costs. Consequently e-books can be published at costs much lower than conventional books. Additional advantages are online availability, keyword-searching capability, cross-referencing, adjustable fonts, electronic bookmarks and imbedded audio. Updating e-books will be easier than re-editing conventional books. From an academic library point of view benefits would include cost savings in terms of shelving, binding, circulation, overdue notices and management of fines. All needed would be a person to maintain the collection and a person to manage user accounts. Print collections in academic libraries are very expensive to acquire and maintain. E-books are also environmentally friendly in the sense that no tree pulping is necessary to for its production. The flaws in current e-book technology will be overcome. When that day dawns e-books being much cheaper to produce and publish than printed books as well as economies of scale will tip the balance in favour of e-books.

Disadvantages

The devices needed to read e-books are relatively expensive, *e.g.*, hand held devices, PC's and laptops. In order to minimize piracy publishers use proprietary hardware devices and software platforms. This lack of universal standards is a problem. The question many ask is whether e-books pose a threat to libraries. Can it eventually put libraries out of business. Although e-books did not take off as well as expected within the public domain, the use of e-books at schools, colleges and universities are rapidly increasing.

Use of e-Books

Falk refers to research done by Forrester that indicated that 4 million e-books were sold at campus stores in year 2000. Forrester forecasted that by year 2005 e-book sales should have increased to 140 million. Research indicates that students are developing a preference for e-books above printed books. At the University of Rochester Rush Rhees Library course reserve section students were exposed to printed books and their e-book equivalents. Statistics compiled on a weekly base indicated a three to one preference in favour of the e-books.

THE EVOLUTION OF INFORMATION TECHNOLOGY

Researcher provide a comprehensive remarks of the evolution of IT where he claimed that during the 1950s, computer systems were used mainly for scientific applications, with scientists the primary users and custodians of these systems. Business use of computers for mainly functional applications, such as accounting, began in the 1960s. The era of the 60s is known for the birth of

Data Processing (DP) or *Electronic Data Processing (EDP),* which created a whole new profession.

During this period:

- The computer was perceived as a number crunching tool.
- Attention was focused on the power of these modem tools to compute, with much less emphasis placed on the overall value of information as a resource.

In the 1970s, more organisations moved towards the use of computers to provide management with information. This concept soon became known as *Management Information Systems (MIS).* Although MIS concepts were considered to be a major breakthrough in the use of computer systems to process information, organisations still emphasised the computer itself rather than focusing on the data and information as major components of the systems.

Many other concepts evolved during this period, examples:

- Database Management Systems (DBMS).
- Decision Support Systems (DSS).

The domination of mainframe computer systems gave way to the introduction of *minicomputers.* This new generation of computers became instrumental in the development of *Distributed Systems (DS).* The introduction of personal computers or microcomputers was another landmark development of this period. The technological advancements of the 1970s paved the way for a new era in the 1980s, which became known as the *Information Age.*

The significant phenomena of this era include the greater recognition of information as a major organisational asset and its importance in a competitive world economy. Another important characteristic of this era is the emphasis on the management of information and related resources utilised to maintain information resources. Furthermore, greater participation by users of information services became a major fact of this age.

The new generation of end users are more knowledgeable than their counterparts of a few decades earlier, and they created many networks of information systems sharing the vast powers of computers, data, information, and knowledge. In addition, technological advancements in telecommuni-cations allowed information users to exchange information more freely than ever. The old dream of developing computer systems that could think intelligently, learn, and make recommendations to decision makers carne closer to reality through many new applications of *Artificial Intelligent (AI)* and its component Expert Systems (ES).

New Information Technology Resources

There are several developments which have lead to a new perception and assessment of the use and management of information technology resources.

These include:

- Recognition of information as a major organisational resource.
- Greater emphasis on utilisation of information as a major driving force in achieving effective strategies.
- New integration of telecommunications and information processing systems.
- A vast array of components comprising information technology resources.

Today, information technology resources consists of all types of information, representing various *functional entities* of organisations. Organisational information now can appear in all forms, which are processed by a conglomeration of computer machinery, examples:

- Mainframe,
- Minicomputers,
- Microcomputers,
- Reprographics, and
- Video discs.

It is communicated through the use of communication systems. The information is generated through the use of many information processing and management systems in diverse organisational structures. In addition to mechanical, procedural, and technical components of information technology resources, one must also consider the human elements.

These human elements can be divided into three categories:

1. Those individuals who are involved in different activities of generating information.
2. Those who are the primary users of information.
3. The management team responsible for the overall management planning functions of information technology resources.

One can argue that the role of the information technology resources management team has become more important to the overall success and growth of many organisations. In addition, the task of managing these resources is far more complex and sophisticated in the information age. Information technology resources are no longer viewed by many organisations as number crunching 'black boxes,' but rather as vital resources for identifying new opportunities and developing strategies.

Information Management in the 1990s

The cost of computing has dropped drastically in the past two decades. There is considerably more advanced information and communication devices available. AB a result, organisations of all sizes and types have been employing this technology to increase their competitive advantages. With the rapid evolution in information technology, the effectiveness of the traditional management techniques to the management of this technology has been the subject of much speculation by both researchers and practicing managers. Clearly, this changing technology is in need of an evolution in its management as well:

- A management approach that is as dynamic as the technology itself,
- Keeping pace in its methods and strategies as the technology matures,
- Making drastic shifts in direction when necessary, and
- Always providing new opportunities for growth, is the essential ingredient for strategic management of information technology resources.

As information technology resources become more important to the overall success of the organisation, its management may not only be limited by technical planning and execution as was true in the past. With the current number of end users and their demands for information technology services, successful organisations will utilise the expertise of their information technology personnel to provide needed support for the end user in order to obtain the necessary competitive edge.

MACHINE UNDERSTANDABLE INFORMATION IN METADATA

Collection of Items are called Data. The additional Information's about the objects stored within our collections may be Traditional or e-format is represented in the form of Metadata, which is nothing but data about data. In General, metadata is machine understandable information.

In Library environment, metadata is commonly used for any formal scheme of resource description, applying to any type of object, digital or non-digital. From Computing Point of View, the content management system contains digital objects. Thus, Metadata is also one of the components of Digital Library. Both Digital objects and Metadata are components of Digital Library. Digital objects are described, structured, summarized, managed and otherwise manipulated in surrogate form through the use of "metadata", which literally means data about data. Metadata is usually produced through a process called "cataloging" that is often carried out by trained librarians.

Collections of such information are commonly stored in "catalogs". In computerized environments, metadata may be automatically or semi-automatically extracted or derived from the original content or the "full text" may simply be indexed and searched.

WHAT IS METADATA

Metadata is "DATA ABOUT DATA" or "INFORMATION ABOUT INFORMATION" Metadata is structured Information that describes retrieval for managing Information Resource. Which states that most data is waste without Metadata. Metadata describes data elements and their attributes such as name, size, data type and also Data Structures like length, field, columns, etc. It also has information about the location of data, how it is associated ownership, etc. Also, metadata describes specific characteristics about spatial data, which provides guidelines with a Standard Format. The Information may includes Name, Ownership, Description, Currency, Status, Access, Quality, Contact Details, etc., It helps us to know where exactly Information locates, Information requirement, relevant Information where exactly locates, even with in another part of your Organization, etc., are the special features of Metadata. Metadata can be encoded in MARC in "keyword=value" pairs or in any other definable syntax.

Many current meta data schemes use SGML or XML. XML is an extended form of HTML which allows for locally defined tag sets and the easy exchange of structured information. SGML is a superset of both HTML and XML and allows for the richest mark-up of a document.

PURPOSE OF METADATA

The purpose of metadata according to Haynes the Purpose may be expressed as information retrieval, management of information services, documenting ownership and authenticity, interoperability.

- Information retrieval is a dynamic process which involves the user, the system and the librarian. The system indicates the usage of the computers, but can also be the manual catalogue. To obtain proper retrieval of relevant documents, the metadata representation is most important and should satisfy the users.
- Metadata also helps in management of various information services like OPAC, SDI, etc.
- It is a vehicle for documenting ownership and authenticity of the information.
- It also focuses importance towards the interoperability of information across continents.

Also, the Purpose extends to:

- Resource Description
- Administration and Management of Resources
- Record of Intellectual Property Rights
- Documenting Software and Hardware Environments
- Resource Discovery
- Preservation Management of Digital Resources
- Providing Information on context and Authenticity.

TYPES OF METADATA

Metadata is divided into different types:

- Descriptive Metadata
- Administrative Metadata
- Structural Metadata and
- Subject Metadata

Descriptive Metadata

Descriptive Metadata are used in the Discovery, Indexing and Identification of Digital Resources by semanting means. It is visible to the User of a system. Descriptive Metadata refers to the author, title content, etc. Preservation information refers to the best way of preserving documents like air conditioning or preserving books in the form of files at Systems, which requires meta fields to maintain with.

Administrative Metadata

To maintain Collections, this Administrative Metadata is used. Administrative Metadata is Managing metadata. Rights management metadata is a form of administrative metadata dealing with intellectual property rights. This Administrative metadata pertains to acquisition, vendor, location, etc., Also, it encompass a variety of data related to viewing, interpretation; use and management of digital objects over time. It includes technical data on creation and quality control, which has rights management, access control and user requirements.

- Management Information: Managing Information according to User requirements and reflects the output.
- Technical Information: Technical Information expresses the Technical details such as Name of the file, its Type, Hardware, Software, Resolution of the Images scanned, Colour space, Pixel dimensions, File relationships, Compressions, etc., Using related Information provides User Tracing Information.
- Structural Metadata: Structural Metadata is nothing but interface which complies individual digital object into more meaningful units for the users. Structural metadata indicates how compound objects are put together. Structural Metadata is used for representing Physical Entity through Navigation, Information Display and Display. Searching Contents among them or with in them. Structural metadata has information about Physical forms of the resources.
- Subject Metadata: To have effective Searching this Subject Metadata is used. For Browsing structure this Subject Metadata is used, with Keywords, Classification Codes, Classification System, Terms from Thesauri and Subject Heading.

HOW METADATA IS USED IN TRADITIONAL LIBRARY CATALOGUING

Traditional Library Cataloging is a form of metadata, and MARC 21 and the rules sets in AACR2 are metadata standards. Other metadata schemes have been developed to describe various types of textual and non-textual objects such as archival materials, visual materials, geographic information, and science and social science datasets. In mid 1990's Schwartz mentions the term metadata, which is used with database management, began to appear in the LIS literature. However, within a short period the topic became very popular in the area of research concentration, giving rise to several hundred publications, including an ARIST chapter in 1998. Lange and Winkler traced the history of the term metadata back to the 1960s, but noted that it began to appear more frequently in the DBMS literature in the 1980s. Vellucci notes that the term metadata transcends boundaries among various stakeholders in the development of the internet and provides a common vocabulary to describe a variety of data structures.

XML (EXTENSIBLE MARKUP LANGUAGE)

XML is a Markup Language in the world of Web Designing and Programming. The markup text is a methodology for encoding data with information about it itself. Examples of markup are universal in the real world. The systematic arrangement of data elements for machine processing contains metadata multiple applications. The *Resource Description Framework* (RDF) is developed under *World Wide Web Consortium* (W3C), which enables encoding exchange and reuse of structured Metadata. RDF is a language for representing information about resources of World Wide Web, which is particularly representing Metadata with Web Resources.

RDF utilizes XML as a common syntax for processing of Metadata. XML is a simple and very flexible Markup Language with a great technology also runs in any platform with any Environment. The XML syntax is a subset of the International text processing *Standard Generalized Markup Language* (SGML) which is meant for Web. The XML syntax provides vendor independence, flexible framework, instant push technologies with *Channel Definition Format* (CDF), Electronic Commerce uses the *Open Trading Protocol* (OTP) and *Mathematical Markup Language* (MML), Pre-defined Tags, User Extensibility, Validation, Human Readability, etc., to indicate complex structures. By exploiting the features of XML, RDF focuses the structure of expression of semantics with machine processing standard Metadata.

WHAT DOES METADATA DO

An important reason for creating descriptive metadata is to facilitate discovery of relevant information. In addition to resource discovery, metadata can help organize electronic resources, facilitate interoperability and legacy resource integration, support digital identification and support archiving and preservation.

HOW TO CREATE METADATA

To encode Information the Data should be expressed in proper way. Create a Single disk file for each metadata record, that is, one disk file describes one data set. Then use some tool to enter Information into this disk file so that the metadata confirm to the standard. The procedure is,

- Assemble Information about the data set.
- Create a Digital file containing the metadata, properly arranged.
- Check the Syntactical Structure of the file. Modify the arrangement of Information and repeat until the syntactical structure is correct.
- Review the content of the metadata, verifying that the information describes the subject data completely and correctly.

DIGITAL IDENTIFICATION

Most metadata schemes include elements such as standard numbers to uniquely identify the work or object to which the metadata refers. The location of a digital object may also be given using a file name, URL, or some more persistent identifier such as a Persistent URL (PURL) or the Digital Object Identified (DOI). Persistent identifiers are preferred because file locations change frequently, making the URL invalid. In addition to the actual elements that point to the object, the metadata can be combined to act as a set of identifying data, differentiating one object from another for validation purposes.

ARCHIVING AND PRESERVATION

Recently created resources are the current metadata. However, there is a growing concern that digital resources will not survive in usable form into the future. Digital information is fragile; it can be corrupted or altered according to the requirement. It may become unusable as storage media and hardware and software technologies change. Format migration and perhaps emulation of current hardware and software behaviour in future hardware and software platforms are strategies for overcoming these challenges. Metadata is key to ensuring that resources will survive and continue to be accessible into the future. Archiving and preservation require special elements to track the lineage of a digital object to details its physical characteristics and to document its behaviour in order to emulate it on future technologies.

RESOURCE DISCOVERY

Metadata serves same functions in resource discovery as good cataloguing does by

- allowing resources to be found by relevant criteria
- identifying resources
- bringing similar resources together
- distinguishing dissimilar resources and
- giving location information

ROLE OF METADATA IN INFORMATION MANAGEMENT SYSTEM (IMS)

The role of Metadata in Content Management is something Interesting and worth interrogating. Metadata is used in variety of Situations and applications with widespread web applications. For "Searching" techniques, the metadata role is very very important. If the user started searching in the name of " Isolation and Purification" one can get number of references for the above said Topic. The associated keywords are analyzed and the related topics may also appear to satisfy the user needs. The terms can be grouped into associative and hierarchically subordinate or super-ordinate terms. This can be represented with the concept of Isolation and Purification. According to Dr. Ranganathan classification, the Personality, Energy, Matter may be defined.

The subordinate terms can be incorporated into the classification schedule and used in assigning subject headings or keywords. This will serve the purpose of the user and the classificationist. However, change of keyword into subject heading is a different procedure. These are all metadata contents. Also, it serves as a good example for Information Retrieval. Finally, the most important fact is that there should be facility in the software for upgradation of the metadata when required. The elements holds related detailed border schema for description, which is enumerated from narrower schema, to increase both recall and precision. This type of Principle is applicable to any type of Information Management System.

METADATA INTEROPERABILITY FOR CATALOGUING OF E-JOURNALS

The content of digital libraries includes data and metadata that describe various aspects of the digital record that consist of links or relationships to other data or metadata, whether internal or external to the digital library. Interoperability, as defined by the IEEE is "The ability of two or more systems or components to exchange information and use the information that has been exchanged. This makes it necessary that every library has to examine the issue of data and metadata required for accessing their documents. Metadata is provided in order to provide richer searching than would be possible using standard free-text indexing. In particular it was desirable to allow users to search on a number of fields including Author, Title and Discription.In addition it was felt desirable to allow users to restrict searches by issues by article type.

METADATA

Metadata Expand the use of data embedded in the digital object or text, and find ways of integrating different kinds of metadata. Metadata has been defined as "data about data". It is information about an electronic resource which may be embedded in the resource. Currently work is being done to define a metadata record which adequately describes a wide range of electronic objects. The aim is to give the authors or information providers associated with electronic resources the means to describe the resource themselves, to a defined standard.

The idea is that in describing the resource you need something which is more informative than an index entry, but less complete then a formal cataloguing record. According to Gilliland-Swetland metadata is more than description; a more inclusive conceptualisation of metadata is needed as information professionals consider the range of their activities that may end up in incorporating it into digital information systems. Repositories also create metadata relating to the administration, accessioning, preservation and use of collections. Acquisition records, exhibition catalogs, and use data are all examples of these, even though they are largely still created in paper form." There are three main types of metadata

- Descriptive metadata: Describes a resource for purposes such as discovery and identification. It can include elements such as title, abstract, author and keywords
- Structural metadata: Indicates how compound objects are put together, for example how pages are ordered to form chapters
- Administrative metadata: Provides information to help manage a resource, such as when and how it was created, file type and other technical information and who can accesses it. There are several subsets of cataloguers decisions about whether a catalogue record should be created for a whole set of volumes or for each particular volumes in the set, so that the metadata creator makes similar decisions

Metadata is structured information that describes, explains locates or otherwise makes it easier to retrieve, use or manage an information resource. Traditional library cataloguing is a form of metadata and MARC21 and the rule sets used with it such as AACR2 are metadata standards. Metadata can be embedded in a digital object or it can be stored separately. Metadata will not be lost and obviates problems of linking between data and metadata, and helps to ensure that the metadata and object will be updated together.

HOW TO CATALOGUE E-JOURNALS USING METADATA

Metadata is used to improve the utility of data by providing a structure of framework for describing that data. Metadata elements are in effect fields of information that can be stored and manipulated in catalogue. Metadata is particularly useful for large collections of documents or other materials, it can be used for managing the resource and for finding specific items. A Catalogue becomes an found by some libraaries is an essential tool for retrieval. Libraries made a commitment to provide users with online access to full-text journals, found in publisher packages and aggregator databases, via Web lists and OPAC with details such as holdings coverage, embargo, source, open access, and local subject headings. The metadata of e-journals were first tracked on spreadsheets in EXCEL for Web lists and were also cataloged in the OPAC, a dual-maintenance system which later proved to be needing improvement as library electronic journal collection expanded. Libraries thus developed an interim solution and a long-term solution for managing e-journals access.

The interim solution is to replace EXCEL with Microsoft ACCESS in processing e-journal metadata, still a dual-maintenance system but with greatly reduced maintenance work and enhanced timeliness of ejournal metadata in the OPAC and on the Web lists. The long-term solution is to generate e-journal Web lists from the OPAC with streamlined e-journal metadata batch-loading process using Innovative's Electronic Resources Management Module. The OCLC/ NCSA Meta Data workshop in Dubin, Ohio held in 1995 proposed the following core set of elements to appear in *Uniform Resource Characteristics* (URC):

- Title,
- Creator,
- Subject and Keywords,
- Description,
- Publisher,
- Contributor,
- Date,
- Resource Type,
- Format,
- Resource Identifier,
- Source,
- Language,
- Relation,
- Coverage and
- Rights Management.

Increasing size and complexity of the digital information available on the web demands for methods of its organization. Uniform and structured meta information which can effectively be employed to achieve this goal. Metadata support efficient and effective organization, access and retrieval of information contents in a digital library. Meta information is used in effective designing of browsing and search interfaces of a digital library. Describing a resource with metadata allows it to be understood by both human and machines in ways that promote interoperability. Most metadata schemes include elements such as standard numbers to uniquely identify the work or object to which the metadata refers. Metadata is key to ensuring that resources will survive and continue to be accessible into the future.

Metadata elements are in effect field information that can be stored and manipulated in a database or a stylesheet. Alternatively the data elements may be embedded in a document, delimited by tags. The marked up metadata tags may also include details of the metadata schema used and the encoding system that has been adopted. Information retrieval is through a combination of key words, menus, and graphic map interfaces. Descriptions include the data custodian, custodian location, data cost, data quality, confidentiality constraints, spatial coverage, time period and a short description of the data set. The next section discuss access to E-Journals via internet.

E-JOURNALS ON THE INTERNET

Using the Web, publishers can easily distribute hypertext documents with multimedia components to a global audience, and they have been actively experimenting with Web versions of new or existing electronic serials. The Journal of Internet Cataloging also looks at:

- Uniform resource identifiers and link-resolve services
- Usability testing
- Interoperability, crosswalks, and mappings among metadata schema
- Learning object metadata
- Using classification and automated assists for organizing Web resources
- Software and hardware for retrieving, reviewing, and describing Internet resources
- Managing the cataloging process of Internet resources
- The problems of maintaining catalogue records for remote electronic resources
- Descriptive and subject cataloging applied to Internet resources
- Education and training
- International issues in organizing/cataloging Internet resources.

The Journal of Internet Cataloging is an essential resource for practicing librarians and information specialists, library and information science educators and students, and systems administrators. The following sections describe individual library/group metadata for cataloguing e- journals

MARC 21

The Library of Congress' Network Development and MARC Standards Office is developing a framework for working with MARC data in a XML environment. This framework is intended to be flexible and extensible to allow users to work with MARC data in ways specific to their needs. The framework itself includes many components such as schemas, stylesheets, and software tools. Library of Congress ' Network Development and MARC Standards Office has developed a schema for a bibliographic element set that may be used for a variety of purposes, and particularly for library applicationsa.

An XML schema, the *"Metadata Object Description Schema"* (MODS) is intended to be able to carry selected data from existing MARC 21 records as well as to enable the creation of original resource description records. It includes a subset of MARC fields and uses language-based tags rather than numeric ones, in some cases regrouping elements from the MARC 21 bibliographic format. MODS is expressed using the XML schema language of the World Wide Web Consortium. Marc also provides url linking facility in its tag. Metadata recorded for Journal of the American Chemical Society.

CONSER PROGRAMME

CONSER is:

- A cooperative online serials cataloging programme
- A source of high quality bibliographic records for serials
- A source of high quality documentation and training materials for the cataloging of serials and the input of serial records
- A group of serial experts who work together in an atmosphere of collegiality and trust
- A promulgator of standards related to serials
- A voice for serials in the library community
- A component of the Programme for Cooperative Cataloging

CONSER began in the early 1970s as a project to convert manual serial cataloging into machinereadable records and has evolved into an ongoing programme to create and maintain high quality bibliographic records for serials. In keeping with its evolution, the name was changed in 1986 from the CONSER Project to the CONSER Programme. In October 1997, CONSER became a bibliographic component of the Programme for Cooperative Cataloging. now in process, serials catalogers will soon be in position to utilize all the computer file bibliographic record elements. CONSER has taken a major step in developing policies for these new elements with the publication. Describing electronic access information is another challenge for the cataloger due to the different areas of the record involved, including the new electronic location and access field. *AACR2* requires catalogers to "always specify the mode of access" for electronic serials in a note. The CONSER "mode of access" note now includes more general information to limit redundancy with the 856 field, which contains the detailed information needed to locate and access documents. Serials catalogers now use the note field 538 for the more general information as the field is newly available through format integration.

METADATA INTEROPERABILITY

Metadata as a tool to facilitate exchange of information between interoperating systems and interoperability of metadata schemas themselves which can help to facilitate systems interoperability. There are three different types of interoperability:

- Semantic interioperability: Achieved through agreements about content description standards
- Structural interoperbility: A data model that is used for specifying semantic schemas

- Syntactic introperbility: Which provides a syntax for expressing metadata: an example is XML

Metadata crosswalks

A crosswalk allows metadata created by one community to be used by another group that employs a different metadata standards. Crosswalks are important for virtual libraries where resources are being collected from a variety of sources and are expected to act as a whole, perhaps with a single search engine applied. While these cross walks are key they are also labour intensive to develop and maintain. Reconciling metadata created in different environments is a major challenge and some effort has been devoted to mapping equivalent metadata elements between different metadata schemas. These mappings can be displayed as tables and are known as crosswalks. They can be used within systems to effect transformations between metadata objects. Crosswalks are a starting point for assessing the suitability of data sources for import.

The library participates in a metadata harvesting protocol to provide extracts of local metadata in a common format to a service provider so that information about the collection is automatically included in a number of relevant tools such as catalogs and portals. The Web page is linked to the library's web site dedicated to resources. Where it is available to researchers in context with archival and visual materials, digitized secondary sources, etc. Administrative, structural, and descriptive metadata for web site also has been created to hold all of its pieces together to allow them to be managed and allow them to be accessed.

FROM MONOLINGUAL TO MULTILINGUAL DIGITAL LIBRARIES

Language is one of the most critical factors in access to information. Information is usable and useful only if it is in a language that can be read or otherwise understood. Communication between people speaking a common language, whether English, French, Mandarin, or Hindi, is influenced by factors such as subtleties of phrasing, vocabulary, regional accents, and knowledge of the subject matter being discussed. In monolingual information retrieval, some of these difficulties are ameliorated through

- Standardising forms,
- Controlled vocabulary, and
- Algorithms that employ knowledge of grammatical structure and word frequency in the language.

People often need information that exists in languages other than those they read or speak, however. Human translators can bridge language in oral and written communication. They can translate between spoken languages in real time, and they can translate texts. Translation is a challenging intellectual task, as no two languages map precisely onto one another. A word in one language may have several meanings in the other, and the interpreter must determine which is most appropriate. Conversely, one word may incorporate multiple meanings in another language and the appropriate subset must be identified. Often, a narrative explanation is needed in place of a single word.

Meaning depends on context as well as on choice of words. Metaphors and idioms are particularly difficult to convey in other languages. Translators are really interpreters of meaning; that is why automatic translation is so limited. Computers can provide approximate translations, particularly of scientific texts, but are far from a reliable substitute for expert human language interpreters. Providing access to information in multiple languages is a challenge inherent in constructing a global information infrastructure. It is also fundamental to tailoring and interoperability trade-offs. Given a choice, people generally prefer to communicate in their native language, both online and offline. Communication in international environments frequently involves multiple languages, however, and people often need information written in unfamiliar languages. The problem of multilingual access to information affects not only users in countries in which several languages are spoken but also all those who search material in information sources or databases containing material in more than one language.

This is the case in the majority of scientific or research databases. In addition, the growth of networks means that we can easily access information/ databases outside our own immediate circle — in another country, another continent. In doing so, we encounter problems concerning not only search interfaces, but also concerning search keys like, subject or even author in another language. Multilingual information access is a pervasive problem in automation, and it is of great concern for anyone exchanging information over computer networks. Multilingual access issues affect e-commerce, information institutions such as libraries, archives, museums, academic institutions at all levels, and those who produce hardware and software for network applications.

However, it is important to understand the connotation of the term 'multilingual access.' Multilingual access is frequently used to cover a variety of topics, and it is necessary to define the use of the term 'multilingual' in the context of this paper.

We frequently hear talk of multilingual systems in reference to search environments, whereas the actual access points themselves are in fact monolingual. Multilingual user environments are now standard in the majority of systems.

MULTILINGUAL ACCESS TO INFORMATION IN A NETWORKED ENVIRONMENT CHARACTER

One of the great benefits of digital libraries is the ability to make information available to a wide audience without geographic constraints. As large-scale digital libraries contribute to the dismantling of the geographic barriers to information access, however, the barrier raised by language considerations becomes apparent. In order to make information available to the widest possible audience, this language barrier must also be tackled. Ideally, a global digital library would provide access to information in all the languages of the world, to all people, all the time. Anyone anywhere could create information in their native language, yet others, wherever they are, could discover that information and have it translated into their favoured languages and formats. Such an ideal situation may well be beyond our reach at the present moment, but it raises issues worthy of investigation.

No single collection, user interface, or set of system capabilities will serve young and old, novice and expert, artist and physicist, in New Delhi and New York. Nor will any single system provide adequate access to books, music, movies, and numeric data, much less serve applications as diverse as ecommerce, weather modelling, census tracking, library catalogues, and virtual classrooms. Yet people with varying backgrounds and skills, speaking in different tongues, have similar information needs. Content of interest may exist in a wide variety of forms and languages, and the same content and collections may be of interest to a wide range of people, for many different reasons. The prospect of a global digital library presents several opportunities like,

- Making information resources accessible to particular user communities while at the same time making those same resources accessible to a broader, improperly-defined, and perhaps unknown audience, and
- Enabling users to bridge the many formats, representations, and languages of individual digital libraries in their quest for information resources.

The issue of multilingual access to information is an example of the tradeoffs between tailoring to local communities and generalising to a global audience. This particular issue is

- Urgent in view of the rate at which new text is being created,
- Long-term — in view of the relative stability of languages compared to the ephemeral nature of new media formats, and
- Broad-reaching — in view of the fact that some form of textual content is involved in most forms of electronic communication, whether alone or as descriptions of other media.

MULTILINGUAL ACCESS TO INFORMATION

Multilingual digital libraries are being created by countries with more than one national language, by the European Union, and by international research consortia and international businesses. Major scientific, technical and medical databases, such as INSPEC and Medline, long have contained metadata in English to represent materials in other languages. Monolingual digital libraries also are being created in many different languages. Many of these digital libraries are of interest well beyond the borders of the countries creating them, and to users who are native speakers of other languages. A fundamental challenge of constructing a global information infrastructure and a global digital library is to provide access to these collections, regardless of the language of the content and the language of the information seeker. The World Wide Web offers access to information resources in many languages. Certain developments facilitate multilingual exploitation of these resources.

Some search engines, for example, allow the user to restrict retrieved sites to those in particular languages; some also provide the searcher with an interface in a chosen language. Many Web sites also offer their information in several languages, one of which typically is English. Systran, a machine translation system available from the AltaVista search engine, can even translate a search statement or a retrieved page from one language to another. Despite these features, however, language also creates obstacles to full exploitation of Web resources. Not all languages are catered for by these multilingual tools. Machine translation output typically is but a rough and ready version of a human translation. The varieties of scripts in which the written forms of the world's languages appear also create major problems in searching, inputting, displaying and printing text in non-Roman scripts. Multilingual access to information is a complex problem. Peters and Picchi have divided it into two basic parts:

- Multiple-language recognition, manipulation, and display — involving matters such as encoding character sets and symbols so that they can be manipulated, and
- Multilingual or cross-lingual search and retrieval — referring to search for content in other languages, otherwise known as "cross-language information retrieval."

The first point addresses the problem of allowing digital library users to access the system, no matter where they are located, and no matter in what language the information is stored; it is a question of providing the enabling technology. The second point implies permitting the users of a digital library containing documents in different languages to specify their information needs in their preferred language while retrieving documents matching their query in whatever language the document is stored; this is an area in which much research is now under way. Let us first have an outline of this second point

Cross-Language Information Retrieval

The interface of a multilingual digital library must include features to support all the languages that will be maintained by the system and to permit easy access to all the documents contained. However, it must also include functionalities for multilingual or cross-language search and retrieval. This implies the development of tools that allow users to interact with the system, formulating the queries in one language and retrieving documents in others. The problem is to find methods which successfully match queries against documents over languages. This involves a relatively new discipline, generally known as *Cross-Language Information Retrieval* (CLIR), in which methodologies and tools developed for *Natural Language Processing* (NLP) are being integrated with techniques and results coming from the *Information Retrieval* (IR) field. Peters and Picchi have identified three approaches that are being studied for solution of the CLIR problem:

- Text translation by machine,
- Knowledge-based techniques, and
- Corpus-based techniques.

Text translation can be divided further:

- Translating the full content of the digital library into another language, or
- Translating only the query.

Translating the full content is rarely feasible except in very small and specific applications. For example, in the area of meteorological reports automatic translation is reasonably successful. For most applications, translating queries appears to be more promising. Queries in English, say for example, can be translated into Japanese and searched in Japanese databases, and vice versa. Knowledge-based approaches involve multilingual dictionaries, thesauri, or ontologies. In these approaches, searchers can construct a query using terms in their own language. The multilingual thesaurus is then used to translate the terms into the target language; they are then submitted to databases in that language. Thesauri can be translated pair wise or among a larger number of languages. In the latter case, a common core of terms would be established, and then the linguistic equivalents in each language would be determined.

Corpus-based techniques involve linguistic characteristics of a language and the distribution of terms in a collection of documents. Information retrieval techniques developed for monolingual retrieval, such as vector-space models and probabilistic methods can be employed for multiple languages. Usually some test databases in each language are required to "train" the algorithms about the relationships between corpora in each language. Each of these methods is both promising and problematic. None are complete solutions, and all are under active study. For any of the cross-language techniques to be effective, however, underlying technical issues in managing multilingual text must be resolved.

Multilingual Recognition and Representation

Despite its name, until recently the World Wide Web had not addressed one of the basic challenges to global communication: the multiplicity of languages. Standards for protocols and document formats originally paid little attention to issues such as character encoding, multilingual documents, or the specific requirements of particular languages and scripts. Consequently, the vast majority of WWW browsers still do not support multilingual data representation and recognition. Ad-hoc local solutions currently abound which, if left unchecked, could lead to groups of users working in incompatible isolation. The main requirements of a multilingual application are to:

- Support the character sets and encodings used to represent the information being manipulated;
- Present the data meaningfully;
- Manipulate multilingual data internally.

CHARACTER ENCODING

Character encoding is at the heart of the data-recognition, data-manipulation, and display components of multilingual information access. The creation of characters in electronic form involves hardware and software to support input, storage, processing, sorting, displaying, and printing. Each character – or ideograph in languages such as Chinese, Japanese, and Korean – needs a unique code to ensure that it sorts, displays, prints, and is matched properly upon searching. Additional codes are required for punctuation, direction of text, carriage returns, and line feeds. The internal representation of each character determines how it is treated by the hardware and the application software. To the dismay of those whose languages have far larger character sets, typewriter keyboards were initially designed for the English language; thus, they contain only 26 letters, 10 numbers, basic punctuation, and a few special symbols.

Only a few more symbols and function keys were added when the typewriter keyboard was adapted to become a computer keyboard. Many versions of the QWERTY keyboard are now in use worldwide, varying the location of letters. Special characters, such as letters with diacritics, can be generated by programming individual keys or by programming key sequences, often using escape key. The same key sequences on two different keyboards may produce two different characters, depending on the encoding system employed. Conversely, key sequences required to generate a character vary by keyboard and encoding system. Effective data exchange is heavily dependent on character encoding. Characters produced from different applications may appear the same on a screen or a printout but have different internal representations. Merging or transferring data between applications requires a common character-encoding standard or software to map variant encoding formats. Searchers need to have the appropriate keyboards and software to generate characters in the encoding standard in which the contents of a digital library are stored, whether locally resident or available through mapping software located at the digital library site or elsewhere. Local printers and displays must have the appropriate software to interpret and produce characters accurately. These factors are not specific to digital libraries; rather, they are issues for all distributed applications on a global information infrastructure.

MONOLINGUAL, MULTILINGUAL, AND UNIVERSAL CHARACTER SETS

For character encoding many standards and practices exist, *viz.*

- Those that are language specific,
- Those that are script specific, and
- The remaining are universal standards that support most of the world's written languages.

Digital libraries employ many different character-encoding formats, and this often leads to problems in exchanging data. After many years of international discussion on the topic, it became evident that adopting a universal character set offered the greatest hope for exchanging text in digital form. If data in all written languages were encoded in a common format, then data could be exchanged between monolingual and multilingual applications, whether e-mail, e-commerce, or digital libraries. Which common format to accept was a matter of long debate, however. In 1991, the Unicode Consortium and the *International Organization for Standardization* (ISO) finally reached an agreement to merge the 16-bit Unicode Standard and the 32-bit ISO standard into a common 16-bit Unicode Standard. Version 1.1 was first published in 1993; version 4.0 is currently the accepted Unicode Standard and the latest revision is numbered as 4.1.0. Unicode can support more than 96,000 distinct characters. Version 4.0 of the standard provides about 96,382 characters from the world's alphabets, ideograph sets, and symbol collections. Version 4.1.0 of the standard has included a further 1273 new characters. A growing number of world's major hardware and software vendors are supporting it and it is being incorporated into popular operating systems and programming languages. A list of such Unicode enabled products can be found from the Unicode Consortium's homepage. As software for e-commerce, digital libraries, automated library management systems, and other applications begin to support Unicode, it will become more widely adopted. Unicode Standard represents a tremendous advance for multilingual computing, but more work is needed in order to achieve a truly multilingual Web.

The impact will be manifold: it will help in the publication and preservation of materials in ancient and historic scripts, facilitate the online teaching of languages using such scripts, and provide universal access to our cultural and literary heritage. As storage costs continue to decline, the storage requirements of Unicode will be an insignificant issue, particularly for new applications. In the meantime, substantial amount of text continue to be produced not only in language-specific and script-specific encoding standards but also in local and proprietary formats. Any of this text maintained in digital libraries may become legacy data that has to be mapped to Unicode or some other universal standard in the future. For the present, digital library designers face difficult trade-offs between the character-set standards in use by current exchange partners and the standard likely to be in worldwide use in the future for a broader range of applications.

TRANSLITERATION AND OTHER FORMS OF DATA LOSS

A long-established intermediate approach to character encoding for languages that cannot be typed on a standard computer keyboard is transliteration, which matches characters or sounds from one language to another but does not translate meaning. Languages written in non-Roman scripts, such as Japanese, Arabic, Chinese, Korean, Persian, Hebrew, and Yiddish, Russian, and Devanagari, are transliterated into Roman characters in many applications. Transliteration is necessary when mechanical devices such as typewriters and computers do not support the necessary scripts. It also is helpful for people without full proficiency in the scripts of the language. The transliteration process may be irreversible, and thus some data loss takes place. Despite the existence of an international standardization body, multiple transliteration systems exist for Cyrillic, Asian, and other character sets. Thus transliteration can be inconsistent, which is why the same Russian name may appear as "Tchaikovsky" or as "Chaikovoskii" depending on which system is used to transliterate Cyrillic characters. Data also are lost when languages written in extensions of the Roman character set, such as French, Spanish, German, Hungarian, Czech, and Polish, are stored without the diacritics that for additional characters, all of which are collapsed into o if the diacritics are omitted).

Data loss is not exclusive to text, however; it is widespread in visual and aural media. Image compression is essential for efficient transmission of either still or moving pictures, and application-specific image compression standards exist for such applications as facsimile transmission, pictures, moving images, and high-definition television. Compression algorithms are made more efficient by discarding some of the data to reduce the granularity of the image. Images subjected to "lossy" compression are legible and suitable for many applications, but the original image cannot be reconstructed. "Lossless" compression retains the full content but requires more storage and more transmission time. Similarly, for music, a popular compression algorithm known as MP3 is used to squeeze digital audio by a ratio of 12:1. MP3 compresses music sufficiently that audio files can be sent via the Internet or stored on a hard disk. Music compressed in MP3 can be expanded and played by an MP3 player with a near-CD-quality sound, yet the files are small enough to be attached to an e-mail message. The music industry is promoting another standard, and Microsoft is promoting yet a third standard named Windows Media Audio for music compression and distribution. The acceptance of technical standards for music and other audio may be determined as much by the availability of playback devices as by the quality of reproduction. The amount of data loss that is tolerable varies by application. Far more data loss is tolerable in e-mail and in teleconferencing than in financial, legal, or bibliographic records. Textual data that have been transliterated or stripped of diacritics are likely to contain variant forms of words that will not match and sort properly, incomplete words that will not exchange properly with digital libraries using complete forms, and incomplete forms that are not adequate for authoritative or archival purposes.. In digital libraries, any kind of data loss can result in information retrieval errors.

INFORMATION COMMUNICATION TECHNOLOGY AND DIGITAL STORAGE IN LIBRARIES

The relatively recent change from the term *Information Technology* (IT) to *Information and Communication Technology* (ICT) due to the convergence of IT and ICT has open up new challenges for libraries. Information Technology is the collective name for a group of technologies that are concerned with the storage, retrieval, manipulation, analysis, and transmission of information. Since the fabrication of the first modern computer in the mid 1940's, computer technology has developed at a tremendous pace to the point where it has penetrated almost all occupations and has spread to the far concerns of the world. Similarly, communication technology has made rapid progress in the post World War II period. But it is the development of this technology in the last 15 years that has made IT so important. The development in this area have been brining about a revolutionary change in the way humans work, and in the way they interact with each others. The spread of telecommunications has brought into limelight the Internet, the global intercommunication of computer networks. This has made available a large store information to all concerns of the world. Information Technology provides the following services for information:

- Storage of large amounts of information in a cost effective manner.
- Structuring of information to enable quick retrieval of what is required.
- Analysis of stored information to help in decision making.
- Sharing of information among people geographically dispersed.
- Quick transmission of information over large distances.

IT consists of five components, *i.e.*, electronic science, computer science, tele-communication science, artificial language and human interface.

3

Evaluation of Library Services

INTRODUCTION

Evaluation data of digital libraries and their services are not yet widely available. In fact, very few evaluation studies of digital libraries have taken place so far. The most prominent publications reporting some digital library evaluation experiments appear in *Library Trends.* Saracevic discusses a number of issues related to the methodology and criteria for evaluation of digital libraries. Arguing that digital libraries were still at the stage of research and evolution, he commented that the best practice standards have yet to develop against which the performance levels are to be measured. Carter and Janes reported a study that analysed the log of over 3,000 reference questions asked of the Internet Public Library (IPL), which is one of the most widely used reference services on the Web.

This study has identified different categories of reference questions, such as common questions, quick questions, regular questions and unanswered questions, which were handled by IPL. The study revealed that users seem to have difficulties in assigning subject categories to their questions, and also in determining whether they are factual or require detailed information searching.

Since, the greatest part of reference and information services in the past has revolved around assisting users in their information search, and because of the fact that in a digital library environment end users need to search information resources all of which are online, it may be wise to take a quick look at some recent studies involving end-users' search behaviour in the online and Web search environment.

Pending any data from large-scale digital library evaluation experiments involving users, findings of these studies may help us assess the users' online information search behaviour. Gordon and Pathak compared the retrieval effectiveness of eight search engines: Yahoo!, Excite, Magellan, HotBot, AltaVista, Lycos, Infoseek and Open Text, and noted, among other things, that there were no statistical differences in the retrieval effectiveness among users for recall, though there were for precision.

Although this study talks about the performance of the selected search engines, this observation is very important as far as the need for personalised help in digital library searching is concerned. It shows that the Web search tools differ in terms of search precision, and who can argue that in an online search environment of today, precision is a very important issue since, no one will ever have time to sift through the hundreds of thousands of documents retrieved by an online search tool at any given instant.

One million Web queries to discern how the public searches the Web and had some astonishing findings, as follows:

- A great majority of Web queries are short, not much modified, and very simple in structure;
- Very few queries incorporate advanced search features, and when they do so, half of them are mistakes;
- Despite gathering a large number of Web sites as answers to their queries, users do not view beyond the first or the second page of results;
- Web users are notmuch interested in relevance feedback.

Yet another study reveals similar findings. The usage of the MelvylWeb catalogue at the University of California at Berkeley. During the 479-day study period users conducted about 2.5 million search sessions, during which about 7.4 million search statements were executed.

The findings of this study reveal that:

- The length of time research searchers spent at a session grew from six to ten minutes during the 16 month study period;
- During the study period, about 7.4 million database selections were made, out of which the catalogue database accounted for 32 per cent (about 2.4 million uses), Medlars for 22 per cent, magazine database for 10 per cent, periodicals database for 8 per cent, Inspec for 4 per cent and *Current Contents* for 4 per cent;
- The time users spent on each database also varied: about 3 minutes per search in the Medlars database, while 2.2 minutes for the catalogue database;
- Users displayed about four to five citations for each search they performed;
- The length of time users spent displaying results was 30-40 seconds.

The observations of these studies are very useful for designing digital library services. One of the major problems of a digital search environment is the absence of human intermediaries who play a major role in traditional online search services. Appropriate online support for query formulation and modification may improve digital library search results. Again, since, most users do not look at more than a handful of records, appropriate mechanisms have to be developed for filtering retrieved output.

VISUAL, INTERACTIVE SERVICES

Students also like self-service, interactive Web sites, and it is surprising that libraries haven't developed visual representations of their services that students could explore. A survey by OCLC found that one of students' top suggestions for libraries was to offer interactive maps, study tips, and guides. An example of that type of environment is a Web site developed by the British Museum as a "student's room" for an exhibit of Mughal, India, an ancient civilisation. Students see an office-style room that they can explore by clicking on components such as a globe, file cabinets, book shelves, and so forth. They are then led to museum resources including an atlas and primary resources from the museum's collections on the Mughal period. This type of model could be used for a library reference room and its resources.

Libraries could add value to key pages of their Web sites by including interactive tutorials on how to find information or how to judge quality information resources. Libraries could use part of their home page to highlight a "resource of the week," to better publicise information content that could likely assist students in their assignments. They could use customised mouse pads to advertise URLs for selected information resources. Libraries also need to think about new services using mobile technology such as cell phones.

They might allow students to reserve group study rooms and be alerted to availability via their cell phones, send simple text-message queries to library catalogs or databases, or check library hours via text messaging. Such services might be particularly valuable for students who live off campus. How will we conceive and design these new services? Librarians should consult with students in the design phase of services and incorporate students on teams that make decisions about the implementation of those services.

Making use of the imagination, creativity, technical skills, and perspectives of Net Gen students is the best way to ensure that new services will be responsive to both their needs and their style.

To summarise, Net Gen information services will:

- Use students on teams that design new services and environments
- Integrate services into course management systems
- Explore services for mobile devices
- Represent services and instruction visually and in multimedia modes
- Focus on partnership models
- Emphasise how to evaluate information resources
- Emphasise information policy issues

WEB BASED LIBRARY SERVICE

A digital Library service manages and develops electronic services, the library Web sites and library staff. According to White, it can be defined broadly as 'an information access service in which users ask questions via electronic means, *e.g.,* e-mail or web forms'. Library service on the internet requires many of the same qualities as traditional references: accuracy, promptness, courtesy, an understanding of the information need. It provides users with the convenience of accessing information in their own time, saving them traveling cost and time and new options for answering reference questions. The provision of these services is not constrained by the traditional opening hours but can be offered on a 24-hour, seven-days-a-week basis known as 24/7. And while there may be a disadvantage in not having a face-to face encounter, there are many advantages to this new medium and the greatest advantage is that many more users can be helped by using electronic library services. Advantages and disadvantages of electronic access over printed form access are showed in table. Web based services are established due to the following reasons.

- Ensuring the needs of users and the accessible information sources are suitable matched at all times.
- Delivering those information sources to the user in a timely and appropriate fashion.
- Ensuring the information provided is high quality, accurate and appropriate.
- Assisting the user in interpreting the materials, if necessary.
- Promoting user awareness of new services and information sources as they develop.
- Providing users with individualised guidance and support as they build their information search and application skills.

DIFFERENT RESOURCES FOR WEB BASED LIBRARY SERVICES

Today, users may have access a variety of textual information resources. There are different kinds of webbased reference resources and services for accessing information from libraries such as OPAC, Gateways, Portals, Subject Portals, Electronic Journals, Online Databases, Subject Directories and Search Engines. These resources overlap considerably in the type of information they cover, and sometimes it is difficult to distinguish between some of them. A library should have a good collection of these resources like selected Web links, subscription resources, and library materials in well-organised pages for serving better services to their users.

Many libraries and organisations are providing digital reference service through collaborative services. Existing library consortia are adding digital reference to current shared services, and networks of libraries. Some regional library consortia are offering member libraries the opportunity to share reference questions with each other using the Internet and other technologies. OPAC OPAS's - On Line Public Access Catalogues, form an important part of many digital library's collections. It allows users to search for the bibliographic records contained within a library's collections. Now days, some OPAC also provide access to electronic resources and databases, in addition to the traditional bibliographic records.

GATEWAYS

A gateway is defined as a facility that allows easier access to network based resources in a given subject area. Gateways provide a simple search facility and a much-enhanced service through a resource database and indexes, which can be searched through a web based interface. Information provided by gateways is catalogued by hand. Gateways cover a wide range of subjects, through some areas, such as music and religious studies, currently lack subject gateways. Some well-known gateways are as follows:

- Internet Public Library (IPL),
- Bulletin Board for Libraries (BUBL),
- National Information Services and Systems (NISS),

PORTALS

In the library community, portals may be defined as an amalgamation of services to the users where the amalgamation is achieved through seamless integration of existing services by using binding agents such as customisation and authentication services, search protocols such as Z39.50, loan protocols such as ISO10161, and e-commerce. The result is a personalised service which allows the individual to access the rich content of both print-based and electronic systems. Portals are either commercial or free web facilities that offer information services to a specific audience. The facilities include web search to communication to e-mail to news ,etc.There are three kinds of portals; Consumer (or horizontal), Vertical and Enterprise.

- Consumer portals are aimed at consumer audiences and offer free e-mail, games, chat ,etc., Examples are Yahoo!, MSN and AOL.
- Vertical portals, target a specified audience, such as a particular industry, and offer many of the consumer portal features. Example includes VerticalNet.
- Enterprise portals on the other hand are similar to consumer portals, but they are offered only to corporations or similar organisations. Examples include Epicentric and Corporate Yahoo! These portals can be best understood as electronic pathfinders for users, pulling together in one place in a web site selected links to subjects or interest-oriented resources located on the WWW.

SUBJECT PORTALS

Web Search Engines had been developed initially by computer scientists, by borrowing techniques from information retrieval search such as best match searching and relevance ranking. Information professional are increasing bringing their skills to help organise the growing wealth of Internet resources.

A good example of their influence is the development of subject-specific web search engines known as subject portals, where evaluation of material covered is a major concern. Two prime UK subject portals are SOSIG Social Science Information Gateway, covering social science resources and OMNI Organising medical networked information covering medical resources. Subject portal sites can be very helpful, but they should be used with care. Users should bear the following points in their mind:

- The aim of the subject portal is to list and review the most important sites on the web relevant to that subject. The sites are usually constantly peer-reviewed to ensure that the site is relevant and up to date.
- New sites are appearing all the time. Relying on a subject portal site to find everything users require may mean that they miss an important site that has recently appeared and has not yet been reviewed by the producers of the particular subject portal.
- A subject portal is a one stop shop for information on the topic it covers. Users don't have to carry out extensive Internet searches in order to find the information require. They can simply go to the required subject portal site.
- Subject portals save users having to have long lists of bookmarks (saved addresses of web pages), which are often, cumbersome and time consuming to arrange and keep up to date. However, if users do prefer to use bookmarks they can arrange them in an order to suit the way they work and not have an order forced on them by the subject portal.
- A subject portal site is only as good as the reviewers who peer-review the site listed. The reviewers need to have a policy of keeping the portal sites up to date and of constantly reviewing the sites they list, to make sure that they are still relevant and still contain good, timely information.

ELECTRONIC JOURNALS

Electronic journals form a large part of the collection of a library for providing web based services. Today many journals are available electronically - some are full text and some contain only bibliographic information with abstract. Major advantage of electronic journals is that they are constantly updated and easy to access but disadvantage is that breaching of copyright law is very easy. They are available as bitmaps, PostScript, PDF, ASCII, SGML and HTML. Library services may be delivering to users on CDRom, through e-mail or through web. Some international societies and associations have developed their own digital libraries through which users can get access to all their publications. Services are available to the members of society or associations through subscription.

ONLINE DATABASES

These are large collections of machine-readable data that are maintained by commercial agencies and are accessed through communication lines. Many libraries subscribe to them for easy access and use of current information. The disadvantage is that only bibliographic data is presented and not full text. The information cannot be accessed when the system is down for any reason. Examples Ei Compendex, SciFinder Scholar, Web of Science, Current Contents ,etc.

SEARCH ENGINES

Search Engines are huge databases of web page files that have been assembled automatically by machines where as the subject directories are human-compiled and maintained. Search engine indexes every page of a Web site and subject directories linked only homepages.

Search Engine is the popular term for an information retrieval (IR) system. A search engine is computer software that searches a collection of electronic materials to retrieve citations, documents, or information that matches or answers a user's query. The retrieved materials may be text documents, facts that have been extracted from text, images, or sounds. A query is a question phrased so that it can be interpreted properly by search engine. Depending on the type of software, it may be a collection of commands, a statement in either full or partial sentences, one or more keywords, or in the case of Non-text searching, an image or sequence of sounds to be matched.

SUBJECT DIRECTORIES

Subject directories differ from search engines in that search engines are populated by robots that finds and index sites whereas humans making editorial decisions that populate subject directories. Subject directories are basically index home pages of sites and can be classified as general, academic, commercial or portal. Among the well known subject directories are the Argus Clearinghouse and Yahoo. Strengths include relevance, effectiveness and relative high quality of content. Weaknesses are that they lack depth in their coverage of the subjects.

NEW WEB BASED LIBRARY SERVICES

VIRTUAL LIBRARY TOURS

Web sites of libraries provides virtual library guide to the physical facilities including collections, services and infrastructure available in the library. The combination of library maps and floor plans, library departments and photographic views are used for the tour. Virtual library tours are also using new technologies such as QuickTime movies etc and are beginning to replace image maps on main campus Web sites.

ASK-A-LIBRARIAN

Ask-A-Librarian services are Internet-based question and answer service that connects users with individuals who possess specialised subject knowledge and skill in conducting precision searches. Most 'Ask-a-Librarians' services have a web-based question submission form or an e-mail address or both. Users are invited to submit their queries by using web forms or through e-mail. Once a query is read by a service, it is assigned to an individual expert for answering. An expert responds to the query with factual information and or a list of information resources.

The response is either sent to the user's e-mail account or is posted on the web so that the user can access it after a certain period of time. Many services have informative web sites that include archives of questions and answers and a set of FAQs. Users are usually encouraged to browse archives and FAQs before submitting a question in case sufficient information already exists.

REAL TIME SERVICES

A new and exciting method of digital reference service that libraries are attempting to provide more and more now is live reference. These are real-time, interactive reference services in which the users can talk to a real, live reference librarian at any time, from anywhere in the world.

User and librarian can interact using chat technologies, and unlike with e-mail reference the librarian can perform a reference interview of sorts by asking the users to elaborate or clarify if needed before proceeding to answer the question. The librarian can perform Internet searches and push Web sites onto the user's browser, and can receive immediate feedback from the users as to whether their question have been answered to satisfaction.

BULLETIN BOARDS

A bulletin board is an electronic communications forum that hosts posted messages and articles connected to a common subject or theme or interest. It allows users to call in and either leaves or retrieves messages. The messages may be directed to all users of the bulletin board or only to particular users. But all messages can be read by all users. Several libraries are using bulletin boards for their web-based library services. The bulletin board system is also used as an interactive interface to invite suggestions on activities and services of a library. It can also be used as an interface to distribute library services.

WEB-BASED USER EDUCATION

Web guides and teaching tools are found everywhere on the Web because they are easily updated, accessed, and printed on demand. The web-based user education provides a high degree of interactivity and flexibility to the users.

The library web sites can use web-based user education for imparting training to users in teaching the basic library skills along with glossary of library terms, using Library OPAC, locating books, magazines, biographical data and other library materials, understanding how to navigate the libraries Web site and how to select the most relevant database, instructions for searching CD ROM and guidance in locating web-based databases and other electronic resources and instructions on subject searching training, using Boolean operators and searching internet resources through search engines.

WEB FORMS

Library web sites have some web forms for suggestions and comments on the Library Services. Different types of Web Forms are available on web that may be an Indent form for acquiring some publications, interlibrary loan request form for document delivery, Ask-a-Librarian forms, on line reservation form or user survey form ,etc.

REFERENCE AND INFORMATION SERVICES ON THE WEB

A number of reference and information services are now available on the Web. Interestingly, many of these services are provided by non-library and commercial organisations. While some are free, others need payment.

Detailed discussions on such services are available in a number of publications, McKiernan maintains a site that provides categorised listing of libraries that offer real-time reference services using chat software, live interactive communication tools, call centre management software, bulletin board services and other Internet technologies. Most of these services are designed for registered users of the libraries concerned.

Researchers categorised online reference and information services into three broad groups:

- Reference and information services from publishers, database search services, and specialised institutions;
- Reference services provided by libraries and/or experts through the Internet; and
- Reference and information services where users need to conduct a search and find information through theWeb.

Researchers discussed several online information services that belong to the first category.

They have listed various current awareness and SDI services such as: the contents page service from commercial publishers, such as Elsevier's

- Contents Direct Service, IDEAL Alert from Academic Press, and so on;
- Information on new books available free from publishers and vendors, such as the *Wiley Book Notification Service* and Amazon.com;
- SDI services fromonline search service providers, such as Dialog;
- *Current Contents* and *ISI Alerting Services* from ISI, and so on.

Some of these services, particularly the contents page services from publishers of journals, are free, while for others, such as *Dialog Alerts* or *Current Contents* from ISI, users need to register and pay.

Table 5.1 provides a quick overview of some online reference and information services currently available. This is not an exhaustive list, but the table shows the different types of services and some of their characteristics.

Service	Subject	Payment	Organisation	Service Providers	Question Input	Mode of Delivery
Ask me	All	Free	Askme.com	Experts (volunteers)	Select a subcategory and input query through a Web-based query form	E-mail
All Experts	All	Free	Allexperts.com	Experts (volunteers)	Select a subcategory and input query through a Web-based query form	E-mail
Inforocket	All	Fee-based (from $5 to $75)	Inforocket.com	Experts (volunteers)	Select a subcategory and input query through a Web-based query form	E-mail
Ask Auntie Nolo	Law	Free	Nolo.com	Subject experts	Input query through a Web-based query form	E-mail
Find/SVP	Business	Fee-based ($250 per question)	Findsvp.com	Business experts	Input query through a Web-based query form	E-mail, phone, fax, courier
Professional City	Law, accounting, marketing	Fee-based ($25 for the first 15 minutes and $18.75 per additional 15 minutes of cybrarian's time)	Professional City.com	Cybrarians	Input query through a Web-based query form	E-mail

It provides the following facts about theWeb-based reference services listed there:

- The listed Web-based reference services are offered by dotcom companies;

- These services use the Web only for communication between the user and the system/answer provider, while the information service is provided by a human expert;
- While most services are free, some charge as high as $250 per question;
- in many cases services are provided by (self-proclaimed?) volunteer experts;
- There are some services offered in specific subject fields.

In addition to those in table, there are also some Web-based reference services where users need to conduct a search for a reference query. Such services provide free access to various online reference sources, and allow users either to select a specific source or conduct a search on a range, or all, of the reference sources.

Examples of such services include the following:

- Internet Public Library.
- Infoplease
- Britannica
- Bartleby Reference.
- Internet Library for Librarians.
- Electric Library.
- Mediaeater Reference Desk.
- ReferenceDesk.
- Xrefer.

While most of these Web-based reference services are available free, some charge a small fee. For example, the Electric Library charges $79.95 for an entire year of unlimited access. Janes *et al.* reported a study of 20 Web-based "expert services". By asking 240 questions to 20 selected expert services, they noted that the sites gave verifiable answers to 69 per cent of factual questions. An interesting observation of this study was that the kind of reference interview that takes place in traditional reference service environments is non-existent in Web-based reference services.

In fact, the sites did not come back for any discussion or clarification after receiving the initial queries. As a justification, the authors suggested that Web-based information services have been built mainly to answer factual questions, and therefore the experts concerned do not need to go through the reference interview process. Nevertheless, the high rate of success of factual questions shows that more and more end-users will move towards these expert services rather than to libraries for answers to simple types of questions.

SEARCH ENGINE SERVICES

Although Ask Jeeves is basically a search engine, many researchers also see it as aWeb-based information service because of two reasons:

- Unlike in other search and metasearch engines, users can ask a question in Ask Jeeves, and in many cases can get an answer right away; and
- Users can ask a question on a given topic, and Ask Jeeves comes up with a list of questions on the same or similar topics; the user can select any of the those predefined questions, and then Ask Jeeves provides answers to that.

This is an interesting service and may be considered as a useful model for digital library reference and information services.

The Ask Jeeves site maintains that:

- Ask Jeeves is a unique question-answering system that allows users to ask questions in plain English, and then delivers the answer. As one of the most sophisticated navigation systems on the Internet, Ask Jeeves combines a unique natural language engine with a proprietary knowledgebase.Taken together, this mechanism processes the meaning and grammar of real questions in plain English; provides intelligent responses for user confirmation; links directly to relevant, high-quality answers; and, perhaps most exciting of all, becomesmore intelligent as its knowledgebase expands with each question asked and each answer delivered.

The site further says that Ask Jeeves processes each query syntactically and semantically, and then Ask Jeeves' answer-processing engine provides the question template response. When the user clicks on a response, the answer-processing engine retrieves the answer template that contains links to the answer locations. Thus, Ask Jeeves helps users select a query from a pre-defined set of queries on a given topic.

However, there is a debate on whether the kind of service provided by Ask Jeeves matches reference services provided by libraries. Kresh reported an interesting finding: "One consortial system in northern California conducted an informal test of Ask Jeeves by sending it 12 questions its libraries had answered. There were no trick questions, none were arcane, just questions typically received by those libraries. Jeeves was unable to answer any of the questions".

Nevertheless, the techniques and the technology used by Ask Jeeves may be very useful for introducing reference services in digital libraries. Webhelp.com is another service that claims to offer "real-time search assistance with a real live expert I any time, day or night". About.com is a service that shows a number of pre-defined categories related to a search topic given by the user.

For example, a simple search on "e-commerce" not only produces a list of sites, but also provides a set of topics related to "e-commerce", such as e-commerce definition, e-commerce security, advantages of e-commerce, e-commerce disadvantages, e-commerce statistics, etc.

CURRENT DIGITAL LIBRARY RESEARCH ON PERSONALISED SERVICES

Researchers have recently reviewed the status of some digital libraries from around the globe. These reviews reveal that while the digital libraries have very good information access and retrieval mechanisms in place, there is almost no provision for quality reference and information services.

However, these studies show that there is a trend towards the personalisation of digital library service, as in case of HEADLINE and GEMS (presently called iGEMS, a digital library developed at Nanyang Technological University in Singapore). Some recent research efforts have been directed at building personalised digital library environments. These studies can be grouped into three categories: user needs assessment, personalised user interface and personalised digital library, researchers reviewed literature on user interfaces, particularly in a digital library environment, and suggested the need for a task-based digital library.

Researcher discussed the personal digital library (PDL) that acts as a front-end to other electronic library systems and manages the user's information needs. Barry and Barbara discussed the creation of personal digital libraries. The North Carolina University Library developed MyLibrary @NCState as a portal application to the NCSU Library's information resources. This portal allows user profiling to build a dynamic, customised gateway to both general and discipline specific resources. MyLibrary is a Cornell University Library initiative to provide personalised library services to their students, faculty and staff on the basis of a focus group study to gauge library users.

The MyLibrary project has two components, MyLink and MyUpdate. MyLink allows patrons to save useful information resource links that they found themselves or those suggested by the librarians via a targeted notification in their personal space. Users can access this personal space from any place. MyUpdate periodically queries the online catalogue and notifies users, utilising a pre-defined user profile. Headline is one of the eLib Programme's Phase 3 projects, developing a hybrid library system called the HeadLine Personal Information Environment (PIE), This PIE uses portal-type technology to present an information environment that is personalised to the user's needs and allows user customisation. This project presents users with pages of resources relevant to their courses/department. PIE users are also provided with an "all resources" page that contains all the library resources.

Users can create their own lists of resources on their own pages. Meyyappan reported on ongoing research at Nanyang Technological University in Singapore on the design and development of task-based digital library organisation and a digital work environment (DWE). The major objective of these research projects is to allow users to personalise digital library access so that they can view their preferred resources, and hence, information is automatically filtered. These projects aim to select automatically a subset of the DL collection based on the nature and characteristics of a user.

The user then can add new resources, or delete recommended resources, to his or her page. The DWE project is somewhat different from others in the sense that the main objective of the DWE is to provide filtered access to the local digital library collections, to remote digital libraries, as well as to traditional libraries, and,most importantly, to the vast information resources on the university intranet. The system also allows users to create their own personal workspace to store selected information resources for future use.

DIGITAL REFERENCE SERVICES AND LIBRARIES

A number of libraries have now begun to offer Web-based reference services and a number of recent studies report the current practice of reference services provided by libraries. Although this is not an exhaustive review of all the Web-based reference services provided by libraries, the following section provides a quick overview of some that are currently available.

DIGITAL REFERENCE SERVICES FOR THE GENERAL PUBLIC

Ask A Librarian is a Web-based reference service, primarily designed for UK residents, provided by a network of public libraries in the UK. The site says: "Mail us your factual question and we'll send you an answer within two working days, if not before". A user has to put the query through an enquiry page, which is automatically routed to one of the participating libraries, which receives it as an e-mail message. Within two days the library sends an e-mail message to the user with its response to the enquiry. The British Library provides special reference services for business, patent, scientific, technical, medical and environmental information. These services range from answering simple questions to finding answers to complex questions involving online database searching, etc. While some of these services are free, for others users need to pay. For example, users can ask simple business questions using a form, and can expect an answer within ten working days. Similarly, users can send e-mails with simple environmental queries.

A typical answer in such a case may include:

- A list of bibliographies from a British Library catalogue literature search; and/or;
- A list of organisations to contact for more detailed information, and/ or
- Information retrieved from Internet sources.

Users are not charged for this kind of service. However, for complex queries users need to pay. For example, the British Library provides a Science Technology Medicine (STM) search service for which users need to pay at the following rate:

- J 82.00 per hour of staff time divided into 15-minute periods;
- Plus costs of online searching;
- Plus Value Added Tax (VAT).

As stated in the Web site most searches take at least 30 minutes and therefore cost J 41.00 for staff time + costs for online searching + VAT. The site also mentions that the average list of references costs J 80.00 for medical subjects, and between J 100.00 and J 150.00 for other subjects.

Users are also charged a fee if the results are to be faxed. In order to obtain an STM search service, the user has to fill in a form that has three parts. In the first part users need to fill in their personal details, etc., in the second part, users need to enter the query, and in the third part they need to specify the modes of delivery, payment, etc. In the second part of the form, users can enter the detail specification of the query using Boolean operators and specifying date, language, etc., as limiting factors.

DIGITAL REFERENCE SERVICES FOR USERS OF ACADEMIC LIBRARIES

Academic libraries have also begun to offer Web-based reference services. Wasik and Wasik and Lankes discuss the value of digital reference and AskA services in the K-12 educational environment. They described how AskA services are built and maintained, and also explain how the service works in the classroom.

Archer and Cast emphasised the importance of the personal touch in reference services and discussed how Web technology and the personal element of reference services can be combined to provide Web-based reference services. Tenopir and Tenopir and Ennis reported a survey of the current practices of digital library services in 70 academic libraries in the USA.

These studies noted that the university libraries allow their patrons to pose reference questions in a variety of ways: 99 per cent offer e-mail reference, 96 per cent offer reference services by appointment, and 29 per cent of the libraries offer real-time virtual reference. Breeding briefly described the various customer relationship management (CRM) software, such as eGain, LivePerson and WebLine, that are used by libraries for providing Web-based reference services. He also suggested that while the CRM software offer a great deal of sophistication to the virtual reference environment, they are more complex and expensive compared to lower-cost chat-based utilities that allow a managed two-way text conversation between the reference provider and the remote library user, thus replacing the need for a face-to-face communication.

Smith discussed the current technologies, such as chat and video conferencing software used by libraries for providing digital reference services. Richardson *et al.* examined the information technology aspects and the key organisational issues involved in establishing an electronic reference desk service in a library. They also reviewed the usefulness of some electronic reference services. Breeding provided an overview of some methodologies and collaborations currently in use to extend assistance to patrons in learning to use virtual resources and in finding the information they need.

DIGITAL LIBRARY SERVICE BY CO-OPERATIVE LIBRARY SYSTEMS

In order to deal with the rising cost of reference sources and staff and also of the huge initial investment required for introducing new services in libraries, many have gone for a co-operative model of digital reference services. Oder and Weissman described the 24/7 Reference Project at Metropolitan Cooperative Library System, a consortia around Los Angeles, and the Bay Area Libraries Project at San Francisco that are co-operative projects for providing Web-based reference services to customers.

One of the advantages of Web-based reference services is that users can ask for such services from a remote location at any time of the day. However, Rogers presented an interesting report of a study analysing Web-based reference services in academic libraries in Illinois.

This study shows a usage pattern that is quite similar to the timing of usage of traditional reference services in libraries, for example, 80 per cent of all usage occurred between 8 a.m. and 10 p.m.; evening use was higher than morning use, and the busiest hour was between 2 p.m. and 3 p.m.

DEFINITION OF DIGITAL LIBRARIES AND PERSONALISED SERVICES

While reviewing the definitions of digital libraries, Borgman noted that "in general, researchers (who primarily come from computer science and/or engineering backgrounds) focus on digital libraries as content collected on behalf of user communities, while librarians focus on digital libraries as institutions or services"'. She further stressed that the current state of digital library research and development, especially in the USA, is influenced by the research definition of digital libraries.

The emphasis on the "enabling technologies" for access to digital resources rather than on the services traditionally provided by libraries becomes quite evident when one looks at the two special issues of the *Journal of the American Society for Information Science*, The two issues contain excellent articles reflecting the state of digital library research but none focus on digital library services *per se*. Even the editor of the two special issues did not discuss reference and information services. He mentioned that "digital libraries have the ability to provide a previously unattainable level of service". He emphasised access to information and suggested the various methods, tools and techniques that facilitate improved access to information in digital libraries. However, this is in sharp contrast to the views of the two editors of the special issue of

Information Processing and Management on digital libraries. Marchionini and Fox in their editorial stated that "digital library work occurs in the context of a complex design space shaped by four dimensions: community, technology, services and content".

The fact that digital libraries should not be regarded only as point of access to digital information was emphasised by a definition of digital libraries given by Borgman as early as in 1992 whereby she contended that a digital library are:

- A service;
- an architecture;
- A set of information resources, databases of text, numbers, graphics, sound, video, etc. and
- A set of tools and capabilities to locate, retrieve and utilise the information resources available.

The definition of a digital library that came up in the March 1994 Digital Library Workshop emphasised that a full service digital library must accomplish all the essential services of traditional libraries and also exploit the well-known advantages of digital storage, searching and communication.

There are many other definitions of digital libraries that mention the services aspect, either explicitly or implicitly. Pointing out the lack of emphasis on reference and information services, Sloan lamented that "human interaction in the digital library is discussed far less frequently. One would almost get the impression that the service tradition of the physical library will be unnecessary and redundant in the digital library environment". He emphasised the point that "technology and information resources, on their own, cannot make up an effective digital library". Emphasising the need for personalised services in digital libraries, Lombardi mentioned that, "helping clients find resources in a digitally chaotic world is the first priority". In a Delphi study of digital libraries it was revealed that "the primary roles librarians play in digital libraries include organisation, selection and acquisition and acting as gateways to the provision of services involving information". This study also revealed that "the best reasons for developing a digital library include: increasing access to information, serving end users' needs and bringing organisation to the unstructured universe of electronically available information".

Thus, this study shows the importance of "serving end users' needs", and the need for the librarians to act as "gateways to the provision of services involving information" in a digital library. Another study conducted by Downs and Friedman indicated that "in the absence of human intermediaries, there is a need for end-user instruction on the use of digital libraries". Covi pointed out that "digital libraries will be used only when workers can readily integrate into social legimitated and legitimatable ways of working". She further suggested that subject specialists, as digital library service providers, help users formulate disciplinary search strategies and provide assistance in developing new resources.

Arms, while trying to answer the question "whether or not we need reference librarians in a digital library", pointed out that automatic tools are steadily reducing the need for reference librarians in fields like medicine that required a significant amount of intermediation in information searching. The essence of Arms' paper is that while computers can do a lot in performing most of the traditional jobs of reference librarians, their skills may be required in case of complex information searches.

Arms, however, believes that there have been significant improvements in the end-user search facilities, provided by electronic database search services and Web search engines, and hence, the need for human intermediaries in information searching has reduced significantly. Perhaps the most comprehensive view of the need for and the nature of personalised services in a digital library has been delineated by researchers.

They maintained that:

- Services reflect the functionality afforded by systems serving the community of users. Access services that facilitate search and browsing have been central to digital library research thus far, but there is great need for attention to reference and question-answering, on-demand help, and fostering of citisenship and literacy and mechanisms to simplify participatory involvement of user communities.

LIBRARY SERVICES: CHALLENGES AND OPPORTUNITIES

REFERENCE

E-learners require more than access to e-resources. Traditionally, a reference librarian acts as an additional type of resource, one who can be counted upon to provide expertise in making sense of library systems and research tools, and to offer a helping hand along that often slippery path known as the research process. Virtual library users face additional challenges in mining relevant information out of a computer system that "obstinately" returns zero hits in response to a query that does not match the character strings in its database files. The most common means of providing electronic reference services to remote users has been e-mail, the advantages and disadvantages of which have been well documented in the literature.

The around-the-clock and around-the-world accessibility of e-mail allows users to connect with librarians beyond the walls of library buildings and outside the usual hours of operation. E-mail provides a written record of requests and responses, permits the electronic transmission of search results, and allows librarians time to reflect on requests. One of the most serious concerns about e-mail reference services is their impact on the traditional face-to-face reference interview, particularly the absence of the verbal and non-verbal cues that typically assist a librarian in effectively responding to a question. Hulshof identifies three issues related to the use of electronic communication in serving virtual patrons: immediacy, intricacy, and interaction. Because it is so easy for a learner to send a request electronically and have it arrive at the library instantly, there is a perception that the librarian's response will be as immediate.

The learner may become frustrated, not realising that the process of locating information and developing a response takes the librarian just as long when the request is made electronically as when it is made in person or in any other way. The more intricate or complex the request, the longer it will take for the librarian to clarify it and respond appropriately: a series of e-mail messages may be required, which will further reduce the immediacy of the e-mail request.

Immediacy and intricacy relate to the lack of interaction: the opportunity to discuss and clarify enquiries that occurs in person or over the telephone is not so easily accommodated by e-mail. There are ways to deal with some of these issues. A welldesigned reference Web form, such as that provided on the Ask AU Library: Ask about a Research Topic Web page, which encourages elearners to include full identifying and course information, to describe clearly their research problem and search terminology, and to state the parameters of the assignment, can clarify requests for librarians and reduce the need to e-mail back and forth.

Automated replies, which are sent out by the e-mail programme in response to the receipt of a message, can be used to reassure e-learners that their messages are being received, and can let them know what to expect in terms of service. E-mail reference service can be enhanced and supplemented with additional technologies that raise the level of interaction with realtime or live communication.Chat technology allows e-learners and librarians to send text messages back and forth instantly, using a form of communication that is familiar to most Internet users. There have been a number of library experiments with Web contact center software, which is modeled on the private sector's online solution to providing customer support. Web contact center software provides a higher level of interaction than does basic chat software, allowing for queuing and routing of messages, as well as enabling librarians to "push" Web pages to users. Providing e-learners with a toll-free telephone number remains an effective and convenient reference services strategy, particularly for intricate enquiries. The telephone reference interview works best when both librarian and e-learner are working in front of computers connected to the Internet.

INSTRUCTION

E-learners are frequently silent and invisible as they search and explore a library's online resources, and they do not have the same access that on-campus learners have to formal library instruction sessions. With the array of digital resources available to them, the multiplicity of interfaces and search tools, and the need for evaluation and critical thinking when using the Internet for research, "information literacy" skills are a must-have for e-learners. Information literacy refers to competencies with information sources in a variety of formats. According to the Association of College and Research Libraries, an information literate individual is able to:

- Determine the extent of information needed
- Access the needed information effectively and efficiently
- Evaluate information and its sources critically
- Incorporate selected information into one's knowledge base
- Use information effectively to accomplish a specific purpose
- Understand the economic, legal, and social issues surrounding the use of information, and access and use information ethically and legally

Supporting the integration of information literacy skills training into the core curriculum has become an important issue for libraries.

As an extension of their traditional role of providing library instruction sessions and developing instructional materials, librarians are designing online tutorials and courses that promote information literacy and encourage active learning.

Particularly fine examples are the University of Texas System Digital Library's *TILT—Texas Information Literacy Tutorial*; and Utah Academic Library Consortium's *Internet Navigator*, a multi-institutional online course developed by a team of librarians and Web developers. The British Open University Library has developed *SAFARI*, a freely available interactive tutorial, as well as an information literacy course called *MOSAIC (Making Sense of Information in the Connected Age)*.

Many libraries provide instruction to e-learners by making information available on their Web pages, including frequently asked questions, library glossaries, research guides, and "how-to" pages. Athabasca University Library's Digital Reference Centre integrates resources with contextual instruction and provides links to instructional resources, including a detailed guide to Internet searching that encourages e-learners to think critically about Internet resources, and library research guides such as the *AU Library Guide to Researching Topics in Women's Studies*. Online tutorials usually operate on a model in which the e-learner interacts in isolation with a computer.

Their effectiveness can be enhanced by the addition of more interactive forms of instruction. The librarians at the Florida Distance Learning Reference and Referral Center, for example, have experimented with chat software to simulate a virtual classroom and open up "live" group instruction to e-learners. Librarians can also work with faculty to develop a library thread in a course discussion area, or to open a discussion forum on the library Web pages.

LIBRARY INFORMATION SERVICE

While forecasting the next must-have library information service can be difficult, it is likely that the service will be available in the cloud. Library IT vendors more frequently offer hosting options along software and are developing new systems that leverage cloud architecture to share data and make adoption and management easier for libraries. In addition, open source projects such as DuraCloud and Omeka are using cloud computing to facilitate adoption and generate income. This means that libraries have new choices to make when selecting information services but also means that they must evaluate IT platforms as well as information services. This stage explores some of the criteria that libraries can use to make these decisions and examines the long term implications of the cloud-computing trend.

WHERE SHOULD LIBRARIES FOCUS THEIR IT RESOURCES

With an understanding of these four factors (cost, expertise/capacity, service quality and policy/legal) libraries can make better informed decions about their IT environments. Libraries operate in a complex information environment comprised of multiple information systems and guided by professional ethics including an interest in ensuring free, open and ethical use of information.

Cloud computing provides both an opportunity and a challenge for libraries seeking to hold onto these principles as they adopt new information systems. It is increasingly common to find software vendors and open source software developers that offer systems on hosted platforms. DuraCloud, Equinox and Omeka are just a few examples of open source software offered by non-profit and commercial hosting organisations that also engage in software development. Many commercial developers offer some form of hosted or cloud-based service as well.

This approach has been successful in growing the market for co-operative library services in the US. For example, the Georgia Pines Library system that led the creation of Evergreen not only succeeded in migrating its branch libraries to a new single-ILS platform, it also led the way for other states seeking the opportunities for data sharing and economies of scale. This is good news for open source projects seeking to find long term viability. A recent Ithaka research report discussed the difficulties associated with finding ongoing support for open source projects including new projects, shifting priorities and lagging community involvement. By leveraging cloud-computing hosting, some open source projects are both expanding their community of adopters and benefiting from a revenue stream to enable ongoing development.

My research on cloud computing adoption in libraries showed that it was more common for libraries who had turned to cloud computing to have turned to a SaaS as opposed to PaaS or IaaS platforms. SaaS solutions also pose a long-term challenge for libraries by eliminating local capacity and expertise and ultimately impacting the ability to migrate to new systems. In contrast, PaaS and IaaS solutions provide libraries with tools that level the playing field by preserving local expertise and expanding capacity. Unfortunately, it can be rather difficult, if not impossible, to implement many current commercial and open source systems in a PaaS or IaaS environment.

Many open source and commercial products operate on very specific IT stacks. Although PaaS providers, including Heroku, Cloud Foundry and Google Apps Engine are expanding support for different programming languages and database platforms, library applications have not been developed using these frameworks or deployment techniques. This means that the redundancy, replication and backup features that come with PaaS platforms is out of reach of libraries who either must rely on a vendor-provided SaaS approach or turn to local or IaaS solutions.

Further complicating the situation is the difficulty inherent in migrating to new platforms for libraries using SaaS or IaaS solutions. While PaaS providers may not always support easy migration, by focusing on building applications using industry standard frameworks, vendors and open source communities could make migration more realistic. Unfortunately, few if any commercial or open source library systems operate in these environments. This limits the range of IT solutions available to libraries and can push libraries towards either largely localised or outsourced options.

While cloud computing offers new opportunities for large and small libraries, it also raises the stakes on information service selection. Libraries are increasingly moving towards network-based data and more complex information services. At the same time they are grappling with constrained resources and a new range of IT platforms. In selecting an information system and IT platform, it is important that libraries choose solutions that improve service while also ensuring that their choices are good for the long-term.

FACTORS THAT INFLUENCE IT ADOPTION

The choice to adopt a particular IT service depends on a number of organisational, technical, and community factors. Differences in funding sources, IT staff expertise, information service needs and policy and legal issues means that there is no one right solution for libraries exploring whether or not to adopt cloud-based IT services. Before we consider the longer-term implications of cloud computing adoption we will consider each of these factors.

COST

Ongoing service cost and requirements of funding sources can be a major barrier to cloud adoption. Many IT organisations are focused on a capital or one-time investment model for technology assets. On the other hand, libraries have a background with subscription-based financial models and may feel more comfortable with lower capital but higher ongoing costs than their IT department counterparts. A way to understand the differences in cost is to complete a high-level return on investment (ROI) analysis comparing the differences between cloud and local IT services.

Reese provides an overview of how to compare ROI on cloud and local IT services including start-up vs ongoing costs, staffing/support costs and direct service vs required infrastructure costs. He suggests comparing cloud and local approaches based on your organisation's capital depreciation schedule to better understand the long term costs. While this enables an apples-to-apples comparison it also masks some of the advantages that cloud platforms offers in service flexibility and scalability.

EXPERTISE

Having a strong understanding of local IT staff expertise and capacity is particularly important when selecting an IT infrastructure. Capacity can be defined as the ability of an IT department to provide technology and staffing resources to ensure quality service. In contrast, expertise can be defined as the technical ability of staff to support a service. While these two factors are often directly correlated (*e.g.* an increase in expertise results in an increase in capacity) this is not necessarily the case. In my own research many libraries cited expertise as either a motivating factor (*e.g.* lack of local organisational IT capacity motivated the library to seek external support) or an inhibiting factor (*e.g.* lack of internal IT expertise limited which cloud solutions were explored).

Expertise and capacity in your organisation can be difficult to quantify but tools such as a time-allocation analysis or skill survey may be useful. If your IT staff's skills typically do not include server or datacentre management skills, then infrastructure as a service (IaaS) based cloud solutions are not likely to be successful. If, in contrast, your IT staff has considerable expertise in software development and tweaking, then platform as a service (PaaS) will provide them tools that may expand their service support capacity.

Defining capacity and current workload can be difficult, but at the least should include understanding your staff's recurring tasks and ongoing workload. Scholars explore capacity planning from a staffing perspective in depth in their chapter on Organisational Structures and discuss tasks including service deployment, ongoing management, end-user support and service decommissioning.

SERVICE QUALITY

Service quality is often where libraries begin their exploration of a new application. Service improvements may include new discovery features, better mobile accessibility, or wider research resources. In deciding whether or not an IT service will be of higher quality in a local or cloud-based platform depends in part on how the data being provided in the service can be managed locally over time. For example some information services depend on rapidly changing data that can only be managed via an outsourced subscription (*e.g.* OpenURL resolvers and journal subscription services).

Because many library services feature large data repositories there are a number of services including journal databases, resource linking applications and 24/7 research support services that are often only available as a cloud-based or at least externally supported service.

In these cases, the ability of the vendor to update the database is an important consideration that may sway libraries towards a SaaS versus a locally implemented approach. Other systems, such as digital library applications, integrated library systems, research support and web site services, however, may be influenced more by other factors including expected uptime and reliability, speed and interoperability. Understanding these issues and how they relate to capacity and skill issues can help libraries understand the essential elements of what will make a service successful.

POLICY AND LEGAL FACTORS

Organisational policy and legal factors should be one of the first areas to explore when considering cloud-based services. Understanding the implications of privacy and accessibility laws on information services and having an appreciation of organisational policy can save time by eliminating solutions that are a poor fit. In addition to speaking with organisation experts about service regulations it is important to evaluate Service Level Agreements (SLAs) of cloud providers to ensure that their services are in compliance. When exploring SaaS providers it is also important to understand which cloud platforms these providers are using to provide their services.

While it is important to be aware of these issues, it is equally important to not get bogged down in them when exploring potential IT solutions. Low risk or low sensitivity services may be entirely appropriate for cloud platforms that do not provide bulletproof SLA agreements while services that have private data or management requirements are best in locally managed environments.

LIBRARY AND INFORMATION SERVICES MANAGER

Rather than roll over and accept this, the City of Edinburgh has chosen to harness the very technology cited as a threat and engage with new audiences in new ways. The primary aim has always been to attract physical users to their facilities, however if this is not possible then the next best thing is to engage digitally with their audience.

If you think about citizens in a new way, as mobile, digitally accessible, yet unique and focused on receiving the service that they want whenever they want it, technology gives them and you the opportunity to build a new relationship. Once in place, it also enables you to market your services free of charge, increasingly important in these austere times. Liz McGettigan, Library and Information Services Manager at the City of Edinburgh Council, realised the requirement to engage with developments in web 2.0 services, or risk being left behind in an increasingly digital world. She saw the opportunities for promotion that social media enabled and created a team of people within the library to pull all electronic resources into one location.

Finally, she employed the best technology available to engage with Edinburgh's citizens, in facilities, on the web, socially and on the go:

- *Your Library*: the Web Portal – This unique portal unites all digital resources including catalogues, databases and other web sites.
- *Tales of One City*: This is an integrated approach to social media, engaging citizens and local communities with Edinburgh's blog, Facebook site, Twitter feed, Flickr and YouTube sites. It's push and pull communication that connects with their audience.
- *SOLUS*: This gives Edinburgh the power to schedule content from their web-based Content Management System to digital signage, web and desktop video players, a library app and to social media channels.

SOLUS, a member of the Capita Partner Programme, provides Edinburgh with a unique digital communications capability and helps maximise efficiency in a market where cost saving and best value is critical. Jim Thompson, Edinburgh's Development and Quality Manager, stated, "The premise behind SOLUS is the ability to create once and schedule many.

SOLUS allows us to use one system to upload a promotional video file to our digital signage network, make it available to view across our desktops, embed it into our web portal and intranet, schedule it to our mobile app and distribute it automatically to all our social media channels."

SOLUS has also fully integrated with the Capita LMS to provide functionality for "Your Library App" and this has enabled additional benefits. Most recently added and most popular stock can now be automatically promoted across other platforms managed by SOLUS, such as digital signage and social media. Neil Wishart, Director of SOLUS, was recently at Downing Street, discussing the potential of "Your Library App" with Nick Jones, Director of Digital Communications for No. 10 and The Cabinet Office.

Following the meeting Neil commented:

- "One of the key requirements for government at all levels is to engage more efficiently and effectively with citizens. The digital citizen is real and their dependency on technology is increasing. Rather than being a threat, it provides libraries with the biggest opportunity in a generation to engage with new users in increasing numbers. At the same time, it will let them do this more efficiently and effectively. For the citizen, libraries can offer easy and immediate access to services that can save them money. If people are cutting back due to their personal budgets being squeezed, libraries can take advantage."

To take advantage, access must be 24/7, slick and with instant gratification. V2 of Edinburgh's Library App will allow users to scan a barcode in a shop and automatically search the library catalogue. This is already reality - the recently launched Haringey Library App, which is powered by SOLUS, allows users to scan, search and reserve within seconds. If they don't know how to get to the reserved item, the app will take them there and if an Ebook is available, users can get that instant gratification!

Of course, the proof is in the pudding and Liz McGettigan has solid evidence to prove this innovative use of technology is working. In the last year digital visits have increased by 135,000, PC usage is up by 145,000 sessions, attendance at events has increased, up 32 per cent, and significantly, the decline in physical visits has been reversed with an extra 30,000 people attending libraries. Wishart stated, "It's a classic case of inbound marketing, where effective online positioning has a direct impact on offline behaviour. It's fantastic for Liz to be able to report back to her stakeholders that she has improved access to services and achieved a direct return on investment, both in relation to time and money."

What's next? Creating an app, using social media and installing a digital signage network are all great foundations, but maximum uptake can only be ensured through effective ongoing promotion. The next step in the partnership between Edinburgh Libraries and SOLUS is to develop a range of collaterals to shout about libraries. Liz commented, "There is no point in having the world's best kept secret, we want as many physical and digital users as we can possibly attract. We are actively working on materials with SOLUS to promote our App and these will be resources that can be shared with other libraries across the UK. There is no point replicating spend - if we can all make further efficiency savings and at the same time develop really exciting material, it benefits the whole library community."

Libraries now lead the way in Edinburgh, with other departments continually looking to implement their successful strategy.

INTERNET TECHNOLOGY AND ITS SERVICES

The Internet has revolutionised our society, our economy and our technological systems. Over the past century, important technological developments have created a global environment that is drawing people of the world closer and closer together. About fifteen years ago, most of the world knew little or nothing about the Internet. The Internet was then a private network accessible only to computer scientists and researchers who used it to interact with colleagues in their respective disciplines.

It is estimated that about 60 million host computers on the Internet today serve about 200 million users in over 200 countries and territories. Also, the total numbers of host computers and users have been growing at about 33 per cent every six months Since, 1988 – or roughly 80 per cent per year. The Internet has revolutionised the computer and communications world like nothing before. The invention of the telegraph, telephone, radio, and computer set the stage for this unprecedented integration of capabilities.

The Internet is at once a world-wide broadcasting capability, a mechanism for information dissemination, and a medium for collaboration and interaction between individuals and their computers without barriers of geographic location. The Internet represents one of the most successful examples of the benefits of sustained investment and commitment to research and development of information infrastructure. Beginning with the early research in packet switching, the government, industry and academia have been partners in evolving and deploying this exciting new technology. Today, terms like 'Yahoo' and 'Google' are common part of our vocabulary. Internet-based communication services, content creation and delivery tools applicable in libraries.

INTERNET-BASED COMMUNICATION SERVICES

Libraries use Internet-based communication system while attending their day-to-day routine works. An Internet-based communication system allows communication between computer users hooked into a network.

Internet-based communication system is used for communication between person-to-person, person-to-group and group-to-group. A document or message sent through electronic system may contain text, graphics, image, speech as well as other types of information.

Electronic Mail (E-mail)

Electronic Mail, or e-mail, is a fast, easy and inexpensive way to communicate with other Internet users around the world. It is the most popular and widely used services of the Internet. E-mail is the term given to an electronic message, usually a form of simple text message that a user types at a computer system and is transmitted over some form of computer network to another user, who can read it.

E-mail offers speedy and economical transfer of messages anywhere in the world. Sending e-mail messages are virtually free even to long-distance destinations. Most integrated library system support e-mail-based communication to library users (for circulation and acquisitionrelated activities) and to the vendors/ publishers (for placing orders, reminders, cancellation, etc).

Listserv

Listservs are electronic groups that typically centre around broad topics such as Digital Libraries or Reference Service, ,etc. Listservers of IFLA with the name IFLA-l, Digilib-l LIBJOBS-l are good example of this. Every e-mail message sent to the listserv is distributed to all members of that listserv, which is potentially hundreds or thousands of people.

It does not cost anything to subscribe to a listserv, but simply requires that the user sends an e-mail message to the appropriate address with the message: subscribe (listserv) Firstname Lastname. Each Listserver has one address where a user sends requests to subscribe, un-subscribe, search the archives, etc., and another address to send actual questions or responses to the readers of the list. Apart from organising discussions, job announcements and conference announcements are popular usage of Listservs.

Chat or Instant Messengers

Chat refers to any live discussions conducted using the Internet, usually between more than two persons using their keyboard to communicate. Chat Programmes allow users on the Internet to communicate with each other by typing in real time. It is a feature offered by many online services or Web sites that allows users to 'chat' by typing messages which are displayed almost instantly on the screens of other users who are using the chat room at a given time.

After entering a chat room, any user can type a message that will appear on the monitors of all the other users. Chatting is one of the most popular uses of the Internet. Generally the users remain anonymous by using nicknames or pseudonyms to identify themselves online. A variation of chat is the phenomenon of the instant messenger. Instant messaging can be used to communicate privately with friends, relatives or co-workers.

To send and receive instant messages, a user needs a connection to the Internet and instant messaging software such as Gmail Messenger, Yahoo Messenger and MSN Messenger. The instant messaging software enables a user to set up a list of contacts who also use the same Programme. Once this list is set up, one can see each contact as they come online. A chat session can be started with them quickly and easily. Most conversations are typed text messages that are sent back and forth, though more advanced users can exchange voice, video, files and more.

Conferencing

One of the most exciting features of Internet is to communicate, talk, and see groups of people in different locations around the world, without the expense of travel. Conferencing can take many forms, such as web chat, audio conferencing, video conferencing, multimedia conferencing, screen-sharing, etc.

The conferencing Programmes, such as the popular CU-SeeMe, allow workgroups to use the Internet to see each others' faces in small windows on the computer screen and to hear their voices through computer speakers. One can use desktop video and audio simultaneously or audio can be used alone, or just use the screen-sharing capability without either audio or video.

Audio Conferencing or Internet Telephony

Internet telephony also called IP telephony is a combination of hardware and software that allows the Internet to be used as a telephone carrier. Internet telephony is the conversion of analogue speech signals used on current telephone systems into digital data, allowing calls to be sent over the Internet, bypassing long distance charges.

While the Internet was first devised as a way of transmitting data, it is now being used to make voice calls. Internet telephony is projected to explode as the costs plummet. After the costs of initial set-up and access to an Internet Service Provider, long-distance voice calls can be made via the Internet free of charge, but current quality of voice transmission over the Internet is not always as good as direct telephone service.

There are also PSTN/ Internet gateways that allow regular telephone callers to make Phoneto- Internet-to-Phone connections. There are PC-to-Phone connections and Phone-to- PC connections.

Video Conferencing

Video conferencing is one of the most exciting areas of development in telecommunications, with applications ranging from business to government to education to home and family. Video conferencing involves sending video signals as well as audio and computer data signals. Conferencing can be done one-to-one, one-to-many (called multicast), and many-to-many (called multipoint). While video conferencing, one can talk as well as see the people sitting miles away as if all are discussing in one room facing each other.

One of the most popular applications is transmission on news from various locations by the TV news channels. It also has enormous potential for enhancing communications for small and mid-sized companies, as well as distance learning. However, video conferencing requires sufficient bandwidth to transfer video files of acceptable quality. Desktop conferencing, therefore, is not yet widely implemented for business and educational use. As bandwidth increases, desktop video conferencing is expected to blossom. The PictureTel and Vtel are two of the largest companies that sell video conferencing equipment.

NetMeeting

Microsoft NetMeeting facilitates a new way of talking, meeting, working and sharing over the Internet. It uses Internet phone voice communications and conferencing standards to provide multi-user applications and data sharing over Intranets or the Internet. Two or more users can work together and collaborate in reach time using application sharing, whiteboard, and chat functionality. NetMeeting can be used for common collaborative activities such as virtual meetings. It can also be used for customer service applications, telecommuting, distance learning, and technical support. The product is based on ITU (International Telecommunication Union) standards, so it is compatible with other products based on the same standards.

NetMeeting supports text chat, video shared whiteboard, transferring of files, directory of connected users. Files, such as documents or pictures, can be exchanged. One of the problems with net meeting is the break-up in audio that sometimes becomes inaudible when using it on the Internet, though it works fine over a high-speed company network.

News Groups

Another Internet service similar to listservs is a newsgroup. News Groups are like an International bulletin board. Each group is a forum for a different subject, where a subscriber can post his/her questions or answers.

There are thousands of groups covering just about every area of interest. The difference between listserv and news group is that when a user joins a group, the mail is no longer automatically deposited into his mailbox. Instead a user is expected to go to the newsgroup himself to read it. Some listservs can also be accessed as a newsgroup. A good analogy to a newsgroup is a bulletin board, *i.e.,* one can go to it, as opposed to having mail delivered to his/ her desk. The mails from newsgroup does not get cluttered and it can be easily regulate how often messages are read.

A drawback of a newsgroup lies in the fact that a user must remember to go out to the newsgroup to look for the information. There are hundreds of newsgroup communities. They centre around topics such as computing, news, recreation, social, and 'alternative' topics. There are newsgroups dealing with virtually every topic under the sun and new newsgroups appear every day.

INTERNET-BASED CONTENT PUBLISHING AND DELIVERY SERVICES

The World Wide Web- know as WWW, W3 or simply, the Web help people to publish, organise and provide access to information on the Internet. The WWW can be defined as a hypertext, multimedia, distributed information system that provides links to hypertext documents, as well as to many other Internet tools and databases. The Web serves as a platform for several specialised content publishing and delivery services. Some of the important tools for content publishing and delivery services applicable to libraries and information centres are described here.

Blogs

A blog (an abridged form of term web log) is a Web site, usually maintained by an individual, with regular entries of commentary, descriptions of events, or other material such as graphics or video. Entries are commonly displayed in reverse chronological order. Blogs are considered as lightweight publishing tools. Blogs provide control to an individual or group of individuals for publishing contents or making commentary on it. Technologically, blogs are easier to use, platform-independent, and accessible online over the Internet. Broadly, blogs can be said to be online dairies, however, thousands of blogs are maintained by experts in different subject areas who are willing to share their knowledge, understanding and opinions with other people. Michael Casey, who coined the term 'Library 2.0', for example maintains a blog on Library 2.0 called LibraryCrunch.

The most obvious application of blogs for libraries is to use it as a tool for promotion, publicity and for outreach services. Libraries can disseminate information to their users, make announcements for its new resources and events through its blogs. Blogs can be used to initiate debates and interaction amongst users and staff. Moreover, library staff and user can be encouraged to use Library blogs to get to know each other and interact at personal level.

Wikis

A wiki is a collection of web pages designed to enable anyone who accesses it to contribute or modify content, using a simplified markup language. Wikis are often used to create collaborative Web sites and to power community Web sites. For example, the collaborative encyclopaedia, Wikipedia is one of the best-known wikis, that has broken down one the golden rules of librarianship, *i.e.,* content validation and authenticity of information. Wikis are also used in businesses to provide affordable and effective Intranets and for knowledge management.

Ward Cunningham, developer of the first wiki software, WikiWikiWeb, originally described it as "the simplest online database that could possibly work". Wikis can essentially be equated to open web-pages, where anyone registered with it can publish on to it, add to it, amend it and change it. As in case of blogs, Wikis do not have reliability as traditional resources.

Inspite of this, their value as information resource cannot be undermined. Wikis are not only popular but de-facto source of information for people inspite of the fact that it is not validated or authenticated. The lack of peer review and editorship in case of Wikis is a challenge to librarians. Wikis as items in a collection, and the associated instruction of users in their evaluation, is certainly an important task for libraries. Libraries can use wiki as a communication tool to enable social interaction among librarians and patrons.

Users can share information, ask and answer questions, and librarians can do the same within a wiki. Moreover, a record of these transactions can be archived for perpetuity. Transcripts of such question-answer sessions would serve as a resource for the library to provide as reference. Furthermore, wikis will ultimately evolve into a multi-media environment, where both synchronous and asynchronous audio and video collaborations will take place.

Podcasting

The word 'podcasting' is derived from two words, namely 'broadcasting' and 'iPod' (popular MP3 player from Apple Computer). Podcasting is defined as "process of capturing audio digital-media files that can be distributed over the Internet using RSS feeds for playing-back on portable media players as well as computers.

Users can subscribe to such feeds and automatically download these files directly into an audio management Programme (such as iTunes, Windows Media Player or MusicMatch) on their PCs. When a user synchronises their portable audio device with their personal computer the podcasts are automatically transferred to that device to be listened to at the time and location most convenient for the user. Podcasts can be used with a variety of digital audio formats and play on almost any MP3 player or portable digital audio device - as well as any brand of desktop computer or laptop.

Though podcasters' web sites may also offer direct download or streaming of their content, a podcast is distinguished from other digital media formats by its ability to be syndicated, subscribed to, and downloaded automatically when new content is added, using an aggregator or feed reader capable of reading feed formats such as RSS or Atom. Several libraries use podcasts to support library orientations programmes. Taking advantage of podcasting and other consumer technologies (*e.g.,* PDAs, iPods and other MP3 players) as a deliver media of Library's content and services is a great leap forward for library profession.

Vodcasting

The 'VOD' in Vodcasting stands for 'video-on-demand'. It is identical to podcasting. While podcasting is used for delivering audio files, vodcasting is used for delivering video content. Like podcast content, vodcasts content can be played either on a laptop or on personal media assistant (PMA).

RSS Feeds

RSS stands for Real Simple Syndication or Rich Site Summary. The technology, on one hand allows a web site (or e-publisher) to list the newest published updates (like table of contents of journals, new articles) through a technology called XML, on the other hand, it facilitates a web user to keep track new updates on chosen Web site (s). Like a personal search assistant, RSS feed readers visit pre-defined web sites, look for updated information and fetch it automatically on to the user's desktop. It provides users a way to syndicate and republish content on the Web. Users republish content from other sites or blogs on their sites or blogs, aggregate content on other sites in a single place, and ostensibly distil the Web for their personal use. Libraries are already creating RSS feeds for users to subscribe to, including updates on new items in a collection, new services, and new content in subscription databases. They can also republishing content from other scholarly web sites on their sites.

DIGITISATION

Digitisation is the process of converting the content of physical media (*e.g.*, periodical articles, books, manuscripts, cards, photographs, vinyl disks, ,etc.,) into digital format. A digital image, in turn, is composed of a set of pixels (picture elements), arranged according to a pre-defined ratio of columns and rows. An images document file can be managed as a regular computer file and can be retrieved, printed and modified using appropriate software. In most library applications, digitisation normally results in documents that are accessible from the web site of a library and thus, on the Internet. Optical scanners and digital cameras are used to digitise images by translating them into bit maps.

It is also possible to digitise sound, video, graphics, animations, ,etc. Further, textual images can be OCRed so as to make its contents searchable. Digitisation is not an end in itself. It is the process that creates a digital image from an analogue image. Selection criteria, particularly those which reflect user needs are of paramount importance. Therefore, the principles that are applicable in traditional collections development are applicable when materials are being selected for digitisation.

However, there are several other considerations related to technical, legal, policy, and resources that become important in a digitisation project. Several digital library projects are concerned with providing digital access to materials that already exists with traditional libraries in printed media. Digitisation of printed material is practically the only reasonable solution for institutions such as libraries for converting existing paper collection (legacy documents) without having access to the original data in computer processible formats. Digitisation is the natural choice for large-scale conversions for major digital library initiatives.

Printed text, pictures and figures are transformed into computer-accessible forms using a digital scanner or a digital camera in a process called document imaging or scanning. The digitally scanned images are stored in a file as a bit-mapped page image, irrespective of the fact that a scanned page contains a photograph, a line drawing or text. A bit-mapped page image is a type of computer graphic, literally an electronic picture of the page which can most easily be equated to a facsimile image of the page and as such they can be read by humans, but not by the computers, understably 'text' in a page image is not searchable on a computer using the present-day technology. An image-based implementation require a large space for data storage and transmission. There are several large projects using page images as their primary storage format, including project JSTOR at Princeton University funded by the Melon Foundation.

The project Jstor has a complete set of more than 1000+ journals scanned and hosted on web servers that resides at the University of Michigan and is mirrored at Princeton University. Using technology developed at Michigan, high resolution (600 dpi) bit-mapped images of each page are linked to a text file generated with optical character recognition (OCR) software. Linking a searchable text file to the page images of the entire published record of a journal along with newly constructed table of contents, indexes, permits high level of access, search and retrieval of the journal material previously unimaginable.

Capturing page image format is comparatively easy and inexpensive, it is a faithful reproduction of its original maintaining page integrity and originality. The scanned textual images, however, are not searchable unless it is OCRed, which in itself, is highly error prone process specially when it involves scientific texts.

ELECTRONIC RESOURCES

Electronic resources can be defined as resources in electronic format or computerprocessible format that provide information or an indicator to the information and are generally accessible over the Internet or stored on media like CD ROM/ DVD ROM or other storage devices.

The emergence of Internet and the World Wide Web (WWW) in early 1990s, as a new media of information storage and delivery, came as a real boon for evolution of electronic resources. While searching bibliographic databases became popular, it created demand for actual content in full-text that became difficult for libraries to obtain.

Coincided with evolution of World Wide Web (WWW), display technology evolved, cost of storage came down drastically and networks became faster. It became possible for publishers to deliver content, either as a bitmap page images or other structured formats such as HTML, PDF or RTF. Increasingly larger number of publishers started using the Internet as a global way to offer their publications to the international community of scientists and technologists given the fact that technology is in a position to deliver more content to more users at a significantly lower cost per user.

Electronic resources on the Internet manifest themselves in numerous flavours and categories, although most of them emulate the traditional publishing while others are revolutionary in their design and approach. While the present trend to imitate and emulate the traditional models of scholarly communication may continue for some time, eventually the capabilities added by the new media would be used in more innovative ways. Some of the important types of e-resources are described here.

ELECTRONIC DATABASES

An electronic database consists of electronic resources integrated in highly organised fashion so as to provide controlled access to it by their commercial providers. The first databases were bibliographic in nature and were online version of existing indexing and abstracting services such as Biological Abstracts, Index Medicus, Chemical Abstracts, ,etc.

By the year 1988, only half of all databases were bibliographic in nature. With introduction of a number of online databases containing textual information, news, statistics, commodity prices, ,etc.,, a third type of databases holding text of full-length documents started appearing. Several full-text of encyclopaedia, directories and articles from journals are now available online.

Most of the publishers now provide access to their full-text journals through their web site or through other electronic publishing platforms.

While there are a number of public-domain databases, most online databases require annual subscription for accessing them. Thousands of databases are now available on compact discs (CD-ROM) as well as on the Web.

ELECTRONIC JOURNALS

Electronic journals, or 'e-journals', are used for those journals and newsletters that are prepared and distributed electronically. Electronic journals may be defined very broadly as any journal, magazine, e-zine, webzine, newsletter or type of electronic serial publication which is available over the Internet and can be accessed using different technologies such as WWW, Gopher, ftp, telnet, e-mail or listserv. Several traditional journals are now being published both on the Web and in print.

Content lists for most of the journals are available on the Web or distributed to subscribers as an e-mail text messages or through technologies like RSS and Atom. Internet-based electronic journals started to appear in the beginning of 1990. These journals were mostly delivered as an attachment to e-mail while their back issues were mounted on anonymous ftp sites and users were required to download them from these ftp sites. The libraries and information centres made them accessible through their gopher site.

1995 witnessed peak of Gopher technology which then dropped suddenly and dramatically by 1997. With advent of WWW technology in 1993, electronic publishing became more than a novelty, the web as a means of delivery of electronic information has grown steadily Since, then. As publishers experiment with different publication modes and models, the very definition of a journal is undergoing change in the electronic environment.

New journals have evolved based on the graphic capabilities of the Internet that are available only in electronic form. Like print journals, current and archival issues of electronic journals can be browsed through their content pages. Moreover, e-journals can also be searched not only on their metadata but also in full-text through sophisticated search interface. Currently, there are more than 50,000 peer-reviewed, scholarly electronic journals that are available on the Internet.

ELECTRONIC BOOKS

An electronic book is digital reading material that a user can view on a desktop or Personal Digital Assistant (PDA), laptop or on a dedicated, portable device with a large storage capacity and the ability to download new titles via a network connection.

More and more traditional book publishers, as well as those catering to the professional and business communities, are launching their e-book collections. The electronic books market consists of two distinct components , *i.e.,* i) electronic books consisting of digital material or contents; and ii) electronic book hardware including ebook reading appliance, PCs, laptop or PDA.

The digital material or content that make an electronic book are simply textual and graphical files consisting of bits that can be transported any digital storage media or delivered over a network connection. It is designed to be viewed on some combination of hardware and software ranging from dumb terminals to web browsers, on personal computers to the new reading appliances. More and more books are now being released on the web through enhanced interfaces that offer features such as increased search capacity within a book or entire collection of books, ability to highlight and flag a page, ability to make notes on text without damaging the book, ability to e-mail quotes from the books to other colleagues, etc.

Most publishers like Springer, Wiley InterScience, Taylor and Francis, Cambridge University Press, Oxford University Press, etc., offer their e-book collections on subscription/ one-time purchase basis. Besides, there are a number of e-books aggregators that make thousands of books available online for libraries and individuals at relatively lower cost. Three major ebooks aggregators are Questia, Ebrary and NetLibrary. However, just like other e-resources, e-books come with restrictions such as limit on downloads, in terms of number of pages, *i.e.,* one page at a time or one chapter at a time or no download at all.

ELECTRONIC THESES AND DISSERTATIONS

Theses submitted to the universities as requirement for the award of Ph.D. degree constitute a useful source of information for the new and ongoing research. Doctoral dissertations submitted to universities and academic institutions are originally created in digital format using one of the word processing software packages like MSWord, LaTex, Word Perfect, Word Pro, etc., or one of the desktop publishing packages like Page Maker, Ventura, etc. These documents are undisputedly highly valuable collection especially in digital format that qualify to be an important component of a digital library. The documents composed on word processing packages/ desktop publishing packages can be easily converted into PDF, Post Script or XML using appropriate software tools so as to host them on the web.

Several universities and institutions have already implemented electronic submission of doctoral dissertations under the overall umbrella of an international digital library initiative called 'Networked Digital Library of Theses and Dissertations' (NDLTD).

AUDIO, VIDEO AND STREAMING MEDIA

Streaming multimedia is sequential delivery of multimedia content, including video, audio or some other learning objects, over a computer network that is displayed (or played back) to the end-user as it is being delivered by the provider.

The advent of the MP3 players and the iPod resulted in a greater effort to deliver downloadable media. Moreover, web documents are now coming with greater integration of text with media. Encyclopaedia now have articles with audio files, video clips and animation to illustrate a given topic. Media can broadly be categorised into three category, namely.

- Commercial movies that have greater copyright restrictions,
- Educational media typically are lesser controlled and many a time are made available free-of-cost; and
- Media targeted for individual users, such as movies and songs, that comes with restrictions in terms of copying and distributions.

SUBJECT GATEWAYS OR LIBRARY PORTALS

The web, being a hypermedia-based system, allows linking amongst electronic resources stored on servers dispersed geographically on distant locations.

The portal sites or gateways redirect a user to the holders of the original digital material. The librarians, being the earliest users of the web, started to gather and organise link to important web-based resources on various subjects. A subject gateway can be defined as facilities that allow easier access to web-based resources in a defined subject area.

The simplest types of subject gateways are sets of web pages containing list of links to resources. Some gateways index their lists of links and provide a simple search facility. More advanced gateways offer a muchenhanced service via a system consisting of a resource database and various indexes, which can be searched and/ or browse throughout a web-based interface.

Subject gateways are also known as Subject-based Information Gateways (SBIGs), subject-based gateways, subject index gateways, virtual libraries, clearing houses, subject trees, pathfinders, ,etc. Subject gateway is an important component of a library web site designed for the library users so as to help them discover high-quality information on the Internet in a quick and effective way. In the traditional information environment human intermediaries, such as publishers and librarians, filter and process information so that users can search catalogues and indexes of organised knowledge as opposed to raw data and information. Subject gateways work on the same principle, , *i.e.,* they employ subject experts and information professionals to select, classify and catalogue Internet resources to aid search and retrieval for the users. Users are offered access to a database of Internet resources descriptions which they can search by keywords or browse by subject area. A description of each resource is provided to help users assess very quickly its origin, content and nature, enabling them to decide if it is worth investigating further.

In the process users get benefited from the expertise of librarians and subject experts with subject gateways rather than having to locate, evaluate, filter and organise the resources themselves. Specialised software are available as freeware or as priced software to create and maintain professionally developed subject gateways.

4

Evaluation of Digital Library

When an animal bred in captivity runs, flaps or slithers into the wilderness for the first time, scientists do not simply wave goodbye, wish it well and move on to the next project. Usually the animal is tracked and observed for a long time thereafter—the point of release is where the research really begins.

However, this has been less true for grant-funded digital library projects. Administrative and institutional barriers tend to confine evaluation to the funding period when the system is being designed, and when its uses and effects can only be guessed at.

In this short paper I will discuss a digital library project in environmental science where some of these evaluation issues arose, the value of eliciting narrative data from users, and some ways to take better advantage of existing but underused mechanisms for long-term evaluation of digital libraries.

Viewing information technologies and society as inextricably co-determined makes it necessary to gather data both on the design process and on how the finished systems are used by people—often in quite unexpected ways.

Iterative design and formative evaluation are ways to introduce user feedback into ongoing design, but while these strategies can serve as an effective translation layer between users, designers and builders, the focus is on how an evolving system *might* be used.

How it is *actually* used can be more accurately determined when the system is in the wild, when the designers and their formal evaluation instruments have gone away. Digital libraries are social entities. They tell stories about a culture, a science, a place or a time, through the items represented and organized in the collection, and in use, they help generate new stories as well.

Manovich has advanced the idea of database and narrative as two ends of same continuum; both structure information, but where a database aims for access, a narrative aims for psychological immersion in the story. From an institutional standpoint, digital libraries are rarely ends in themselves.

The social missions of the funding organizations—the stories they wish to tell— often drive the creation of digital libraries, but how well a finished system supports the mission can't be fully evaluated until the digital library has had some time to develop a user base. This line of research began with a participant observation of the design of a digital library of environmental science collections. Funded by an Library Services and Technology Act (LSTA) grant, the project involved diverse designers, content, metadata and institutional participants.

As one of the participants in the environmental science digital library noted, "Part of the art of grant writing is interpreting vague language in a way that lets you do what you want to do," or in other words, making project proposals and achievements dovetail with the mission and goals of the funding agency.

These goals included outreach and evaluation, so a usability component was included in the grant proposal. My initial role in the project was to develop the instruments and conduct the evaluation.

Understandably, digital library designers tend to create evaluation instruments that demonstrate in a measurable way the work they've done, a tacit statement of the value produced for the grant funds received. For example, the design of the interface, the appropriateness of descriptive metadata, and user success at canned search tasks are classic evaluative measures.

However, in an analysis of the Perseus Digital Library (PDL), Marchionini writes: "Operational data are powerful components in a chain of inferences that address impact but the PDL evaluation illustrates the value of anecdotes and "stories" that illustrate new effects, i.e., how DLs augment existing capabilities with new ones. These augmentations garner public support for a DL and should not be underestimated in assessing impact.

Integrating multiple views is more naturally done with narratives than summary statistics and integrating these forms of evidence can aid in assessing complex change." In the evaluation, statistical and demographic data were not hard to come by.

Observation, interviews, document analysis, narrative analysis and social network analysis were effective ways to construct as complete a picture as possible about the interactions of the designers. But the usability component needed to be completed at the same time as the digital library, in time for the results to be included in the final LSTA grant report (though the exact LSTA grant regulations vary by state, most LSTA grantees must submit a final grant report within 15-30 days of project completion).

Participants in the usability study were evaluating a still evolving system, and had to project potential uses into their responses to open-ended interview questions. By the time they might integrate the collections into their professional lives, and perhaps surprise themselves with unexpected dimensions of usefulness, the evaluation would be long over. This is certainly not to say that there is no such thing as continuing evaluation of grant-funded digital libraries.

But the mechanisms for long-term evaluation are usually little more than Web forms or e-mail links, not organic components of the digital library. In practice, designers are more concerned with present and future digital library projects than with continuing evaluation of those of the past.

Digital library researchers have an opportunity to conduct this longer-term research, to question and reveal the impacts of digital libraries as social entities, and to apply the resulting knowledge to future projects.

The good news is that in some situations, a mechanism for longer term evaluation already exists. For example, the State Library of Ohio's LSTA grant process makes use of a "year-after" evaluation form (http://winslo.state.oh.us/publib/lstayraft.html), which includes questions such as "Did the project produce any unexpected results?" and encourages narrative ("Please provide a success story of how your project has impacted someone's life or had a positive impact on the community.").

This is precisely the sort of openended data collection instrument that can reveal how a digital library is actually being used—but even this document is only the length of a one-page questionnaire. Subsequent research will attempt to evaluate the usefulness of this and other longer-term evaluation instruments, and how they might be expanded.

While longer-term evaluation should include quantitative data such as transaction logs and perhaps a list of external sites that link to collection content, evaluation instruments should also be open-ended, designed to encourage narrative expressions of unexpected use, the kind of data that reveal to funding agencies the real impact of their grants.

Iterative digital library design philosophies have always had at their core the sense that user input should feed back into ongoing system design. I propose here simply a wider iterative design circle, one that allows for more naturalistic data about longer-term use to be fed back into future systems.

In sum, lessons learned that will be explored in future research include an increased emphasis on:

- Long-term evaluation of digital libraries
- Narrative data; allowing users to tell stories
- Unexpected uses
- Evaluating social outcomes, not just the design process or product
- Linking findings more directly to the higherlevel goals of funding agencies

DIGITAL LIBRARY INFORMATION APPLIANCES

Although digital libraries are intended to support education and knowledge work, current digital library interfaces are narrowly focused on retrieval. Furthermore, they are designed for desktop computers with keyboards, mice, and high-speed network connections. Desktop computers fail to support many key aspects of knowledge work, including active reading, free form ink annotation, fluid movement among document activities, and physical mobility.

This paper proposes portable computers specialized for knowledge work, or *digital library information appliances*, as a new platform for accessing digital libraries. We present a number of ways that knowledge work can be augmented and transformed by the use of such appliances.

These insights are based on our implementation of two research prototype systems: XLibris, an "active reading machine," and Tele- Web, a mobile World Wide Web browser.

Fig. XLibris Prototype in a Reader's lap.

The standard platform for accessing today's digital libraries is a desktop computer with a keyboard, a mouse, information retrieval software, and a network connection. Unfortunately, desktop computers are not suitable for many types of knowledge work.

Studies of people using electronic and paper documents show that desktop systems fail to support four important activities:

- Active reading
- Free form ink annotation
- Fluid movement among document activities
- Physical mobility

As a result of focusing on the desktop, today's interfaces for accessing digital libraries support retrieval in isolation, without addressing these broader work practices. We propose a new platform for accessing digital libraries: specialized portable computers designed for knowledge work, or *digital library information appliances.* In this paper, we draw on our experience designing and building two research prototype information appliances— the XLibris "active reading machine" and the TeleWeb mobile Web browser— to show how these devices can support a broad range of activities in the digital library.

READING AND DIGITAL LIBRARIES

The first and most fundamental document activity is reading. "Reading" encompasses a broad range of complex and poorly understood practices involving documents, including skimming, searching, browsing, speed-reading, surfing, reviewing, and rereading. Although we often take it for granted, reading can be hard work. We use the term *active reading* to distinguish this rich collection of activities from simply looking at words on a page.

Desktop computers do not support active reading. Once expected to create a paperless office, computers have instead produced ever-increasing quantities of paper documents. Dataquest predicts printers and copiers will generate over 1012 pages in the U.S. in 1997.

This statistic suggests that people do not use computers to read. The reason for this is obvious: paper supports extended, focused, deep reading practices better. Current research on digital libraries does not address a broad range of reading activities. Instead, as David Levy points out, digital libraries support shallower, more fragmented, and less concentrated reading.

The research focus in this field is on tools for search, selection, and distillation, tools that promote identification and extraction of information fragments. Because digital library interfaces do not support active reading, people search online and then print documents to read them. This "search and print" reality contrasts with the "search and read" ideal held by researchers.

Although a dual online/paper system is not *a priori* undesirable, we will show the many advantages of an online system that enables a variety of reading practices. The XLibris active reading machine supports a broad class of reading activities by employing a "paper document metaphor" (as opposed to the desktop metaphor) that imitates the physical experience of reading and marking on paper. The paper document metaphor follows lessons learned from a number of studies comparing reading online to reading on paper, summarized below.

TANGIBILITY

Readers often move paper documents to avoid glare, to speed up handwriting, or to adjust their perspective of a text. In contrast, most computer displays are stationary while in use, so that readers must move themselves— their heads, their bodies, and their arms— rather than their display. XLibris supports paper document-like tangibility by running on tablet displays. Although XLibris has not been deployed for real use, people say that holding a page-sized display in their lap and being able to easily reposition it changes their online reading experience. The tangibility of paper documents also supports navigation. Turning paper pages seems easy and natural, and the weight and thickness of a paper document convey length and location. In XLibris, pressure strips on the case of the device provide a tangible interface for page turning: pressing on one side of a sensor moves to the next or previous page, and holding down initiates riffling through pages. The harder you press, the faster you move. A quick animated transition indicates the direction of turning.

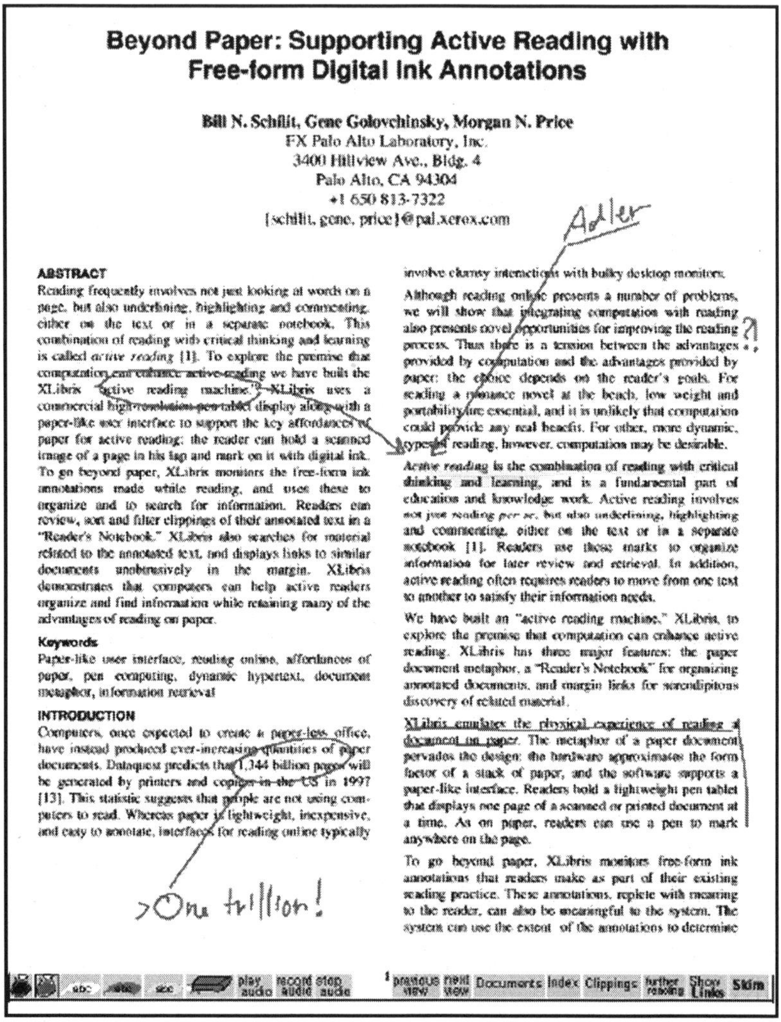

Beyond Paper: Supporting Active Reading with Free-form Digital Ink Annotations

Bill N. Schilit, Gene Golovchinsky, Morgan N. Price
FX Palo Alto Laboratory, Inc.
3400 Hillview Ave., Bldg. 4
Palo Alto, CA 94304
+1 650 813-7322
{schilit, gene, price}@pal.xerox.com

ABSTRACT
Reading frequently involves not just looking at words on a page, but also underlining, highlighting and commenting, either on the text or in a separate notebook. This combination of reading with critical thinking and learning is called *active reading* [1]. To explore the premise that computation can enhance active reading we have built the XLibris "active reading machine." XLibris uses a commercial high-resolution pen tablet display along with a paper-like user interface to support the key affordances of paper for active reading: the reader can hold a scanned image of a page in his lap and mark on it with digital ink. To go beyond paper, XLibris monitors the free-form ink annotations made while reading, and uses these to organize and to search for information. Readers can review, sort and filter clippings of their annotated text in a "Reader's Notebook." XLibris also searches for material related to the annotated text, and displays links to similar documents unobtrusively in the margin. XLibris demonstrates that computers can help active readers organize and find information while retaining many of the advantages of reading on paper.

Keywords
Paper-like user interface, reading online, affordances of paper, pen computing, dynamic hypertext, document metaphor, information retrieval

INTRODUCTION
Computers, once expected to create a paper-less office, have instead produced ever-increasing quantities of paper documents. Dataquest predicts that 1,344 billion pages will be generated by printers and copiers in the US in 1997 [13]. This statistic suggests that people are not using computers to read. Whereas paper is lightweight, inexpensive, and easy to annotate, interfaces for reading online typically involve clumsy interactions with bulky desktop monitors.

Although reading online presents a number of problems, we will show that integrating computation with reading also presents novel opportunities for improving the reading process. Thus there is a tension between the advantages provided by computation and the advantages provided by paper; the choice depends on the reader's goals. For reading a romance novel at the beach, low weight and portability are essential, and it is unlikely that computation could provide any real benefit. For other, more dynamic, types of reading, however, computation may be desirable.

Active reading is the combination of reading with critical thinking and learning, and is a fundamental part of education and knowledge work. Active reading involves not just reading *per se*, but also underlining, highlighting and commenting, either on the text or in a separate notebook [1]. Readers use these marks to organize information for later review and retrieval. In addition, active reading often requires readers to move from one text to another to satisfy their information needs.

We have built an "active reading machine," XLibris, to explore the premise that computation can enhance active reading. XLibris has three major features: the paper document metaphor, a "Reader's Notebook" for organizing annotated documents, and margin links for serendipitous discovery of related material.

XLibris emulates the physical experience of reading a document on paper. The metaphor of a paper document pervades the design: the hardware approximates the form factor of a stack of paper, and the software supports a paper-like interface. Readers hold a lightweight pen tablet that displays one page of a scanned or printed document at a time. As on paper, readers can use a pen to mark anywhere on the page.

To go beyond paper, XLibris monitors free-form ink annotations that readers make as part of their existing reading practice. These annotations, replete with meaning to the reader, can also be meaningful to the system. The system can use the extent of the annotations to determine

Finally, "location guides" of varying thickness drawn in the top cor- ners of each page provide feedback about the length of the document and the reader's current location.

Page Orientation & Fixed Layout

Paper documents are laid out on fixed-size pages. The page layout often communicates the type of the document (e.g., business letter versus technical article) and where to find important information (e.g., a return address). The fixed layout also supports spatial memory and helps readers find old information. In these and other ways, paper pages give readers an excellent "sense of the document." This sense of the document is often lost online.

Most CRT monitors cannot display a full page of text legibly, leading to awkward scrolling and zooming. Word processors and Web browsers commonly re-flow the text on a "page." And hypertext versions of paper documents can lead to disorientation and a sense of being lost. XLibris respects pages by displaying the image of a single page at a time.

Because the LCD panels we use are designed for landscape viewing, XLibris rotates the image 90° to approximate the portrait orientation of a typical printed page. XLibris stores the image of each page and the underlying text; this "image + text" file format is compatible with printed and with scanned documents.

Multiple Displays

People often work with multiple pieces of paper simultaneously, either with several pages from one document or with several documents. Most of today's computers provide multiple virtual displays through use of a windowing system. Unfortunately, the effort of managing window layout and switching among windows can interfere with reading.

Therefore XLibris displays a single page image and does not support windows. Since limiting the digital library information appliance to a single page image is problematic, we have considered a number of ways to address the need for collateral displays. Presenting two full-page images side by side, as in Book Emulator, makes text unreadable on current tablet displays, but may be feasible as LCD technology evolves. A form factor with multiple physical displays is another approach.

(Bush's vision of a Memex desk included multiple displays). In our case, to maintain mobility, a book (instead of a tablet or desk) with two opposable LCD panels may be appropriate. Weiser presents an enticing vision of ubiquitous computing with devices so cheap they can be scattered and used as paper.

In the near term, however, a small number of pen computers in conjunction with nearby desktop displays or even paper may provide the most practical solution to the problem of collateral document work. In summary, XLibris employs tangibility, page orientation, and fixed layout to provide an online reading experience comparable, in many ways, to reading from paper.

FREE FORM INK ANNOTATION

"Until we provide support for smooth integration of annotation with reading, it is likely that people will continue to annotate paper materials, even as they read materials in a digital library." – Cathy Marshall The second key document activity is annotation. Knowledge work involves reading combined with categorizing, speculating, remembering, judging, or, more broadly, critical thinking.This active reading process is facilitated by underlining, highlighting and making notes on the text or in a separate notebook. Marking on paper helps readers "make the text their own" and is a common practice associated with deep understanding of written information. In a nutshell, readers write.

Unfortunately, annotation online is quite different from its paper-based cousin. Interfaces for annotating often involve selecting a command, pointing with a mouse, and typing on a keyboard. They generally require much more effort than scribbling with a pen.

Text annotations are not as visually distinct as ink marks, and online annotations often cause changes in the layout of the document.

We believe that the ability to make unstructured, free-form, idiosyncratic ink marks is a crucial feature of any interface to digital libraries.

Although such marks may not have explicit meaning to the computer, they have rich semantic meaning, supporting visual and episodic memory. An essential aspect of ink on paper is its lack of modality: users can write anything they want, anywhere on the page.

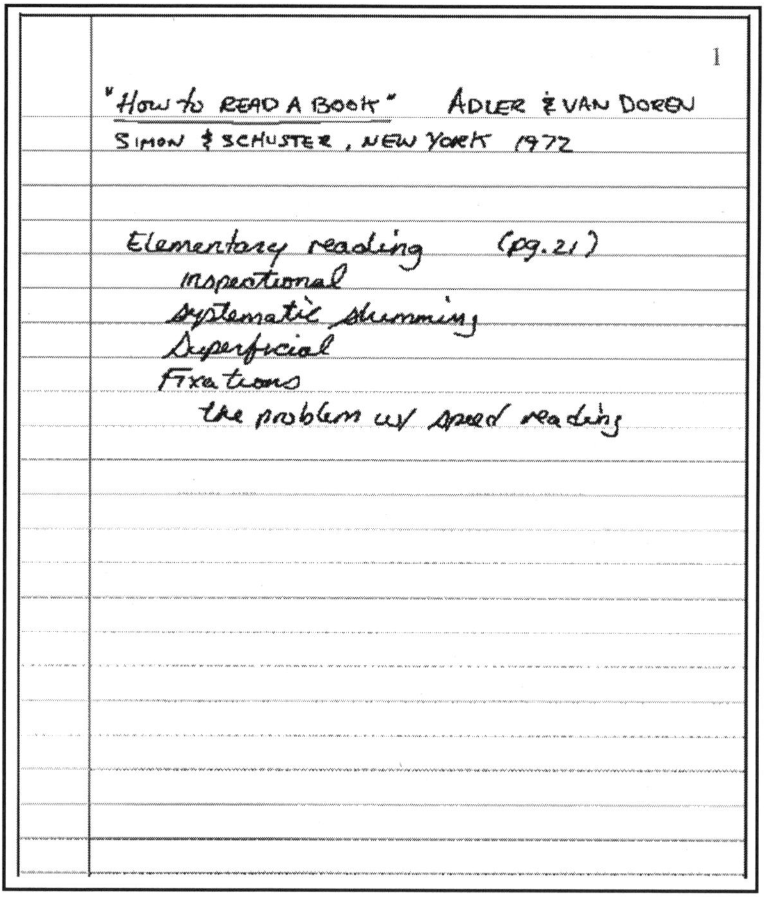

Fig. A Notebook page from XLibris.

In XLibris, we followed this principle by letting users scribble notes, draw figures, highlight, or annotate text, all without switching modes or applications. Readers highlight and mark-up document page images as they read or flip to a blank page in a lined notebook for more space. XLibris provides several colors of ink, several highlighter pens, and a stroke-based eraser.

FLUID MOVEMENT AMONG DOCUMENT ACTIVITIES

The third key aspect of knowledge work is fluid movement among different styles of reading and different document activities. As an example, consider the process of "information triage" where an analyst skims through a pile of search results and reduces them to a manageable set.

The current practice is to fire off a query to a search engine, retrieve the 100 top-ranked documents, print them out, mark them up with highlighters, and put them into piles. Analysts then read the most relevant passages to answer the original question. Consider an alternative scenario where the analyst owns a digital library information appliance. After conducting a search, the analyst skims the documents online. The appliance enhances skimming by emphasizing important material. As on paper, the analyst marks up important information as it is found. Instead of reviewing the collected information by thumbing through piles of paper, the analyst views a concise collection of his or her text annotations. If any of the annotated material is worth reading in greater depth, the analyst can do so comfortably online. If the analyst needs more information, the text that has already been highlighted can be used to generate the next query. At a high level, this scenario demonstrates fluid movement among document activities. The analyst quickly moves among searching, skimming, annotating, reviewing, and deep reading.

There is no waiting for a printer. Because skimming and deep reading are tightly integrated with retrieval, analysts can determine if the information they are collecting is useful before they invest much effort. This scenario also demonstrates how computation can enhance skimming, reviewing, and searching. Because the interface is based on a paper document metaphor, the reading and annotation activities remain much the same as on paper. In our design, the "computer" remains in the background and, when requested, rises to the surface to assist the reader with the tasks of skimming, reviewing, and searching. Below we describe how XLibris supports and augments these three activities.

Skimming Mode

Skimming is one way readers gain a quick impression of a text. When skimming, the reader's eyes typically search for and alight on key words or sentences and take in short passages before moving on. Sometimes the reader becomes engaged and shifts into deep reading, or is distracted and moves into quicker skimming or into riffling.

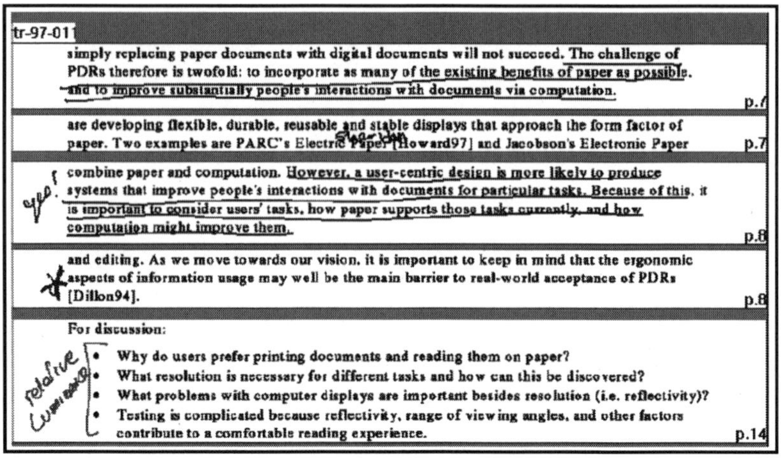

Fig. The Reader's Notebook shows annotated clippings of documents laid end-to-end. Clippings are labeled with document title and page number and are linked to the corresponding pages.

XLibris' "skimming mode" highlights phrases and sentences that are characteristic of the document being skimmed. We call out key phrases because they can be read at a glance and tend to reflect the topic of the nearby text.

This assists with the activity of scanning the text for relevant portions to read. The *Wall Street Journal* and *People Magazine* use a similar technique of boldfacing company names and Hollywood celebrities' name to help readers find information. We also highlight summary sentences to support a speedreading– like activity. Skimming mode uses a commercial text summarizer to identify summary sentences that are emphasized. Skimming through a document of highlighted summary sentences provides a narrative overview that is not available by just reading key phrases.

Both of these highlighting techniques permit a smooth transition from skimming to deep reading: key terms and sentences can help readers decide whether a passage is worth reading and are likely to be appropriate places to transition to deep reading. Skimming mode uses shades from gray to black to indicate term importance. Meaningful terms are identified by heuristics that select noun phrases.

The shade for each term is then based on a statistical information retrieval measure: terms that occur frequently in the document but occur rarely in other documents are colored black, while terms common to many documents are colored light gray. For example, the term "digital library information appliance" would be colored black when it appears in this document. Skimming is a common practice: a study of college students' reading habits reported that skimming occupied 32% of their reading time, and that "86% of the descriptions of skimming strategies mentioned a selection process based on key words and/or particular sentences and paragraphs in certain text locations". Although our design requires empirical evaluation to confirm its utility, from our experiences thus far, we are optimistic that computers can improve the skimming activity and that augmented skimming is a useful function for a digital library information appliance.

Reviewing the Reader's Notebook

Reviewing paper documents is facilitated by the marks made during reading: marks not only record information but are also used to organize it for later review. There are three common venues for marking: annotating on the page, taking notes in a notebook, and writing on loose-leaf paper. Annotations on the page highlight key information but tend to be lost in piles of paper. Notebooks are compact and can be reviewed quickly, but taking notes can be tedious and error-prone.

Unbound notes can be reorganized flexibly, but require even more effort by the note taker. XLibris' Reader's Notebook combines the best features of annotating directly on the page, of taking notes in a separate notebook, and of organizing index cards. As with paper documents, readers mark on the page in the context of the document, yet without the laborious and imprecise step of copying.

As with a bound notebook, readers can review concise annotations by time. Finally, as with note cards, flexible filtering and sorting of the view allow readers to reorganize their information as needs change. The Reader's Notebook extracts "clippings" of annotated text and lays them end to end in a separate, multipage view.

Each clipping is linked to the corresponding annotated page, so readers can move fluidly between notes and documents. Each clipping includes some surrounding text, and is labeled with document title and page number to help readers understand the meaning of the marks. In designing clippings, we had to decide how much of the document should be shown for each annotation.

Starting with the bounding rectangle of each ink stroke, we expand it horizontally to the width of the page and vertically to include complete words. Snippets that overlap are merged together resulting in reasonably sized clippings of annotated text.

The Reader's Notebook can display, sort, and filter clippings from one document or from all documents. By default, clippings are sorted by document page number, which is analogous to rummaging through a pile of paper, but should be faster because readers do not see the less important (i.e., un-annotated) information. Clippings can also be sorted by time so that new information appears at the end, as in a paper notebook.

Finally, readers can filter the clippings by ink colour to search for different kinds of marks or to group related items together. Many readers already use different pens to mark different types of information. For example, some lawyers highlight "pro" information in green and "con" information in red.

Finding Information Related to Readers' Annotations

Readers often search for related material and move from one text to another. For example, an ecology student studying the effects of acid rain in the Appalachian Mountains decides to search the Internet for information on the economy of West Virginia. A doctor reading up on a drug she has never prescribed decides to follow a reference to a study of its side effects.

Unfortunately, in both online and offline situations, finding related materials and reading are not well integrated. Typical information retrieval interfaces force users to stop reading, to identify related documents, and then to print them. References found in paper documents are even more timeconsuming to track down. Although hypertext was designed to address some of these problems, authors cannot anticipate the information needs of all readers. Ironically, despite the fact that readers' interests may change rapidly, interfaces for moving from reading to finding and back to reading again are time consuming and disruptive. Clearly this is another example where fluid movement across document activities is desirable. XLibris facilitates fluid transitions among reading, searching and browsing by creating a dynamic hypertext from readers' marks. The system observes readers' annotations and the text of the underlying document and generates hypertext links (margin links) to related documents: no additional effort from readers or authors is required. Because XLibris suggests links of interest to particular readers at particular times— based on the passages they are marking— people can discover useful information *serendipitously*. This type of serendipitous retrieval is a benefit of paper libraries: as people walk to the shelf for a particular book, walls of related books surround them, making it possible to find interesting material accidentally. Although serendipity in the library is often a rewarding experience, it is generally lacking in online systems. XLibris provides two user interfaces that integrate reading, searching, browsing, and serendipity. These are described below.

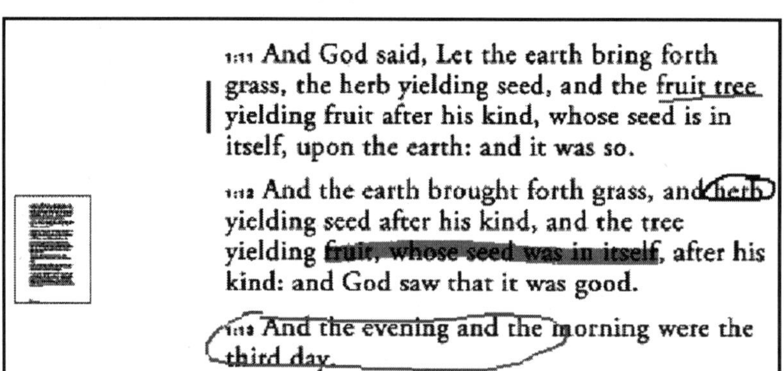

Fig. Examples of Highlighting, Underlining, Circling, and margin Annotations. Each Annotation Generates a Query. If a good match is found, XLibris adds a margin link (Rectangle on the left) that shows the thumbnail of the Destination page.

MARGIN LINKS

Margin links provide serendipitous access to related documents *during* the active reading process. As readers mark up passages, the system finds related documents and presents links unobtrusively in the margin; our intent is to provide a modeless link suggestion mechanism. Because margin links persist, readers can follow links at their leisure.

We use thumbnail images of the target page as anchors. The reader taps on an anchor to move to that page. For the most part, link creation does not disrupt the reading process since the reader is free to disregard the suggestion and to continue reading. In the current design, however, margin links intrude on the reading process more than we would like.

One problem is that XLibris computes a separate query for each stroke (although strokes often do not result in margin links because of a similarity threshold). We have begun to address this by adding a button to turn links off and by designing ways to manage the frequency with which margin links appear.

FURTHER READING LISTS

When readers reach the end of a document, they often want to know more. The document may not emphasize the topic they are most interested in, or it may spark an interest in a new topic without providing enough depth or detail. Sometimes this need is addressed. For example, articles in *Scientific American* typically describe an area of research at a high level, without providing much technical detail. To help readers go into more depth, the editors create a further reading list at the end of each article.

Further Reading

LEGALLY SPEAKING: REGULATION OF TECHNOLOGIES TO PROTECT COPYRIGHTED WORKS. Pamela Samuelson in *Communications of the ACM*, Vol. 39, No. 7, pages 17–22; July 1996.

FORUM ON TECHNOLOGY-BASED INTELLECTUAL PROPERTY MANAGEMENT: ELECTRONIC COMMERCE FOR CONTENT. Edited by Brian Kahin and Kate Arms. Special issue of the *Interactive Multimedia News*, Vol. 2; August 1996.

LETTING LOOSE THE LIGHT: IGNITING COMMERCE IN ELECTRONIC PUBLICATION. Mark Stefik in *Internet Dreams: Archetypes, Myths, and Metaphors*. Edited by Mark Stefik. MIT Press, 1996.

SCIENTIFIC AMERICAN March 1997 81

Fig. A Further Reading list from *Scientific American*

The *Scientific American* example illustrates the limitations of authored reading lists. The article describes a technological vision for protecting digital copyrights. Consider a reader with a narrower interest, such as "how digital copyright affects librarians." The reference to a six-page article on digital copyright law may help track down this information, but the reference is unlikely to answer the question directly. Furthermore, by the time the reader scans the further reading list, more appropriate articles may have been written. XLibris augments this traditional editorial practice by automatically generating further reading lists for each document. Unlike static references, these lists reflect the interests of a specific reader at a specific point in time. As with margin links, the reader's interests are inferred from annotations, and no additional intervention from the reader is required.

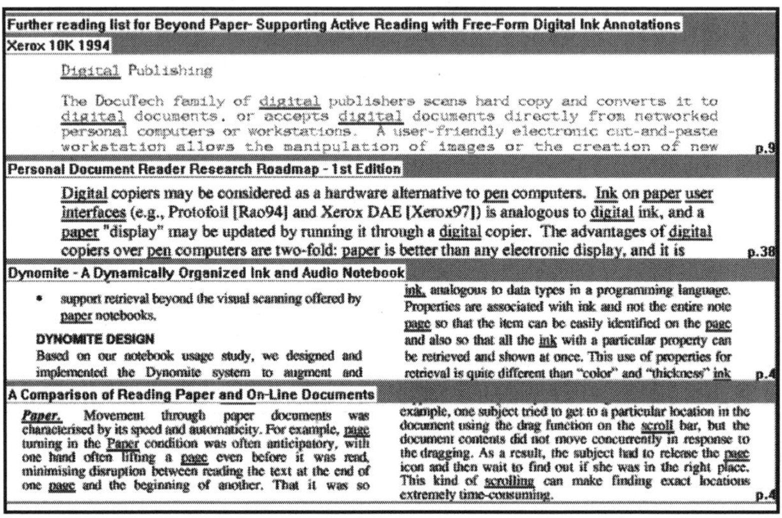
Further reading list for Beyond Paper- Supporting Active Reading with Free-Form Digital Ink Annotations

Xerox 10K 1994

Digital Publishing

The DocuTech family of digital publishers scans hard copy and converts it to digital documents, or accepts digital documents directly from networked personal computers or workstations. A user-friendly electronic cut-and-paste workstation allows the manipulation of images or the creation of new p.9

Personal Document Reader Research Roadmap - 1st Edition

Digital copiers may be considered as a hardware alternative to pen computers. Ink on paper user interfaces (e.g., Protofoil [Rao94] and Xerox DAE [Xerox97]) is analogous to digital ink, and a paper "display" may be updated by running it through a digital copier. The advantages of digital copiers over pen computers are two-fold: paper is better than any electronic display, and it is p.38

Dynomite - A Dynamically Organized Ink and Audio Notebook

- support retrieval beyond the visual scanning offered by paper notebooks.

DYNOMITE DESIGN

Based on our notebook usage study, we designed and implemented the Dynomite system to augment and

ink, analogous to data types in a programming language. Properties are associated with ink and not the entire note page so that the item can be easily identified on the page and also so that all the ink with a particular property can be retrieved and shown at once. This use of properties for retrieval is quite different than "color" and "thickness" ink p.4

A Comparison of Reading Paper and On-Line Documents

Paper. Movement through paper documents was characterised by its speed and automaticity. For example, page turning in the Paper condition was often anticipatory, with one hand often lifting a page even before it was read, minimising disruption between reading the text at the end of one page and the beginning of another. That it was so

example, one subject tried to get to a particular location in the document using the drag function on the scroll bar, but the document contents did not move concurrently in response to the dragging. As a result, the subject had to release the page icon and then wait to find out if she was in the right place. This kind of scrolling can make finding exact locations extremely time-consuming. p.4

Fig. A Further Reading list in XLibris. Each related Document is Presented as a Clipping of the most Relevant Sentence with key Phrases Underlined.

Further reading lists are presented as a separate set of pages, or *view*, associated with each document. Readers can access this view at any time, whether or not they have annotated the current document.

Of course, the more annotations the user has made, the more focused the resulting list is on the reader's interest as opposed to the document as a whole. Visually, the further reading list looks like a Reader's Notebook of annotations except that each clipping is a segment of a related document obtained from a search engine. These clippings, with matching terms underlined, help readers understand the destination of the link and also make the target passage more recognizable if they choose to follow the link.

Query-mediated Links

Both margin links and further reading lists use a technique called *query-mediated links*. Query-mediated links derive a query from a user's interaction with a document and use that query to identify related documents. Golovchinsky has shown that query-mediated links based on explicitly selected words and passages are effective in supporting information exploration tasks.

XLibris computes margin links from the words, phrases and passages that are implicitly selected by the reader's marks. (We do not expect readers to make marks for querying explicitly, but rather as part of their existing annotation practice.) Marks are converted into text selections, which are then expressed as full-text queries that yield a best-matching passage. The system adds a margin link to the best match if its similarity value (or belief score) is above a threshold. For further reading lists, each annotation is interpreted as a text selection and is transformed into a list of word scores.

The scores for each word are then summed across all annotations. If several annotations select the same instance of a word, then the maximum score for that instance is used. The words along with their scores are used to generate a query. If not many words have been included, then terms that are most characteristic of the document can be added. This padding reduces the chance that a query based on a small number of annotations will return documents that are entirely unrelated.

Ink Annotations as Queries

XLibris recognizes several distinct ink patterns from which queries are computed. These include underlined words, highlighted words, circled words, circled passages, and margin annotations. We emphasize that there is no "vocabulary of marks" that readers must learn; rather, our heuristics are based on general annotation practices. Each type of annotation results in a slightly different query for the search engine. Marks that select specific words translate into queries that retrieve other instances of the same term. Marks that select longer passages generate queries that search for similar passages.

PHYSICAL MOBILITY

The fourth and final document activity supported by digital library information appliances is mobility. Until now we have discussed reading in XLibris; in this section we describe mobile information access in TeleWeb. Desktop access to digital libraries is not adequate for mobile workers.

A doctor making hospital rounds has no desktop with her to access a digital library. This could have grim repercussions: a recent study concluded that patients for whom prompt MEDLINE searches were conducted have significantly lower costs and shorter hospital stays. Mobile work is not limited to physicians and traveling salespeople; even office workers often work with documents away from their desks. For these people, portable information appliances can provide access to digital libraries anywhere, anytime. Unfortunately, it is not possible to give mobile people the same network access that they would have in their office. Compared to wired desktop networks, wireless networks are slow, expensive (with different billing schemes), and only intermittently available. As workers move from place to place, they are likely to experience three levels of connectivity: high quality connectivity from an office network, lower quality connectivity from a wireless network, and no connectivity at all when disconnected. How can people use digital library appliances to access distributed information sources across this range of operating conditions? Aside from the variable networking conditions, there are two other issues that affect mobile access to digital libraries.

First, downloading a document over a wireless network can be very expensive, and current interfaces for search engines and Web browsers do not help people manage these costs.

Second, user interaction is punctuated by surprises: an information request may return right away (when data is locally stored), take a while (when data is remote), or take forever (when the network is down). The TeleWeb mobile Web browser was designed and built to explore these three issues.

TeleWeb runs on a laptop computer with multiple communication channels: it may be docked to an office Ethernet, used from home over a telephone line, used while traveling over a wireless network such as a cell phone, or operated while not connected to a network. The lessons learned from TeleWeb apply not only to the Web but also to digital libraries.

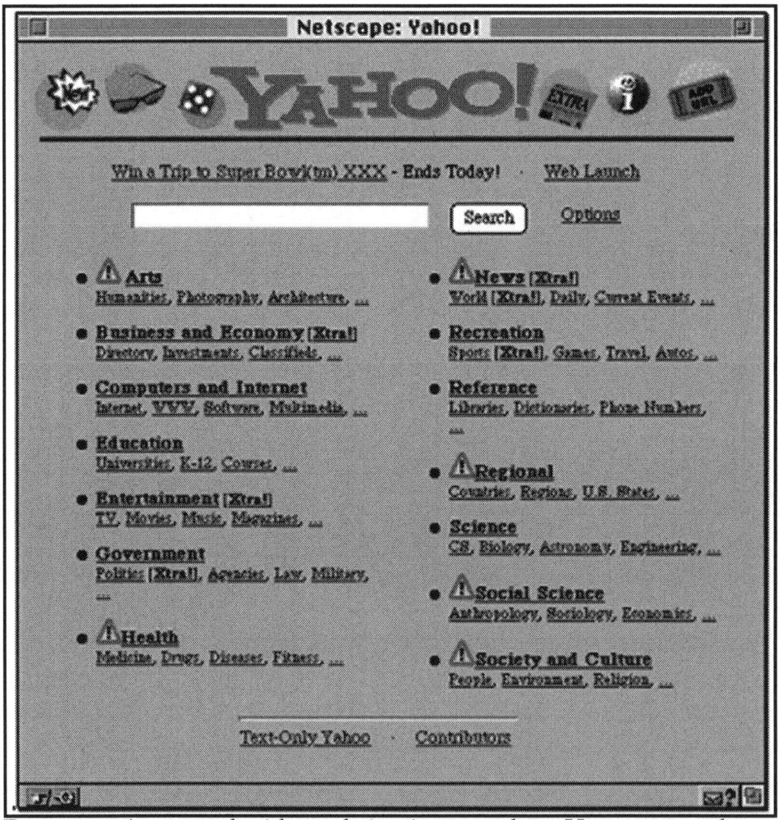

Fig. A Document Annotated with road sign icons to show Hypertext anchors Absent from the cache. *Networking not ubiquitous*

In the design of TeleWeb, we assumed that at least some of the time users would be disconnected but would still want to browse the Web. Some mobile networks are so limited in bandwidth compared to office networks that users may feel like they are disconnected. How can people browse the Web when disconnected? TeleWeb uses "caching for availability," the standard solution for this problem. This means that the system loads documents into a local cache when fully connected. Later, if the user needs the document while the network is not available, the locally cached copy is returned. Caching for availability only works if the system knows the user's information needs ahead of time. The system can use past history to predict future needs. In addition, the user can tell the system what documents belong in the cache; unfortunately, in practice people find it difficult to articulate which documents they need.

Furthermore, both techniques share the drawback that information needs often change in unpredictable ways. Overall, caching for availability often works, but is frustrating when it does not. An alternative solution is to replace synchronous interaction (a user request followed immediately by a response from the network) with asynchronous interaction. For example, when the user requests a document not in the cache, TeleWeb asks the user if the system should download it later.

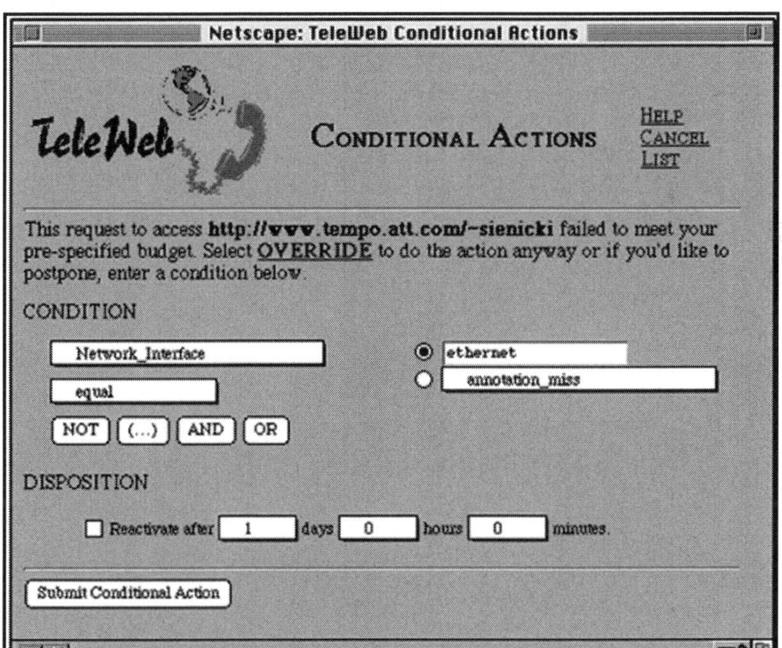

Fig. Creating a Conditional Download to fetch documents when Reconnected. *No feedback on cost*

If so, Tele- Web downloads the information the next time the user connects and adds the document to a "to read" list that the user can browse. This interaction style is analogous to sending a request for a book from an out of state library, and eventually receiving it in the mail. There are other reasons to postpone downloading a document. For example, if a user is connected over a cellular telephone, downloading a large document is going to be expensive, and can tie up the network connection for hours. Given the choice, the user might be happy to download this document overnight or upon returning to the office. There is a tradeoff here between how urgently people need information and how much they are willing to pay for it in time and money.

With a mobile information appliance, users should be able to decide how much they are willing to pay for each document and how quickly they need that document. With this principle in mind, TeleWeb includes a budget monitor that sits between the user and the network. If a request is made for a document that is not in the cache and downloading the document will break the user's budget, then TeleWeb presents a "conditional download" form instead of the document. Users can override their budget to fetch the document immediately, or they can request that the document be fetched at a later time.

UNPREDICTABLE SYSTEMS ARE FRUSTRATING

The third problem of mobile appliances is unpredictable behaviour. Those using computer networks already know this problem: sometimes they hit a key and nothing happens. In wireless computing, this experience is magnified many-fold. TeleWeb's solution is to show the user what is going on inside the cache and network manager. Specifically, Tele- Web labels links that will be slow to download with a "road work" icon.

If there is no road sign, then either the link destination is cached, or a high-speed connection to the information superhighway is available. This simple change— essentially exposing the state of the system— makes mobile Web browsing much more predictable. This contrasts with the traditional approach of trying to simplify the user's view of the system by concealing the state of the network.

THE FUTURE

The development of tomorrow's digital library information appliances is an iterative process. Our current cycle, however, is not complete until we evaluate the ideas presented in this paper.

Towards this end, we have begun a series of laboratory user interface experiments and are in the planning stage for a real-world deployment. One experiment suggests that free-form ink marks made while reading are better for query formulation than traditional relevance feedback.

People who have tried XLibris agree that our approach of taking a work practice and augmenting it— rather than redefining it— makes the system immediately accessible. Information *appliances* must be accessible. The digital library community must decide whether digital libraries should, as we propose, support users throughout the process of turning information into knowledge.

If so, there are many issues that must be addressed. One reviewer of this paper asked: "Where is the digital library?" We purposely avoided describing protocols, services, and architectures because we believe infrastructure should *support* the vision of working with a digital library information appliance, not *define* it. The next step is to understand how users of digital library information appliances should interact with external repositories. For example, should users pay authors to cache documents on their devices, even when they do not read them? How should users search repositories that are not always accessible?

How should searches be distributed between local and remote databases? These and other issues require further investigation. We have shown how information appliances based on the paper document metaphor can support active reading. Because these systems allow people to work on digital documents much as they would on paper, this provides an alternative to the standard "search and print" model of digital libraries.

Furthermore, by integrating a wide variety of document activities, and by allowing fluid movement among them, disruptive transitions between paper and digital media can be eliminated.

The combination of the paper-like and the digital allows us to augment these activities without redefining them. Finally, the mobility of a digital library information appliance supports work away from the desk.

With all these benefits, digital library information appliances can create a rich, universally accessible, digital library experience that improves the way we work. Clearly there is an exciting future for digital library information appliances in the digital library.

THE FUTURE OF PUBLIC LIBRARIES IN AN INTERNET AGE

With the Internet reshaping so many aspects of our lives, it has become common for prognosticators to speculate about the ultimate demise of all sorts of institutions that many of us have come to take for granted. So when Public Agenda set out to investigate public and civic leaders' thinking about public libraries today, we were not at all certain what we would hear. The first message that came was loud and clear: there is a future for public libraries in the Internet age. Even with the vast and growing amount of information available on the Internet and more competition for public funding, Americans say that public libraries will continue to play a vital role in communities.

A strong majority say that if their public library were to shut down, they would feel "that something essential and important has been lost, affecting the whole community" (78 per cent). The feeling that libraries are central to healthy communities is even more common among those who are most actively engaged in communities: the voters, volunteers, and contributors who make communities strong and can usually be counted on to raise a ruckus when things go wrong. In our recent report on the research, "Long Overdue: A Fresh Look at Public and Leadership Attitudes About Libraries in the 21st Century", Public Agenda documents the strong beliefs people have that their communities must have wellfunctioning public libraries in order to be healthy and strong. Large majorities said that all children should have a good, safe, appealing library in their neighbourhood; that libraries play a crucial role in preserving permanent and unalterable records; and that government should support the wiring of libraries so that low-income people can have access to the Internet.

AMERICANS SAY LIBRARIES ARE A GOOD PUBLIC INVESTMENT

At a time of broad concern about wasteful public spending, and as we hear of communities refusing to pay more taxes for public education or "essential services", 71 per cent say that libraries spend public money well. Fifty-two per cent say that if their local library needed additional funding, they would favour a tax increase to generate the necessary resources— significantly more than the number who favour charging users (32 per cent) or reducing services (16 per cent) as options for solving a financial shortfall. In many ways, people believe that libraries are more essential now than ever before. Americans say that since so many businesses are selling information, we absolutely need public libraries to provide vital information free of charge to anyone who needs it.

They also strongly agree that libraries are an important, quiet oasis from fast-paced, stressful lives. In an age when people are often deeply cynical about the performance of all sorts of public services, from public education to the police to cultural institutions, public libraries are rated A more often than any other public service we asked about. Indeed, public libraries seem almost immune to the distrust that is associated with so many other institutions. More than one hundred years ago, the philanthropist Andrew Carnegie saw the potential of the public library to be the center of enlightened learning in every community. He offered to build libraries if communities would contribute land, furnish money for annual maintenance, and exercise governance and oversight.

He gave communities the incentive to participate in a national movement and between 1881 and 1917 invested the equivalent of $3 billion to build 1,689 libraries across the nation. The result of Carnegie's investment and the involvement of communities helped educate generations of Americans. His commitment helped fix the library in the American consciousness as a significant public institution that needed and deserved broad public support. A century after this compact with American communities, nearly 90 per cent of library funding derives from local public dollars—which can be seen as either a curse or a blessing.

LIBRARIES FOR TODAY, LIBRARIES FOR TOMORROW

When people think about their expectations of libraries today, they generally think about the traditional services that most libraries carry out so well. Topping the public's list of priorities is that the basic services they have come to expect from libraries remain free of charge to the public. They also expect libraries to have enough current books for children; numerous reference materials; and friendly, knowledgeable librarians available. Libraries should offer convenient reading hours and special programmes for children, and they should have well-maintained buildings along with books and information that are organised for easy self-service. The top-ten list of public priorities for libraries also includes making available safe and productive gathering places for teenagers, being open on evenings and weekends, and having plenty of current books for adults.

For the most part, these public expectations are matched by libraries' performance, the public told us. People give especially high grades to their public libraries for having buildings that are well maintained; comfortable places to read; and enough friendly, knowledgeable librarians to supply help when needed. Although people clearly want libraries to ace the basics—materials, hours, and service—they also expect more and more from libraries in this age of the Internet. "Long Overdue" reveals a great deal about libraries and technology. Libraries are anything but relics of the past. They are viewed as key players in our digitised future.

Two-thirds of survey respondents say that having enough computers and online services for people should be a high priority for their local library. Seven in ten favour wiring libraries so that those who might not be able to afford a computer in their home can learn computer skills and get online. Those who think that libraries are merely becoming "information resources of last resort" for those who can't afford a home computer seem to be mistaken. Advanced computer users and families with higher income are even more likely to use public libraries and the technology services they offer. But, not surprisingly, people with few computer skills are the most likely to say wiring libraries to provide for "have-nots" should be a high priority.

WHERE IS THE LOVE

Public libraries are beloved institutions, but they can't survive on accolades alone. With the advent of computers and search engines, digital libraries, and the Internet, some question if libraries are essential and whether they should command priority in the competition for public dollars. Public Agenda's research shows public libraries are not seen as objects of nostalgia, but rather as essential community players in the effort to increase equity, opportunity, and community development in the information age. A growing number of communities are determined to keep their libraries at the leading edge of technology: affording small businesses the resources to compete globally; giving residents access to credible, current health information; and making libraries vital information access points for everyone.

These communities reveal the vast potential of libraries for the future. But only a small percentage of communities invest in public libraries to the extent necessary to produce maximum dividends. In those communities where the case for libraries is less clear and competition for public funds is high, there are disturbing indicators that support for libraries is slipping. The precarious financial condition of the nationwide public library system (to the extent that there is a cohesive system at all) that we heard about from library advocates was reinforced in our interviews with civic leaders across the nation.

Civic leaders do see the great strengths of the public library as being an information center in the digital age, an important resource for those who have the fewest resources available to them, and the "go to" place for all manner of public functions (including health information, job services, immigrant acculturation, and adult literacy training). But they also see challenges for libraries that need to be addressed by library supporters. Many civic leaders pointed to public libraries' seemingly infinite variety in governance structure as a major stumbling block. Public libraries' lack of marketing, impassive advocacy, and isolation from the community were also cited as shortcomings in library performance. Our research identified four specific areas where civic leadership, public citizens, and library leaders all seem to agree that there is a major opportunity for public libraries to step in and address community needs:

- Developing better programming and services for teens,
- Addressing illiteracy and poor reading skills among adults,
- Offering ready access to information about government services (including making public documents and forms quickly and easily available), and
- Permitting much greater access to computers for all.

Yet venturing into these areas would likely require financial resources that many libraries do not currently have. The civic leaders we spoke to questioned whether a groundswell of citizen support for public libraries would emerge in their communities. "Long Overdue" suggests that there is, in fact, strong potential for vocal support from activist citizens who could argue effectively for consistent and reliable financial support for public libraries. But library supporters, especially leaders with governance responsibility, must take the steps necessary to harness this potential and make it a reality.

LEVERAGING PUBLIC GOODWILL FOR FINANCIAL SUPPORT

There are people in every community who make things happen but don't necessarily hold any official post. These are the folks we refer to in our research report as "community soldiers", because no battle can be won without them. The good news for libraries is that these citizens—who nearly always vote in local elections and involve themselves in community organisations and activities—are heavy users and big fans of libraries. But even though they may be considered champions of libraries, currently they are not very aware of the potential financial vulnerability of their local libraries. Although 45 per cent of the civically engaged think their local government has not furnished enough money and assistance to the public libraries in their communities, 42 per cent think they have, and 13 per cent say they simply do not know. It appears that those citizens who can be counted on to rally to the cause if libraries are in financial peril are no more likely than the general population to be aware of the challenges facing libraries today.

Public lack of awareness of the financial challenges libraries face aside, there are other reasons everything is not milk and honey in the land of libraries. Libraries face real challenges today. Only 35 per cent of survey respondents say their local library gets an A when it comes to having convenient hours so people can use the services; only 28 per cent give libraries an A for offering access to catalogues and databases through the Internet; 26 per cent give an A for having enough computers and online services in the library for the people who want to use them; and just 24 per cent give an A for making available reading hours, homework help, and study space for children and teenagers. These are services that the public rate among the highest priorities for libraries. Clearly there are opportunities to improve service delivery on the part of local libraries. Library leaders would like to do much more in the way of customer service and innovative programming. But as our interviews with public leaders attest, finances are always a challenge. The civic leaders we interviewed generally share the public's high regard for libraries but are more conscious of the tenuous financial condition of many public libraries. Some public libraries are comfortable with the funding they receive, but the vast majority are not so well supported. Though the public remains largely unaware of the fiscal pressures on libraries today, civic and business leaders believe that public libraries are often first on the chopping block when state and local budgets are cut. Recent history in Salinas, Calif., a community that closed almost all of its libraries (and is profiled in our study), points to the passion for libraries that can emerge when a funding crisis imperils a treasured institution. But since the vast majority of the public do not sense that their own libraries may be at risk, most people do not see a reason to raise their voice in concern. It is simply not something on their radar screen today. The "canary in the coal mine" metaphor has a place here. Leaders have pricked up their ears to the distressed calls of the canary, but the public seems to hear only a sweet song and no hint of impending trouble.

LIBRARIES: ESSENTIAL COMMUNITY PROBLEM SOLVERS

To identify the most favourable potential opportunities for libraries to strengthen public support, Public Agenda asked the public about their priorities for urgent action in their communities and in which areas they think government should be more effective because current performance is relatively poor.

Researchers explored the same terrain in the interviews with national and local leadership.

Four areas of opportunity resonated most with the public and leaders alike:

- *Providing stronger services for teens*: The public is greatly concerned about teenagers and feels (72 per cent) that offering safe and productive activities for teens should be a high priority for their communities. This is also an area where the public potentially holds local government accountable, believing local government both can and should do more for teens. In the public's reckoning, libraries can potentially fill the gap: three out of four Americans (74 per cent) believe providing services for teens should be a high priority for libraries.
- *Helping address illiteracy and poor reading skills among adults*: Another major opportunity for libraries to fill community needs is with supplying literacy and reading programmes for adults, which many civic leaders tied to strengthening workforce skills and economic development. Sixty-eight per cent of the public said adult literacy programmes should be a high priority for the community, very few said it was something their community was doing a very good job of providing, and a large majority (68 per cent) said it should be a high priority for their local library.
- Affording ready access to information about government services, such as making available government forms or information on literacy programmes.
- Ensuring even greater access to computers for all. Almost two-thirds of Americans say having enough computers and online services for the people who want to use them should be a high priority for libraries.

For public libraries today, the greatest challenge is not in convincing the public of their worth—in the present or for the future. People clearly see many valuable roles for libraries to play. Our research yields ample evidence that libraries are highly valued public institutions serving multiple needs that, the public notes, will certainly continue to be needed with changing times.

A TIME OF RECKONING

America's public libraries are facing a pivotal time in their history. There is a rich tradition of public service that infuses citizens with great respect for the mission of libraries. Libraries have received significant public and private financial support over the years, ranging from local property tax support to state budget funding and a high level of private philanthropic funding. But funding level and mechanisms vary tremendously from one community to the next—and that's part of the problem. During the past several decades, there has been a major effort to upgrade technology and Internet access to bring the benefits of these new technologies to all citizens, regardless of economic circumstances. This has added further to public approval of the allimportant contributions of libraries.

Of course, libraries have also long held a position of special importance in educating schoolchildren and older students. The kind of action required for libraries to position themselves securely in the future will demand active and engaged governance. When change happens in communities, it is often a product of the passion of engaged citizen leaders who demand change from elected officials. But our research into a variety of library environments would suggest that libraries may suffer in some cases from a kind of "benign neglect" on the part of those who are most civically engaged. The reasoning here may be a variation on the theme that if it ain't broke, don't fix it. Although the public's strong feelings about how well libraries are doing their job make clear that libraries aren't broken, this doesn't mean there aren't cracks in the foundation.

Those who are most passionate about the importance of libraries in communities, if they are to secure their future, must make certain that the local and state governance structures that determine funding understand all that libraries are able to do for citizens and just how successful their constituents perceive them to be.

DIGITAL LIBRARIES OF THE FUTURE AND THE ROLE OF LIBRARIES

Research on digital library (DL) systems started in Europe in the mid-nineties. At that time DLs were seen essentially as repositories of digital texts accessible through a search service which was operating by indexing information stored in a centralised metadata catalogue. The construction of a DL was very resourceconsuming since, for each new DL, both the content and the software providing the DL functionality were built from scratch.

As a result of this development approach, only powerful user communities or user communities with in-house computer science technical skills could afford the building up of DLs. These DLs were created to serve end-users only as consumers of information. They did not provide any functionality for submitting the documents. The submission was usually performed either by the author or by a librarian operator by means of specific procedures residing outside the DL. Today, the requirements imposed on DLs are very different from that early time. A novel notion of DLs, also referred to as "knowledge commons" has recently emerged, whose fulfilment requires new technologies and new organisational models. This paper focuses on such new DLs by first discussing the motivations for their introduction, then presenting an innovative DL technology, called DILIGENT, and, finally, illustrating the role that libraries can play in this new scenario.

DIGITAL LIBRARIES OF THE FUTURE

According to the most recent understanding, the DLs of the future will be able to operate over a large variety of information object types - far wider than those maintained today in physical libraries and archives. These information objects will be composed of several multi-type and multimedia components aggregated in an unlimited number of formats. These, for example, can mix text, tables of scientific data and images obtained by processing earth observation data, or they can integrate 3D images, annotations and videos. These new information objects will offer innovative and more powerful means to researchers for sharing and discussing the results of their work. In order to be able to support these objects, the DL functionality has to be appropriately extended far beyond that required to manipulate the simple digital surrogates of the physical objects. In order to support these objects the DL may need considerable resources.

For example, the creation and handling of the new documents may require access to many different, large, heterogeneous information sources, the use of specialised services that process the objects stored in these sources for producing new information, and the exploitation of large processing capabilities for performing this tasks. New DLs are also required to offer a much richer set of services to their users than in the past. In particular, they must support the activities of their users by providing functionalities that may range from general utilities, like annotation, summarisation or co-operative work support, to very audience-specific functions, like map processing, semantic analysis of images, or simulation. The availability of this new DL functionality can, in principle, change the way in which research is conducted.

By exploiting such types of DL, for example, a scientist can annotate the article of a colleague with a programme that extracts useful information from a large amount of data collected by a specific scientific observatory. This programme, executed on demand when the annotation is accessed, can complement the content of the paper with continuously refreshed information. In the new DLs users are not only consumers but also producers of information. By elaborating information gathered through the DL they can create new information objects that are published in the DL, thus enriching its content. The new DLs are thus required to offer services that support the authoring of these new objects and the workflows that lead to their publication. In parallel with the evolution of the role of DL systems, we are now observing a large expansion in the demand for DLs.

Research today is often a collaborative effort carried out by groups belonging to different organisations spread worldwide. Motivated by a common goal and funding opportunities, these groups dynamically aggregate into virtual research organisations that share their resources, *e.g.* knowledge, experimentation results, or instruments, for the duration of their collaboration, creating new and more powerful virtual research environments. These virtual research organisations, set up by individuals that do not necessarily have great economic power or technical expertise, more and more frequently require DLs as tools for accelerating the achievement of their research results. This new potential audience demands less expensive and more dynamic DL development models.

They want to be able to set up new DLs that serve their needs for the duration of their collaborations in an acceptable timeframe and with an acceptable cost. The current DL development model cannot satisfy this large demand; a radical change is needed if we want to be able to address these new emerging requirements. A great contribution towards the satisfaction of all the requirements can certainly come from the introduction of mechanisms that support a controlled sharing of resources among different organisations. Sharing in this context is not only applied to repositories of content, as is usually meant today, but can be extended to any type of resource needed to build a DL, *i.e.* language and ontology resources, applications, computers and even staff with the necessary skills for supporting the DL development, deployment and maintenance.

Supporting this type of sharing requires the introduction of appropriate solutions at both the technological and organisational levels. These two levels are not independent; instead they strongly influence each other. In fact, the availability of a good technological solution favours the creation of an appropriate organisation, and vice-versa, a successful organisation stimulates the development of new supporting technologies. We present the DILIGENT infrastructure as an example of a technological solution for these new DLs. The organisational aspects stimulated by the introduction of this technology are briefly discussed afterwards.

DILIGENT

DILIGENT (DIgital Library Infrastructure on Grid ENabled Technology) is a three-year Integrated Project funded by the European Commission under the 6th Framework Programme for Research and Technological a Digital Library Infrastructure that will enable members of dynamic virtual research organisations to create on-demand transient digital libraries that exploit shared resources. Resources in this context are multimedia and multi-type content repositories, applications, and computing and storage elements. Following the understanding of DLs expressed in Borgman *et al.*, this project focuses on the development of DLs that "are not ends in themselves; rather they are enabling technologies for digital asset management, electronic commerce, electronic publishing, teaching and learning, and other activities".

From an abstract point of view, the DILIGENT infrastructure can be understood as a broker serving DL resource providers and consumers. The providers are the individuals and the organisations that decide to publish their resources under the supervision of the broker, according to certain access and use policies. The consumers are the user communities that want to build their own DLs. The resources managed by this broker are content sources (*i.e.* repositories of information searchable and accessible through a single "entrance"), services (*i.e.* software tools that implement a specific functionality and whose descriptions, interfaces and bindings are defined and publicly available) and hosting nodes (*i.e.* networked entities that offer computing and storage capabilities and supply an environment for hosting content sources and services).

Providers register their resources and give a description of them by exploiting appropriate mechanisms provided by the infrastructure. The infrastructure also automatically derives other properties of the resources that are used to enrich the explicit description. The infrastructure manages the registered resources by supporting their discovery, monitoring and usage, and by implementing a number of other functionalities that aim at realising the required controlled sharing and quality of service.

A user community can create one or more DLs by specifying a set of requirements. These requirements specify conditions for the information space (*e.g.* publishing institutions, subject of the content, document types), for the operations that manipulate the information space (*e.g.* type of search, tool for data analysis), for the services for supporting the work of the users (*e.g.* type of personalised dissemination, type of collaboration), for the quality of service (*e.g.* configuration, availability, response time) and for many other aspects, like the maximum cost, or lifetime.

The broker satisfies the community's requirements by selecting, and in many cases also deploying, a number of resources among those accessible to the community, gluing them appropriately and, finally, making the new DL application accessible through a portal. The composition of a DL is dynamic since the DL broker continuously monitors the status of the DL resources and, if necessary, changes them in order to offer the best quality of service. By relying on the shared resources many DLs, serving different communities, can be created and modified on-the-fly, without big investments and changes in the organisations that set them up.

In order to support the transactions between the providers and the consumers, the DILIGENT infrastructure exploits the virtual organisations (VOs) mechanism that has been introduced in the Grid research area. This mechanism models sets of users and resources aggregated together by highly controlled sharing rules, usually based on an authentication framework. VOs have a limited lifetime, are dynamically created and satisfy specific needs by allocating and providing resources on demand. Through the VOs mechanism the DILIGENT infrastructure glues together the users and the resources of a DL.

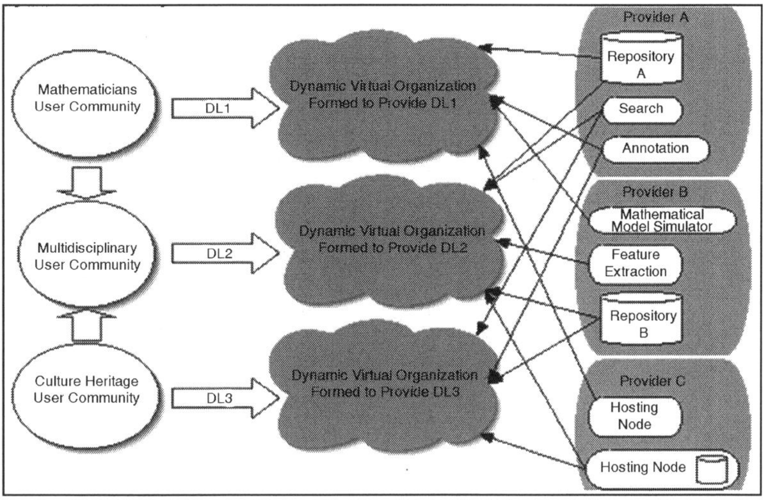

Fig. The Role of Virtual Organisations in DILIGENT

Figure graphically illustrates the role of VOs in supporting the brokerage model. The consumers, *i.e.* the user communities that require DLs to support their needs. The providers, each of which makes a number of resources available, are on the right. The infrastructure acts as a mediator by maintaining a framework where multiple virtual organisations, active on the same shared resources, can co-exist. The DL development model proposed by DILIGENT is radically new. Within the described framework each DL consumes the required resources only for the time it needs them.

This opens a lot of new opportunities for the creation of the functionalities required by the new "knowledge commons" environments. In particular, the exploitation of more effective, but also very computationally expensive algorithms becomes viable at an acceptable cost for many communities. For example, thanks to sharing, the use of the high processconsuming algorithms that automatically extract features from multi-media objects can be exploited in a large number of DLs. Moreover, in the framework established by the new development model, the user communities can easily, and in a timely manner, create and maintain their own DLs with limited resources since the management of the DL is automatically and transparently carried out by the infrastructure. The system that implements the functionality of the DILIGENT infrastructure is being built by integrating DL and Grid technologies. The motivation for this design choice relies on the similarity between many of the problems encountered through our new notion of DLs and the issues addressed by the most recent research in the Grid domain.

From the functional point of view, the DILIGENT system is divided into five functionality clusters:

- *DL Creation and Management:* is responsible for the dynamic construction and maintenance of the transient DLs and for the controlled sharing and management of the resources that are used to implement them. The functionalities offered by this cluster allow users to express the requirements that the DL must fulfil. Moreover, they automatically identify and arrange the pool of resources needed to satisfy these needs.

- *Content and Metadata Management:* implements the handling of DL content and related metadata, the consistent and distributed management of annotations, and the integration of external content and metadata sources.
- *Process Management:* manages the creation of user processes composed of existing services, the validation of their correctness, the automatic optimisation of their definition according to the resources available and the service characteristics, and their reliable execution. Thanks to this feature, the DILIGENT system can easily be enriched with additional operational workflows to meet new user requirements.
- *Index and Search Management:* is responsible for enabling cost-efficient search and retrieval of information in DLs, while satisfying the level of quality required for the overall data retrieval and delivery operations.
- *Application Specific Functionality:* provides the functionality needed to support user-specific scenarios, like portals, document visualisation, or features extraction.

From the architectural point of view, the DILIGENT system is designed as a Web Services Resource Framework (WSRF) application built on top of the gLite Grid middleware released by the Enabling Grids for Escience in Europe (EGEE) project. gLite hides the heterogeneous nature of the computing elements (*i.e.* services representing a computing resource) on the one hand and storage elements (*i.e.* services representing a storage resource) on the other hand by providing an environment that facilitates and controls their sharing. The DILIGENT services are being initially deployed on a project-proprietary gLite infrastructure. Architecturally, this infrastructure is completely interoperable with the EGEE infrastructure. EGEE is currently the largest European Grid infrastructure ever built.

A number of other recently funded projects will extend this infrastructure to other geographic regions, like Mediterranean countries, Latin America, or China. The interoperability with the EGEE infrastructure will allow any authorised virtual community that wishes to create DLs to also exploit the resources made available by this vast Grid infrastructure. During the project timeframe, the DILIGENT infrastructure will be populated with a number of important archives and software applications provided by the two communities that are participating in the experimentation with the results of the project, one from the environmental e-science domain and one from the cultural heritage domain. The first community is ImpECt (Implementation of Environmental Conventions) and includes leading players in the environmental sector. This community will use DILIGENT to support the organisation of conferences and the preparation of projects and periodical reports. Through DILIGENT this community expects to improve accessibility, interoperability and usability of environmental data, models, tools, algorithms and instruments, integrating the distributed data sources with specialised data handling services. The second community, ARTE, is a community of scholars located in different parts of the world, working together to establish a new discipline that merges experiences from research in medicine, humanities, social sciences and communication.

In order to achieve their objectives, these researchers require instruments to ease the construction of multimedia artefacts and to improve support for education. At the time of the writing of this paper initial experimentation with the features of a DILIGENT DL has already been conducted by implementing simplified services for preparing environmental reports, as required by the ImpECt environmental agencies. Through the exploiting of rich information sources, ranging from raw data sets to maps and graphs archives, these agencies periodically prepare reports on the status of the environment. Currently, this task is performed by first selecting the relevant information from each of the multiple and heterogeneous sources available, then launching complex processing on large amounts of data to obtain "products", like graphs, tables and other summarised information and, finally, producing the required report by assembling all the different parts together.

This process, which is repeated periodically, requires a lot of work due to the complexity of interfacing the different sources and tools. Despite the effort expended, the resulting reports do not completely fulfil the requirements of their readers, who would like to have a picture of the environmental status which is updated at the time the report is accessed. A DILIGENT DL offers a more effective framework for the creation and maintenance of these reports. In our experimentation, for example, we have built a DL which exploits content maintained in both repositories including textual documents and archives of Earth observation raw data provided by the European Space Agency. In this DL, which is accessible through a single user interface, all the different kinds of information necessary for creating the reports can be found.

By combining this information and by defining how to derive the associated "products" (images, tables, or graphs) from raw data, the users can create their reports much more easily. Moreover, a specialised user interface allows authorised users to access these composite reports by choosing static or dynamic generation. The selection of dynamic generation triggers associated process workflows which, by combining appropriate applications, generate the required products on demand by processing both the raw data and other intermediate products stored in the DL repositories. The dynamically generated products are obtained by running those applications that are computationally intensive on the Grid.

In this way the complex processes required to generate the products are executed in few minutes at a limited cost to the community that is exploiting them. In order to obtain the same performance without the Grid, an institution would have to equip its digital library with a great number of computers, while in the case of DILIGENT the institution can also exploit computer capabilities made available by third party organisations. The same is true for storage capacity. Maintaining raw data, intermediate products and high resolution images requires a large amount of storage capacity. By exploiting the Grid technology, part of this information, especially the temporary part, can be maintained in third-party storage systems.

THE ROLE OF LIBRARIES IN FUTURE DLs

In the framework envisaged by DILIGENT, libraries play an important role at the organisational level. In particular:

- As providers of resources, they can help to enhance the amount of available resources by making stakeholders aware of the importance of sharing. In particular, as far as the sharing of content is concerned, they can operate by promoting digitisation campaigns and the Open Access approach. These actions may result in a vast amount of new digital information accessible online which can be exploited by advanced services.
- Also within a digital framework, libraries are certainly the best candidates for carrying out content description, maintenance and preservation of resources. By exploiting their large experience acquired in the past, they can contribute to the long-term availability and to the quality of the resources disseminated by the DLs.
- Long-term availability also requires the implementation of models able to support the sustainability of the resources provided. Libraries, either alone or as members of library consortia, can also act as the organisations deputed to define and put in place these models.
- As main resource providers, libraries can work jointly on the definition of common policies and standards. An agreement on these aspects would strongly contribute towards facilitating the design and development of the new complex services required to fulfil the emerging user needs.
- In the future envisaged by DILIGENT, libraries can also play an important role as mediators between the infrastructure and the user communities. In particular, they can proactively promote and facilitate the creation of DLs that respond to the needs of the user

communities. They can also assist users by providing, if necessary, the skills required to select, update and exploit the DL content and services.

So we can expect to see a shift from a service *provided* to a community to one in which *local people are more active and involved* in its design and delivery. Libraries will be recognised as connecting individuals, communities and organisations to innovate, create and provide new library based services and ideas. People will be using libraries to do more with each other and this activity will cross over between physical and virtual spaces. They will be creating new content, having conversations and using new technology for their own benefit, for their community or their business. Those working in libraries will be less occupied in straightforward transactions and more involved in linking people and organisations together in using library spaces and resources for new activities.

There will be a greater emphasis given to community, digital and entrepreneurial skills. In this context, volunteers offer new ways to add capacity and skills. Libraries' role out in the community, reaching vulnerable and excluded people, will extend to popping up temporarily as local circumstances demand and allow. This might involve using vacant spaces, or being invited in to other community services or workplaces to meet particular needs. If the library of the future will look different from those of the past and present, their enduring role and purpose means that some things will feel familiar. A high value will continue to be placed on the importance of quality leadership, professional skills and experience.

Books will sit comfortably alongside digital and other cultural resources in a rich and diverse library collection. Finding the information to answer any question, books to satisfy the never-ending desire for pleasure, learning and knowledge, and the practice of literacy as one of life's basic skills, will remain at the heart of what makes a library, and what will place the library at the heart of the community. Our national role means that we are well-placed to stimulate debate and offer support to the development of public libraries, and we want to work with our partners based on the thinking that has emerged in our research.

How that is reflected locally will be determined by each council based on their own priorities and the needs of their communities. It is this combination of enduring values, new thinking, collaborative leadership and flexibility that will equip public libraries to create economic and social benefits for this country and its communities long into the future.

NEW OPTION FOR LIBRARIES IN THE DIGITAL ERA

In the electronic information environment one of the responses to the problem of bringing large amounts of information together has been for libraries to introduce portals. A portal is a gateway, or a point where users can start their search for information on the web. There are a number of different types of portals, for example universities have been introducing "institutional portals", which can be described as "a layer which aggregates, integrates, personalises and presents information, transactions and applications to the user according to their role and preferences".

A second type of portal is a "subject portals". A third type of portal is a "federated search tool" which brings together the resources to a library subscribes and allows cross-searching of these resources. They work using the Z39.50 protocol used by database suppliers to enable communication between computers. This protocol is not always effective because database suppliers have not always adopted it consistently so other protocols are also used such as HTML, XML and SQL. Since, these tools access resources that the library pays for, some type of authentication is required to ensure. Well before the launch of the World Wide Web, librarians recognised the need for establishing a common interface to search multiple sources. The ANSI/NISO gives the international search-andretrieval protocol, Z39.50, which was originally proposed in 1984 as a standard means of interrogating bibliographic databases. Since, then it has gone through three versions, the latest of which was issued in 1995.

Federated search compliments the Z39.50 facility, it offers the ability to extend search beyond the online catalog virtually to any electronic resources that can be authenticated at the point of access. This means that users no longer need to jump from one search interface to another.

Information integration over distributed sources is an urgent problem to be solved for providing access to a variety of Digital Libraries through a common search interface and portal. Federated or cross-database search tools now available on the market are the correct solution for unifying access to a variety of information resources.

These tools can search not only library catalogs but also commercial abstracting and indexing databases, web search engines, and a variety of other databases, while often merging and de-duplicating results. Federated searching started in 1998 when Webfeat Team took the initiative to connect any or all of their databases at the same time through a simple, common user interface and turned this idea into a product called Webfeat.

WebFeat, the original federated search engine, used by over 15,000 leading public, academic, government and Global 1000 libraries and information centers — including over a third of the largest 100 U.S., public libraries, 18 statewide library systems, and 2 out of every 10 Association of Research Libraries (ARL) institutions, brings you the next frontier in federated search technology.

Originally founded in 1992 as an information technology consultancy. The WebFeat concept is simple: search any or all of your library's databases simultaneously with a single intuitive interface. WebFeat can search any database, including licensed databases, free databases, catalogs, Z39.50, Telnet, proprietary databases, anything! And with SMART, WebFeat's next generation usage tracker, you can report detailed database usage within your library with just a few mouse clicks.

FEDERATED SEARCH

Federated search is the simultaneous search of multiple online databases and is an emerging feature of automated, Web-based library and information retrieval systems. It is also often referred to as a portal, as opposed to simply a Web-based search engine. It is sometime termed as broadcast search, parallel search, cross reference search, etc. Various terms are used to refer to these tools in the literature including: metasearchers, crosssearchers, cross-database searchers, portals, broadcast searchers or parallel searchers.

The term metasearcher is particularly prominent and is the term adopted by the United States National Information Standards Organisation (NISO), which has developed a Metasearch Initiative. However as Fryer explains, the term metasearcher can cause confusion due to its association with web Metasearch engines such as Metacrawler which function in a different way to federated search tools.

The term federated searching is the function of search tools, which search a number of databases, particularly subscription databases, simultaneously with one interface. The content searched by federated search tools is content that could not normally be searched via a web search engine.

DEFINITIONS

Researcher defines federated search as, "Transforming a query and broadcasting it to a group of disparate databases with the appropriate syntax, merging the results collected from the databases, presenting them in a succinct and unified format with minimal duplication, and allowing the library patron to sort the merged result set by various criteria". In simple words, Federated searching will be defined as a search system using a common interface that enables the simultaneous searching of databases from a variety of vendors. Federated search technology enables users to search multiple information resources simultaneously through one search query. Users can then view search results in a single integrated list. In other words, users do no longer need to consult each information resource individually.

Instead, they can search multiple library catalogs (OPACs), Web sites (e.g. Amazon.com, Google, etc.), subscription and citation databases all at once. Federated search technology is an integral component of an Information Portal, which provides the interface to diverse information resources. Once the user enters his or her search query in the search box of the Information Portal, the system uses federated search technology to send the search string to each resource that is incorporated into the Portal. The individual information resources then send the Information Portal a list of results from the search query. Users can view the number of documents retrieved in each resource and link directly to each search result.

Metasearch, this word is synonymous to federated searching, people find no difference between federated searching but there is slight difference between federated and meta searching.

DIFFERENCE BETWEEN FEDERATED SEARCH ENGINE AND META SEARCH ENGINE

Federated search engine and Meta search engine seems to be synonymous but we found slight difference between them. Some of them are as follows:

Table 11.1. Federated Search Meta search.

Federated Search	Meta Search
* Federated search engine have cost. More, depending upon the seats, design, functionality and targets or databases and subjectc ategories and thesauri	* Meta searc h engines are a vailable "free" of cost on internet.
* Federated searches concentrate mostly on textual inforrmation and offer subscription-based premium content database searching ignored by Web oriented meta search engines that miss these invisible Web Sources.	* Meta search engine commonly found on internet. The Public at large uses meta Search engines because they run Searches via multiple web search engines that spider the open Web, including multimedia sources.
* Federated searching refers to the ability to issue a single query that concurrently searches multiple disparate and heterogeneous collections of information. This is especially important to library patrons and staff that are interested in locating resources that exist within, or are licensed by libraries or library consortia.	* This technical part is lacking in meta searching.
* Typically, these collections include the library catalog(s), commercial databases *(Ebsco, Gale, ProQuest, etc.)*, digital collections, specialised collections, and even third party systems and content (Library of Congress, Web search engines, etc.). Single-search access to multiple resources enables	* Web meta-search tools such as and MetCrawler run across multiple web search engines at once, returning sets of results grouped individually in each search source. Names such as VIVISMO and IXQUICK also spring to mind in this context. In this context. meta-search vendors are Muse Global's Muse Search, Web

libraries to offer value added services that Web savvy patrons have come to expect. These include a single login, personalisation features, and the ability to remotely interact with your library Value added services not only enhance end user experience, but help ensure that the library continues to be the epicenter for information discovery in the ever-increasing digital world.

Feat's Prism that is used by Dynix, and Sirsi uses Muse Search, just to name a few common vendors

NEED AND PURPOSE OF FEDERATED SEARCH TOOLS

The need and purpose of the federated searching are as follows:

- The growth of different types of databases, produced by different suppliers, with numerous interfaces and logins means that library users can find it confusing when attempting to access information;
- Library OPACs and web-pages have been alienating users with their use of library terminology and by including long lists of databases that users find it difficult to select from and search;
- The needs and expectations of library users, particularly students using academic libraries. The growth of different types of databases, produced by different suppliers, with numerous interfaces and logins means that library users can find it confusing when attempting to access information.

There are certain purposes which can be served by the federated search are as follows:-

- Transforming a query and broadcasting it to a group of disparate databases with the appropriate syntax.
- Merging the results collected from the databases,
- Presenting them in a succinct and unified format with minimal duplication,
- Providing a means, performed either automatically or by the portal user, to sort the merged result set.

In traditional search engines such as Google, only sources that have been indexed by the search engine's crawler technology can be searched, retrieved and accessed. The large volume of documents housed in databases is not open to traditional Internet search engines because of limitations in crawler technology.

Federated searching resolves this issue by the technique described above and makes these deep Web documents searchable without having to visit each database individually.

ADVANTAGES OF FEDERATED SEARCH

There are certain advantages of using Federated Searches. Some of them are as follows:

- The reduced time it takes to do a basic search is benefit enough.
- Unified access to diverse content sources.
- Simultaneous searching across all sources.
- Ability to Simple search as well as advanced search.
- Integrated results which are easy to view and use.
- Direct links to the native source for further searching.
- Ability to filter, sort, save, print, export and e-mail search results

SEARCH MODELS

Search on data bases starts with simple search formulation using single keyterm and combinations of terms. The search results thus obtained can be listed in simple predefined format or using user customised format to get desired information. Various search models indicate the interactions of users search formulations and its interface with databases in a Library or online web access to aggregated databases.

OLD SEARCH MODEL

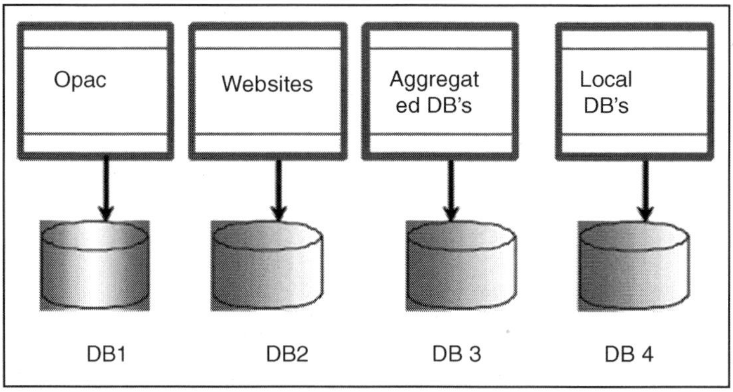

Fig. Old Srearch Model.

Without a federated search tool, each database requires its own unique search tool - significantly complicating and slowing the search process for patrons. In this kind of search model user submit their search query to individual database or search engines etc and individually they get their required information. This kind of search tools are very time consuming and most of the time user didn't get their desired information.

FEDERATED SEARCH MODEL

Using federated search, a single tool searches and accesses all databases with one, easy to use interface.

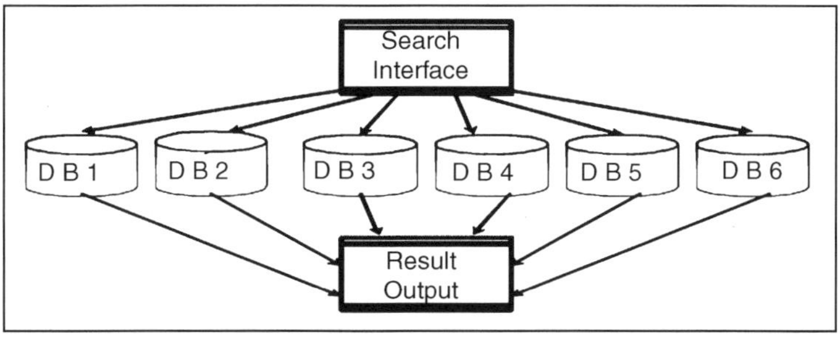

Fig. Federated Search Model.

It provides opportunity to the users that they get their desired information from various databases, search engines, etc.

FEDERATED SEARCH TECHNOLOGIES

There are mainly four technologies used for federated searching.

- Screen scraping or HTTP
- Z39.50 protocol
- ZING - SRW protocol
- XML gateway

SCREEN SCRAPPING OR HTTP

"Hyper Text Transport Protocol" - HTTP is the single most important technology that drives the web and yet remains virtually transparent. Without this protocol HTML and XML via the web would not be able to perform the myriad of tasks that we put them to daily.

The Hypertext Transfer Protocol (HTTP) is an application-level protocol for distributed, collaborative, hypermedia information systems. HTTP has been in use by the World-Wide Web global information initiative since, 1990. The HTTP protocol is a request/response protocol.

A client sends a request to the server in the form of a request method, URI, and protocol version, followed by a MIME-like message containing request modifiers, client information, and possible body content over a connection with a server.

HTTP communication usually takes place over TCP/IP connections. TCP guarantees that packets arriving to and from the web server are error free and in the right order. It doesn't however guarantee that packets arrive no matter what the network conditions are. When communications are congested or unavailable web page delivery is slow and can time-out.

Z39.50 PROTOCOL

Z39.50 is an American national standard for information retrieval. It is formally known as ANSI/NISO Z39.50-1995 - Information Retrieval (Z39.50): Application Service Definition and Protocol Specification.

This document specifies a set of rules and procedures for the behaviour of two systems communicating for the purposes of database searching and information retrieval. As a network application standard, Z39.50 is an open standard that enables communication between systems that run on different hardware and use different software The Z39.50 standard was developed to overcome the problems associated with multiple databases searching such as having to know the unique menus, command language, and search procedures of each system accessed.

Z39.50 simplifies the search process by making it possible for a searcher to use the familiar user interface of the local system to search both the local library catalogue as well as any remote database system that support the standard. In libraries, the Z39.50 protocol is most often used for searching OPAC sources.

The important facilities offered by Z39.50 are as follows:

- *Browse*: Allows the client to scan the contents of wordlists or indexes on the server. This can be particularly useful in the case of controlled keyword lists or facets.
- *Access and resource control*: Allows authentication of users, and cost control and online charging for commercial services.
- *Sort*: Allows the client to request different orderings of query results, eg. relevance ranking, sorting by date or version number, etc.
- *Explain*: Allows the client to interrogate the server about a number of details about its contents and its level of support for the application profile.
- *Item Order*: Allows offline ordering of materials in cases where they cannot be delivered electronically, or where per-unit charging (eg. online charging) is required. Such services are being supplied in an ad-hoc fashion by online Web-based component repositories such as ASSET. The item order service provides a ready-made and semantically standardised version of this service.
- *Item Update*: Permits an authorised client to update the contents of the remote database.

SRW (SEARCH/RETRIEVE WEB SERVICE)

Search/Retrieve Web Service is a new HTTP-based information retrieval protocol providing broadly the same facilities as Z39.50, but by means of very different technology. SRW is designed to be a low barrier to entry solution to performing searches and other information retrieval operations across the internet. It uses existing, well tested and easily available technologies such as SOAP and XPath in order to perform what has been done in the past using proprietary solutions. The protocol has two ways that it can be carried, either via SOAP or as parameters in aURL.

This second form is called SRU – Search Retrieve by URL. Other transports would also be possible, for example simple XML over HTTP, but these are not defined by the current standard. The primary function of SRW is to allow a user to search a remote database of records. This is done via the search Retrieve operation, in which the client sends a search Retreive Request and the server responds with a search Retrieve Response. The request has several parameters, most of which are optional. The response is primarily a list of XML records which matched the search, along with the full count of how many records were matched.

XML (EXTENSIBLE MARKUP LANGUAGE)

XML stands for EXtensible Markup Language. XML is a markup language much like HTML and was designed to carry data, not to display data. XML tags are not predefined. You must define your own tags. XML is designed to be self-descriptive and it is is recommended by the World Wide Web Consortium. It is a fee-free open standard.

XML is not a replacement for HTML. HTML is about displaying information, while XML is about carrying information. In simple words, XML is a software and hardware independent tool for carrying information. It is used both to encode documents and serialise data.

It supports Unicode, allowing almost any information in any written human language to be communicated. XML is now as important for the Web as HTML was to the foundation of the Web.

XML is everywhere. It is the most common tool for data transmissions between all sorts of applications, and becomes more and more popular in the area of storing and describing information. XML simplifies data sharing as in the real world; computer systems and databases contain data in incompatible formats. XML data is stored in plain text format. This provides a software- and hardware-independent way of storing data. This makes it much easier to create data that different applications can share.

SELECTION OF FEDERATED SEARCH ENGINE

In selecting a Federated search engine, one needs to bear in mind the following:

- The maximum number of resources the software can include
- The ease of setting up resource targets
- Availability of simple search options
- Speed of search results
- Limiting and refining searches
- Ranking results by relevance
- Export options, *i.e.,* print, e-mail, download
- Adequate statistics and reporting features

STANDARDS AND DEVELOPMENT

NISO – (US) National Information Standards Organisation launched and continue to develop initiatives in order to develop and adopt standard search and retrieval protocols for federated searching. XML – Web protocol and SOAP (Single Object Access Protocol)

ACCESS ISSUES WITH FEDERATED SEARCH

Verification, authentication and certification can be difficult for the federated search vendor. Since, federated search engines don't hold the data locally, *i.e.,* the engines perform the search, and send the results back to the portal.

The federated search engine must be able to access multiple passwordprotected databases behind the scenes, or IP validate all at the one time, and show users their results in one easy navigable interface.The challenge for federated search vendors is to provide only licensed users access to databases, as specified for each license agreement that is in place for the organisation.

AUTHENTICATION

Authentication sets federated search engines apart form other expensive and highly sophisticated search software such as Verity and Autonomy. The latter usually restricts searches to internally generated information, ignoring subscription databases that enterprises have bought in-house. All the user needs with federated searching is ID, password or IP validation along with files to be searched, and the federated search engine do the rest..

THE SET–UP PROCESS

The set up process is lengthy and time consuming for both the Library and the vendor. This is not the end of the process either! It continually evolves as databases change, or new resources are acquired and links are added to the federated search portal.

INTERFACE ISSUES

We need to decide how much time is to be devoted to design, who is the audience and should this audience be able to perform multiple searches, without having to do more than input their ID and password or IP authenticate, and type in the search query.

REMOVING DUPLICATES (DE-DUPING)

Most federated search engines will de-dupe some only when requested. However this opens up a Pandora's Box about how the results are returned. User habits indicate that the end user views only the first ten hits or results.

How do the vendor and the interface designer ensure that the highest hits are returned? This area is continually evolving, and it is up to the federated search engine provider, to provide what they can, to the best of their technological ability in this regard.

HOW FEDERATED SEARCH WORKS

Federated search computer programmes allow users to search multiple data sources with a single query from a single user interface. The user enters a search query in the portal interface's search box and the query is sent to every individual database in the portal or federated search list. Access details for the individual databases must be preset in the portal by its owner.

Federated search systems either rely upon vendors to create commercial portal systems, or they rely upon government or other organisations to provide open access portals. How federated search is implemented depends upon which of the two types of organisations is providing the portal. Federated search portals, either commercial or open access, generally search public access bibliographic databases; public access Web-based library catalogues (OPACs), Web-based search engines like Google and/or open-access, government-operated or corporate data collections.

These individual data sources send back to the portal's interface a list of results from the search query. The user can review this hit list. Some portals will merely screen scrape the actual database results and not directly allow a user to enter the data source's application. More sophisticated ones will de-dupe the results list by merging and removing duplicates. There are additional features available in many portals, but the basic idea is the same: to improve the accuracy and relevance of individual searches as well as reduce the amount of time required to search for resources.

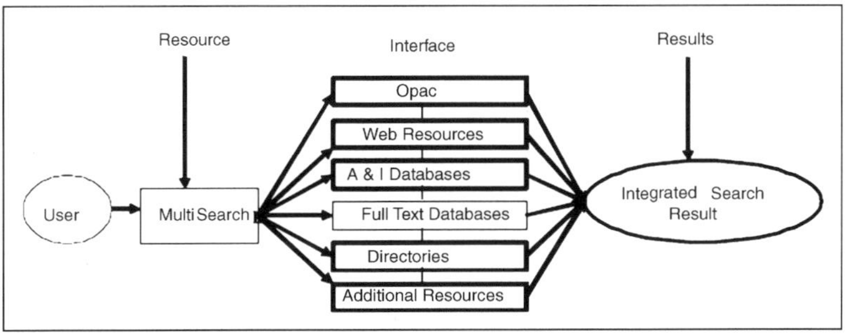

Fig. Diagrammatic Representation of Federated Searching.

In federated searching, a wealth of information is incorporated into a single repository that can be searched. In this model, the information is processed prior to the user's search. From the enduser's point of view, federated searching and metasearching may seem similar, because both provide a single interface to multiple resources, but they actually differ in many respects.

The pre-processing taking place in a federated searching environment, which we can describe as just-in-case processing, offers new opportunities regarding search methodologies and the presentation of results. For example, a ranking algorithm can be applied to each data element stored in the repository, unrelated to any future user query. Such an algorithm can take into account the number of times that an article has been cited, the number of articles that the author has published, the number of times that a book has been borrowed, a journal's impact factor, and other parameters.

A federated searching system can use the calculated rank to better evaluate the relevance of the specific item once it has been retrieved as the result of a query.The system searches a local repository that was created earlier through the accumulation of data from numerous resources. Looking back a few years, we can see that the need for a single search interface to multiple resources arose some time ago, and, in fact, metasearching and federated searching have been available for quite some time.Such systems originated in a variety of environments; for example, Elsevier, a publisher offering numerous journals, created a federated search mechanism enabling its users to search all its e-journals through its ScienceDirect service.

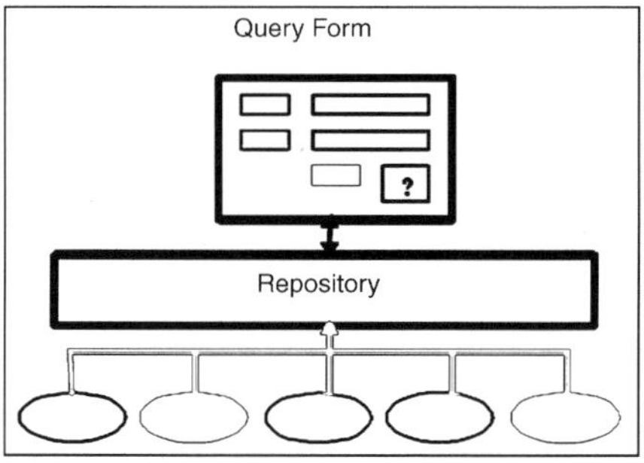

Fig. Diverse in Form Mation Resources.

As Elsevier acquired other publishers, it was able to add their journals to the same platform. Database vendors developed similar mechanisms. For example, Ovid provides a single interface to a few hundred databases that it publishes, and still retains them as separate databases.

Commercial organisations were not the only ones that addressed the need for a single search interface; several large research institutions created a local environment based on federation.

For example, the Los Alamos National Laboratory and the Ohio Link consortium in the United States, the University of Toronto in Canada, the Technical Knowledge Center of Denmark (DTV), and the Max Planck Society in Germany all offer large, diverse collections of e-journals that they store locally. These institutions have implemented federated searching to provide a single search interface across their electronic collections. However, not all organisations have the resources to adopt this just-in-case approach.

Furthermore, with the rapid increase in the number of heterogeneous resources that institutions offer their users, a single federated searching system can serve only as a partial solution.

IMPLEMENTATION

When a federated search engine is implemented at a particular library, it then becomes a unique service. Federated-searching software allows customisation, so no two implementations are exactly the same. For example, a library may choose to include all of its online resources as targets for a federated search engine or it may choose to create subject groupings first, each of which leads to a federated search service for a narrow topic. Gerrity, Lyman, and Tallent discuss implementing a federated search system at Boston College, where they promoted the new service as "MetaQuest".

One application of federated searching is the metasearch engine; however, this is not a complete solution as many documents are not currently indexed.

This is known as the deep Web or invisible Web. Many more information sources are not yet stored in electronic form.

'Google Scholar' is an example of a project trying to address this.When the search vocabulary or data model of the search system is different from the data model of one or more of the foreign target systems the query must be translated into the each of the foreign target systems.

This can be done using simple dataelement translation or may require semantic translation.

FEDERATED SEARCH PROVIDERS

Individual institutions have their in-house Federated option and other institutions uses global federated search options, following are the popular federated search providers:

- Google Scholar
- Scopus
- Liberty

GOOGLE SCHOLAR

Google Scholar is seen as the competition for both campus institutional repository systems (at least in terms of search and discovery) and academic library federated searching. Google Scholar provides a simple way to broadly search for scholarly literature.

From one place, you can search across many disciplines and sources: peer-reviewed papers, theses, books, abstracts and articles, from academic publishers, professional societies, preprint repositories, universities and other scholarly organisations. Google Scholar helps you identify the most relevant research across the world of scholarly research.

FEATURES OF GOOGLE SCHOLAR

- Search diverse sources from one convenient place
- Find papers, abstracts and citations
- Locate the complete paper through your library or on the web
- Learn about key papers in any area of research

Google Scholar gives various option to the user so that they can search according to their equirements, such as time period, author wise search, subject wise, publication, institution wise etc and after giving the key term by the user, it searches that key term to various databases, search engines, journals etc and display the result on interface with name of author along with its full bibliographical description and it also provide citation information.

SCOPUS

Scopus is the largest abstract and citation database of research literature and quality web sources. It's designed to find the information scientists need. Quick, easy and comprehensive, Scopus provides superior support of the literature research process.Scopus is updated daily and it offers 15,000 peer-reviewed journals from more than 4,000 international publishers, over 1000 Open access journals, 500 Conference proceedings, over 600 trade publications and over 125 Book series.

It also covers 33 million records, out of which, 16 million records include references going back to 1996 and 17 million pre-1996 records go back as far as 1869.

LIBERTY: QUEST

Liberty is a total web based library automation software which allows federated searching. In Liberty federated searching refers as "Quest" it capitalises our investment in online databases by providing library users with a single search point from with in Liberty.

Benefits of Quest:

- *Single Search Point for Multiple Databases*: Include databases that your organisation subscribes to in your Liberty3 search. Quest simplifies searching and access for your users.
- *Easy to Use*: Quest offers basic or advanced searching options, interleaves search results, and represents search results graphically. Quest allows a number of refine and sort options including sort by relevancy.
- *De-duplicate Searches*: Easily remove duplicates from search results by title or URL.
- *Customisable*: Quest offers you the option to include the library catalogue in the federated search. You can also select the databases you wish to search in your federated search.

- *Local Soft link Support and Service*: Quest is supported locally and hosted on Soft link servers. There is no need for you to worry about installation or maintenance.
- *The biggest players* in the federated searching industry are MuseGlobal (Muse Search), Fretwell- Downing (Zportal), and Webfeat (Knowledge Prism). These product offerings allow a user, regardless of vendor, to access multiple databases through one search interface. Endeavor (ENCompass) and ExLibris (MetaLib) are also in the federated search engine.
- Scirus, Wikipiedia, Pub med central, these are public domain site which provide federated searching.
- Publishers offering numerous journals created a federated search mechanism so that users are able to search their all journals. A good example is Elsivers Science Direct. As Elsivers acquired other publishers, it was able to add their journals at the same platform.
- Database vendor develop the same mechanism such as Sliver Platter provide a single interface for more than 300 databases that they published SCOPUS, etc.
- Proquest, Ebsco, Gale Cengage and Elsevier etc are such databases who offer federated search. In Gale Cengage "federated search" refers as "Power Search".
- The NISO Metasearch Initiative seeks to develop industry standards for one-search access to multiple resources that will allow libraries to offer portal environments for library users offering the same easy searching found in Webbased services like Google.
- Many public and academic libraries also utilise Auto-Graphics' federated search solution AGent Search.

DRAWBACKS OF FEDERATED SEARCH

Limitations of the current generation of federated search engines. These include:

- The lack of a uniform authentication standard means that some databases are inaccessible to federated search engines.
- True, full, deduplication is impossible because databases download results in small sets and metadata standards vary by resource.
- Relevancy ranking is limited by the quality of the metadata, which usually does not include abstracts or full-text information.
- Although federated search systems are fundamentally software, they must be implemented and managed as a service, which takes a great deal of resources.
- Federated search engines cannot improve on the native interface in terms of search accuracy and precision.

- Federated searching is not for power searching needs. Just as with searching metasearch engines, only basic Boolean commands can be used.

The federated search has some other issues as well. First, it cannot cover all online library resources. The goal of one-stop shopping cannot be achieved completely by any federated search.

There are various reasons for this:

- Some databases do not work with any federated search at all, such as SciFinder Scholar. SciFinder Scholar does not use a web browser but rather requires its own internet client. Neither MetaLib nor WebFeat can cover SciFinder Scholar.
- If databases require a login, they will not work with the federated search.
- Some databases work with one federated search product but do not work with the other. MetaLib cannot search LexisNexis databases because LexisNexis does not allow Z39.50 or XML gateway access. WebFeat cannot search databases that do not have a search box on their front page because WebFeat counts on the search box on the native interface to search.
- Many libraries have databases on a pay-per-search basis, and libraries normally do not want them to be searched by a federated search for budgetary reasons.
- Some databases have a limited number of concurrent users, and if these databases are included in a federated search, the limited seat(s) is/are taken immediately whenever someone logs into the federated search, and no other users can use these databases. Libraries normally do not want to include databases with a very limited number of concurrent users in the federated search.

It may not make sense to add to a federated search menu the very specialised databases that most general users would not be interested in, or the databases that require special software. One example is Inter-university Consortium for Political and Social Research (ICPSR) that requires statistics software such as SPSS to view data.

ROLE OF STORAGE DEVISES IN DIGITAL LIBRARY ENVIRONMENT

Storing documents is one of the foremost jobs of present digital library and it's professional. In order to store a large number of digital collections and to retrieve them at any point of time, the necessity for having a computerized system in this regard was felt; digitalization of printed material was the result. It is highly valuable for storing the information in an organized manner and retrieves the same quickly. Managing documents in the proper order is very much necessary in library to provide better services to the user community and some permanent solution to preserve the library material was needed. The permanent solution will be digitalizing the printed materials, which can be transmitted and received anywhere in the world where the infrastructure to send and receive is in place. This new access of technology will help to preserve the information in digital form for future use for future generation.

WHAT IS DIGITAL LIBRARY ?

Although Metrics for traditional libraries such as precision and recall can be directly applicable to some aspects of a digital library and have been widely accepted, the digital library is much more complex and there is much more to be considered. Matrices are required to deal with issues such as the distributed nature of the digital library, the importance of user interfaces to the system, and the need for systems approaches to deal with heterogeneity among the various components and content of the digital library. The main activities of users can be classified into five categories:

- Locating and selecting among relevant sources
- Retrieving information from them
- Interpreting what was retrieved
- Managing the filtered-out information locally, and
- Sharing results with others

Definition of Digital Library

Digital Library can be define as "Computer-based information system for acquiring storing, organizing, searching, distributing and displaying digital materials for end-user access; not necessarily network-based but designed and constructed so as to be capable of attaching or being attached to a network" It means it is clear that fundamental mission of libraries for the users are not changed, *i.e.*, easy access to knowledge and information but the processes tools, techniques are totally changed. Digital Libraries are viewed as systemic providing a community of users with coherent access to a large, organized repository of information and knowledge. This organization of information is characterized by the absence of prior detailed knowledge of uses of the information. The ability of the use to access, recognize, and utilize this repository is enriched by the capabilities of digital technologies. More people are recognizing that digital library is not a topic only computer and information science, but advances in digital library also depend on efforts from legal community. Digital libraries are libraries extended and enhanced through digital technology. Important aspects of a library that may be extended and enhanced include:

- The collection of the library
- The organization and management of the collection

- Access to library items and the processing of the information contained in the items
- To communicate information

PURPOSE AND FUNCTION OF DIGITAL LIBRARY

Purpose of Digital Library:

- To speed up the systematic development of the means to collect, store and organized information and knowledge in digital form, and of digital library collection
- To promote the economical and efficient delivery of information to all parts of society
- To encourage cooperative efforts which leverage the considerable investment in research resource, computing and communications network
- To strengthen communication and collaboration between and among the research business, government and educational communities
- To contribute to the lifelong learning opportunities of all people

Function of Digital Library:

- Provide access to very large amount of information resources to the users wherever they are and whenever they need.
- Focus on providing access to primary information apart from the secondary sources
- Support multimedia content along with the text makes the information more useful and understandable to the users.
- Network accessibility in an Internet and Intranet environment
- Provide user-friendly interface to enable the users for access information comfortably
- Provide hypertext links for navigation through the required reference
- Support client server architecture
- Support advanced search and retrieval for better output to the users
- Integration with other digital libraries

WHAT IS STORAGE TECHNOLOGY

Computer technology may conveniently be grouped into: processor technology, storage technology and software aspects. In storage technology considering advances in devices for digital information storage it may be stated that most of the primary storage in computers is now supplied by semi-conductor circuits. There have been significant developments in memory technology affecting three areas of performance spectrum; the high speed, high performance the midrange and the low speed bulk memory systems. It is now possible that even a small computer system might have cache memory, a small associative memory retaining most recently referenced information and in a readily available place. In some cases, cache memory may be at the top of a hierarchy of memories having a wide variety of characteristics. Memory management, dynamic memory allocation, and virtual memory schemes, generally found in large computer systems, are now appearing on computers which are small and less costly. The development of *charge coupled devices* (CCDs) and bubble memories have filled the gap which previously existed in the continuum of memory devices such as Fixed-head magnetic disk and these are slower than other semi-conductor memories.

These memories have advantage over magnetic disk in that they contain no mechanical parts and could be used to store significant amount of information and can be treated as a structured file system. There has been continuous improvement in recording densities of magnetic media. Floppy disk and microfloppies provide a convenient media to store data. The development of video disk has added a new dimension to the information storage technology. Video disks could be used to store large volumes of information in digital form. These kinds of mass storage are believed to be very useful in the development of information storage and retrieval systems. It may be stated that all these innovations in storage technology provide us a variety of alternatives depending on the requirements of speed of operation.

TYPES OF COMPUTER STORAGE

Computers systems include two types of digital information storage: internal storage, within the CPU and the Backing storage on external devices such as disks or tapes. Different types of storage media differ according to a number of criteria such as speed of operation, capacity cost, reliabilities, the degree to which information is immediately accessible, etc. The various types of storage devices are available in computer market like Network Storage, Backup Storage, Internal Storage and PC Storage Products but we think the manufacture wise classification are different.

Internal Storage Devices: Internal storage is also known as main, primary or core storage, or memory. It is used to hold those instructions and data required at any moment while a programme is running, which must be available instantaneously. Silicon semiconductor chips are now invariably used for internal storage; these are categories as either RAM or ROM chips. ROMs are used for data which is never altered for example, a computer's operating system instructions, while RAM is used for data which is liable to change often, and instructions used in the execution of a programme Backup storage: Backup storage, also termed external storage, is used to hold programmes ad data which are read into internal storage when required. The most common form now, as for the last thirty years, is magnetic storage media, either tapes or disks. With both of these, data is recorded onto a plastic surface, coated with a varnish containing an oxide which can be magnetized in one or two directions; each magnetization representing one bit of data. Data is written or read with the help of read/write heads. Small electromagnets, close to the surface. Magnetic Tapes are very commonly used for storing large quantum of data for which rapid access is not necessary; especially for archival data backup, etc. Tapes are cheap means of storing data but access is generally slow. Small cassette tapes, of relatively low capacity are used with microcomputers. Magnetic Disks are most widely used form of baking storage, suitable for holding information required rapidly for example, data for running programme.

In the type of disk drive in large computer system, data is recorded on the flat surfaces of circular disks revolving on a common spindle, with one read/ write head for each disk.

Access times typically 0.01 second, although much faster than tape, are rather slow by comparison with other computer operations and disk access times are one of the main limiting factors in the speed of operation of retrieval system with information stored on disk. Disk capacities have increased greatly, from original values of about 10 MB to present units with 1 GB which is one thousand million bytes. Smaller computer systems use Winchester disks, with a single hard disk in a sealed unit, floppy disks, which are compact, cheap and convenient for transfer of programmes and data. They are limited in storage capacity, with relatively slow access times, and less movement than a hard disk in day to day use.

Floppy disks are available in two sizes, 1.44 MB and 1.2 MB but now-a-days 1.2 MB floppy are not used. So, we would mention only two types one is Internal Storage and External Storage. In Internal Storage device it may be Network Storage, Internet Storage, Hard Disk Storage, etc. and External Storage devices like Floppy, CD ROM, CD Writer, DVD, USB Port, Pen drive and many more but we discuss only external storage drives. The contents of a digital library get to the readers via direct physical transmission: one person talked to another. These kinds of transmission have so many disadvantages. The other transmission methods like physical objects computer network technologies can perform the duty in a better way. The mainly used physical objects are books and CD ROMs. Books are the permanent version of information. The economics of scale in modern publishing are such that it is difficult to issue a book today in a small press run. Since so many to the costs of printing a book are incurred before the first copy comes off the press, a small press run means high costs and thus high prices. Scholarly journals are even more affected by the push by authors to see their names in print. Their prices have been raised to levels that no one could have imagined 30 years ago; today a journal subscription can cost as much as a new car. Since the authors are not being paid for their contributions, and since journals do not carry a retailer's mark-up, these prices reflect the very small number of libraries that are still willing to subscribe.

CD ROM

The first product in evolutionary optical storage of information is CD ROM. It is a permanent optical-based storage device that in conjunction with an associated drive becomes a powerful peripheral for the PC. The CD ROM puts multi megabytes permanently store data bases at user front end of a PC. Its only drawback is that the end users cannot put his own information on it. CD ROM stands for Compact Disc Read Only Memory.

A compact disc is a 12cm diameter disc made from polycarbonate substrate and a reflective metalised layer. A disc weighs 16 grammas. A typical CD ROM can store about 650 MB data. One would get a better idea of the size of the data that a CD ROM can hold if we say that a CD ROM can hold about 250000 pages of text of 5000 handling systems and services CD ROM can store full motion video, animation, graphics, text and high resolution audio. One should keep in mind that a floppy drive cannot run a CD ROM. For running a CD ROM one would require a CD ROM drive. The time taken by a CD drive to find and grab a piece of information is known access time. This is usually in milliseconds. The smaller the access time, the better the drive; the amount of data transferred form the CD ROM to the computer in unit time is known as transfer rate.

The basic rate is 150 *kilo bytes per second* (kpbs) and "4x" drive transfers at the rate of 600 (4*50) kbpsz. Today "16 xs" become the normal CD drive. However, in the market "24 xs" is also available. One would require more the 450 high density floppy diskettes to store an equivalent amount of information on CD compared to hard disc or floppy diskettes. Read Only Memory means that the information stored on a compact disc can only be read but it cannot be modified. As CD ROM stores text, graphic or still images audio and video or moving images, one would need to install a sound card and speaker to enjoy the world of multimedia that a CD ROM offers. The music CDs were followed by CD ROMs. CD ROM can hold a variety of multimedia information. At one point of time, it was called CD-I or compact disc interactively to the user's instructions. Of course, today such terminology has become irrelevant as almost every CD ROM available in the market is interactive. The benefits of storing data in the CD ROM are:

- High storage capacity
- No head crash
- Low error rate, correctable data
- Long life
- Random access
- Early transportable
- OS independent file system
- Low cost
- Reliable medium
- Less shelf space

This benefits that made CD ROM practically attractive in today's competing information environment are:

- Multi-Media: the ability to deliver unlimited end users access to over 600 MB information delivered using ordinary post means. It can be used for text, graphics, data, audio and video in one simple purchase.
- Multiplatform: It is the first truly system independent media with appropriate SWI, CD ROM allows equal access to information regardless of the computer HW or SW platforms used by the end users.
- Multilingual: Sophisticated CD ROM systems today allow the end users to select the operating language at choice and change it on-the-fly.

The technology which will most characterize the nineties is multimedia, Multimedia technology integrates text, images, graphics, video, animation, sound or music. It is interactive on the lines of technological barriers, for examples, extra disk space required to store multimedia formats and broad bandwidth to transmit the text.

5

Electronic Publishing in Library Evolution

INTRODUCTION

The scope of the term 'electronic publishing' can be interpreted in many different ways. For example, it could be considered to include all forms of electronic aids to authors, from simple word processing capabilities to actual typesetting and/or mark-up tools as well as networking support to collaborative authorship and electronic communication among authors, editors, referees, and other participants in the publishing process.

Since, 'publishing' implies production and distribution, however, the term refers most obviously to the generation of publications in electronic form or, at least, with the aid of electronics. In this more restricted sense, electronic publishing can be considered to have evolved gradually over a period of about thirty years, the evolution having the following manifestations. Use of computers to generate conventional print-on-paper publications. This development can be traced back to the early 1960s.

The use of electronics to print on paper is not a completely pedestrian application since, it allows new capabilities such as printing on demand and even the production of customised publications tailored to individual needs:

- The distribution of text in electronic form, where the electronic version is the exact equivalent of a paper version and may have been used to generate the paper version. For secondary publications, electronic distribution began early in the 1960s. For primary journals, the development occurred somewhat later. Today there is considerable activity and interest in projects that make electronically accessible the text and/or graphics of journals that are also sold in print-on-paper form. Major projects of this kind include ADONIS, Red Sage, CORE, and TULIP. Moreover, the full text of a significant number of journals is now made accessible online by vendors such as DIALOG.
- Distribution in electronic form only but with the publication being little more than print on paper displayed electronically. Nevertheless,

it may have various 'value added' features, including search, data manipulation and alerting capabilities.

- The generation of completely new publications that exploit the true capabilities of electronics. This phase of development can actually be subdivided into:
  - — The presentation of existing text and graphics in innovative ways, and
  - — The production of publications designed *ab initio* to exploit full electronic capabilities.

ELECTRONIC PUBLISHING

For the purposes of this resource guide electronic publishing is defined as:

- Making the content of the journal available online.

This chapter will also address the use of electronic tools to facilitate the processes of, publication, for example online electronic editorial processing.

WHY DO ELECTRONIC PUBLISHING AT ALL

Many journals around the world struggle to attract authors and readers, and frequently suffer from a lack of resources—both human and financial. In addition, research habits are changing and researchers increasingly expect any information to be found online, which means that a journal which cannot be located on the web may be effectively invisible. Online publication can help to address some of these issues. At the same time, many readers still seem to prefer print so you may not feel you can stop producing a print edition as well.

Publishing a journal electronically sounds very attractive. There are a number of good reasons for doing so, but it does have disadvantages too. Before committing yourself and your organisation to the effort and expense involved, it is sensible to look carefully at both the advantages and disadvantages. In the end, the decision will depend on what your main objectives are, so it is important to be clear about why you are publishing, or planning to publish, in the first place: what information you want to disseminate, and to whom. Electronic publishing is often considered to have six advantages over print: international reach, speed, additional capabilities, lower cost, new publishing opportunities and sustainability.

INTERNATIONAL REACH

If a journal is available on the Internet, it is true that readers all over the world can obtain and read your journal; you do not have to arrange for printed copies to be mailed to different parts of the world, which can be both expensive and slow. However, if readers are going to obtain and read your journal they need to know of its existence, and they must want to read the articles you publish. To enable readers to discover your articles/journal, you need to be visible on the main search engines and to encourage use, you really need to carry out some international promotion to raise awareness and trust in your publication.

SPEED OF PUBLICATION

An online journal has a great advantage over a print journal, as it is possible to publish an issue as soon as it is ready, and not wait for it to be printed and bound, then despatched. What is more, you do not need to wait until you have enough articles to make up a complete printed issue. You can, if you wish, publish articles individually as soon as they are ready. These time savings can be very helpful to authors, particularly in fast-moving subjects such as some of the sciences where speed of publication is extremely important. Many of the important processes of publication, however, cannot be speeded up if you want to produce a quality journal. If it is a research journal, you will still need to arrange for peer review to be carried out—and peer review is often the most time-consuming step between submission of an article and its eventual publication.

The transmission of papers to referees, and of their reports to the editorial office, can be done instantly by electronic means, and make some time savings, but the reading, thinking and writing of reports will take exactly the same amount of time. It is also important to recognise that even online publication is not instantaneous; preparing the files correctly, loading them online and maintaining the online service all take time—further time is inevitably introduced if you are working with a third party host.

ADDITIONAL CAPABILITIES

The online environment offers the potential to provide readers with more functionality. One key feature of online publications is the ability to search for articles—at a minimum within one journal, and frequently across multiple journals Another feature commonly added to online journals is that of linking. This refers to the ability to go from one place online to another, at a click of a button—the most common example being the link from a citation within the body of an article to the relevant reference at the end of the article, and from there to the actual article which is being referenced.

Reference linking in scholarly journals is now increasingly being undertaken using DOIs, which are unique identification codes assigned to online articles, and which provide permanent links for the user. This is one of the international standards being developed to assist different systems to communicate and link with each other, to help with visibility and discovery of online material. The methodology of using DOIs in scholarly journals is being managed by an organisation called CrossRef. Electronic publication also makes it possible to include material which you would not include in a print journal, either for space reasons or because the material is difficult, costly or even impossible to print.

Research articles online can be accompanied by the full data-sets from which the results were reached—ideally in a form which readers can manipulate for themselves. Colour illustrations may be prohibitively expensive in a printed journal, but present no such problems in an electronic journal. Moving images, sound, or animations may also be included, although relatively few authors automatically think of providing such material at present and the technical comple-xities may outweigh the benefits. Before introducing any additional features within the online journal, you must consider whether your readers are likely to have the necessary software to make use of the additional material.

It is also worth noting that linking is generally rated very highly by readers, who find it an invaluable way of enhancing their research; however, other additional features are much less highly valued. It may, therefore, not be worth spending a great deal of time and money on these. One final consideration is that the additional capabilities which online publishing can offer may be of particular relevance to you, as the publisher, and not so much use to the user. These may involve the ease with which you can upload your content, and streamline your working practices.

One particularly important new facility which online publishing can provide you with, is a tool to measure and monitor online use. Most commercial hosts will automatically offer sophisticated usage statistics, and most of these will be COUNTER compliant, which is another increasingly important international standard which online publications should comply with.

REDUCED COSTS

It was originally assumed that publishing online introduced immediate cost savings. However, this is only true if the journal is no longer printed at all; continuing to print even a few copies removes most of the cost savings.. If you decide to cease printing altogether, you may save a significant percentage of your total direct costs, although many costs will be unchanged—however, most readers still seem to want print copies. The cost of administering an electronic version will also be considerably lower if you are able to make it available to everyone, free of charge.

Depending on the way the journal is funded, however, you may need to replace subscriptions income by raising author-side charges; this will require an administration system, which will reduce the savings. The costs of publishing a journal can be split into direct costs and indirect costs. Direct costs are those where an invoice is received from an external supplier, and the journal needs to find the money to pay them. Indirect costs are those costs which are covered by the parent organisation, and the journal may be unaware of them. Introducing online publishing may provide an opportunity to reduce direct costs but is likely to increase indirect costs.

ELECTRONIC RESERVE AND ON-DEMAND PUBLISHING

The term 'electronic reserve collection' may be a misnomer as it implies rationed access whereas 'the digital environment removes the need for this form of rationing as a single digitisation can simultaneously be accessed by any number of readers'.

Nevertheless, the term is used to describe collections of resources, including journal papers and extracts from texts and newspapers, that have been digitised and mounted on campus networks to be accessed by students.

The rationale for this is that hard copy can be accessed by only one person at a time but access to digital copy is limited only by the infrastructure required to use it. Electronic reserve collections (ERCs) have been developed with a view to meeting more effectively the needs of large undergraduate classes which rely increasingly on the library for core reading materials. Development of ERCs is more widespread in the US than it is in the UK. In the early 1990s, many of those developing ERCs in the US considered it 'fair use' to digitize copyright resources and make them available electronically.

The Conference on Fair Use (CONFU) guidelines were intended to formalise this reading of the law but publishers and librarians were unable to agree on guidelines for electronic reserve use of copyright materials (http://www.utsystem.edu/ogc/intellectualproperty/confu.htm).

Nevertheless, many libraries continue to interpret the law in this way (follow links from the following URL for examples http://www.cc.columbia.edu/~rosedale/#Sites). Use of copyright resources in ERCs in the US must now be licensed just as it is in the UK. In the UK, HE ERC developers have assumed that ER use of copyright materials is not 'fair dealing' and guidelines published recently by the Publishers' Association and the JISC confirm that this is so (http://www.ukoln.ac.uk/services/elib/papers/pa/licence/fairnote.html).

Clearly, the cost of obtaining permissions is important to the economic viability of the whole exercise. This cost includes not only the price for using copyright material but also time spent identifying right sholders, seeking permission to use their copyright material and, often, chasing that request. The total figure can be as high as ten times the actual copyright fee. The cost to rightsholders of administering permissions requests is also significant.

At present the Association for Computing Machinery (ACM) grants blanket permission to copy its copyright materials for educational use because the cost of administering applications exceeds the revenue generated. This suggests that if licensing digital use of copyright materials is to become a viable revenue stream for publishers, copyright fees must be relatively high. Although publishers have been willing to grant permissions free of charge to limited life

ER projects, i.e. during development, they charge fees to use their material in ongoing ER services. This may not be a viable revenue stream but many publishers consider ER use of their material to be a threat to their core business. Charging deters widespread adoption of ER as an alternative to text provision or recommendation. On the other hand, as long as ER systems do not cannibalise publishers' primary income, a streamlined process may actually generate incremental revenue for them.

Another significant cost associated with ERCs is the cost of digitising text. Odlyzko cites an example of a company that will digitise text for $0.60 per page but recent eLib supporting study established £2.50 as a reasonable estimate. Obviously, cost varies with a number of factors such as the cost of identifying and obtaining the original, the condition of the original, the presence or otherwise of special characters, i.e. the degree of manual intervention required to produce a useful file.

If publishers begin to supply their texts in electronic form and offer the facility to buy subsections of texts, then the need for HEIs to digitise a significant amount of text will vanish. However, unless publishers digitise all back runs of journals and text back lists, there will be a need to digitise older material.

At present, developments in delivering texts in electronic form are embryonic, so material selected for reserve collections from texts must almost always be digitised if it is to be delivered in electronic form. However, duplication of effort may be avoided if institutions collaborate.

Very little has been published on the economics of running an ERC. The ACORN Project at Loughborough University compared the costs of traditional and electronic reserve collections of journal papers.

A more comprehensive study of the costs and benefits of ERCs was published as an eLib supporting study in 1998. This study was informed by all eLib studies in the electronic reserves (ER) and ondemand publishing (ODP) programme areas, including ACORN. Another relevant study comparing charging mechanisms was conducted on behalf of a JISC/PA working party following a seminar on pricing in July of that year.

This study arose from debate among and between librarians and publishers regarding appropriate pricing mechanisms that would not cannibalise publishers' primary income stream. It considered only licensing of digitised copy from printed books and journals; not licensing of electronic products.

The report from the study called for a pricing mechanism that is 'simple and therefore inexpensive to administer ... susceptible to centralised administration [and produces] predictable costs for users and revenues for rights holders'. Furthermore, the report recommended that two models be adopted to reflect different types of use of digitised material; a 'textbook substitution' model and a 'library substitution' model. The former would be applied to materials that, in print, publishers would expect students to buy.

The pricing mechanism would be based on student numbers and a licence would be granted for a fixed period; probably an academic year. The latter model would be applied to material that, in print, publishers would have expected libraries to buy. In this case, a licence would be granted in perpetuity.

The report referred also to the high cost of digitisation and commended the idea of a central repository of digitised text which would avoid duplication of effort among HEIs and would make it easy for HEIs to identify material for which permission is likely to be granted, as it had been in the past. The report from this study is particularly useful because it resulted from an ongoing collaborative attempt by publishers and HE representative to resolve many issues that hindered progress with ERC developments.

Many of the recommendations in the report appear to have informed the Copyright Licensing Agency (CLA) Higher Education Digitisation White Paper which details the terms on which copyright materials are now licensed by the CLA for digitisation and distribution.

The CLA will continue to require institutions to request rights on a transactional basis and prices will be set individually by publishers. Publishers will differentiate between material that is likely to substitute for sales of texts to libraries and material that is likely to substitute for sales of texts to students. The latter will be more expensive to compensate for many more 'lost sales'.

This differentiation will refer to specific titles; it will not vary between institutions depending on their patterns of use of that title. Thus, although institution A may refer students to title X for further reading while at institution B it is required reading for all students in a class, both institutions A and B will be required to pay at the prescribed rate, be it 'text substitution' or 'library substitution'. This system is not ideal but the alternative, i.e. setting prices with reference to both the title and the institution requesting permission to digitise it would be extremely complex and thus expensive.

The CLA White Paper also specifies the format of digitised text; it should be an 'exact page representation' of the print original. As pages designed to be printed tend not to be suitable for on-screen reading students can be expected to print.

At present, students tend to photocopy materials borrowed from a reserve collection so the library could recover print costs from students without increasing student expenditure. However, support for networked printing is likely to be a significant cost associated with the introduction of an ER system.

The CLA does not expect institutions to comply with the 'exact page representation' criterion by creating and delivering bitmapped images from printed originals. The White Paper acknowledges that bitmapped images are large files and thus are bandwidth hungry.

However, licences may specify the degree of qualitative and quantitative accuracy in digitised text. It may be possible to comply with terms by using suitable software and including disclaimers regarding accuracy (and the CLA anticipates that this will be the case) but there is no guarantee that this will be the case. As OCR programs tend to generate errors, it may be necessary to proof-read digitised text.

This adds considerably to the digitisation cost. It is not immediately apparent that the eCLA (the name of the new CLA service) will be more efficient than the often criticised CLARCS system for clearing rights in materials to be used in course packs (containing photocopies).

A transactional payment mechanism is expensive. The Copyright Clearance Centre in the US has operated a transactional system for electronic reserve materials since 1997. In addition to any permission fee it charges $5 per request regardless of whether or not permission is obtained and claims that this charge is required to cover costs. The CLA requires from each publisher a mandate to license that publisher's material for use in electronic form in HEIs. The Publishers Licensing Society (PLS) has published a template which publishers can use to mandate the CLA

Some of the terminology in this template differs from that used by the CLA, i.e. the PLS refers to a 'Bookshop Materials' model and a 'Library Materials' model instead of, respectively, a 'text substitution' and a 'library substitution' model. One more substantial difference between the CLA White Paper and the PLS mandate is that the latter restricts a licence for 'library materials' to 5 years rather than granting it in perpetuity.

The PLS mandate also sets the 'Bookshop Materials' model as default and recommends a default price of 5 pence per page. Thus, libraries will be expected to pay for copyright at a rate of 5 pence per page per student in a class. A single 20-page extract for a class of 200 students would cost £200 (£235 inc. VAT) in copyright fees alone. If widely adopted, the terms of this mandate will probably render ER prohibitively expensive.

HERON

HERON is an eLib-funded project developing a national database and resource bank of electronic texts to be selected and accessed by HEIs throughout the UK. HEIs will supply details of materials that they require in digital form. HERON will obtain permission for their use and will digitise these materials. HERON is collaborating with rights holders and representative bodies to determine appropriate fee levels and conditions of digitised text and to streamline copyright clearance procedures.

The Project will normally clear rights through the CLA and when an institution requires permission to use material that is owned by a publisher or other person who has not mandated the CLA, HERON will seek to secure an agreement directly with the rightsholder. Thus, when HERON has agreed terms with a publisher and an institution seeks to use material owned by that publisher,

HERON can approach the company with confidence not only that permission will be granted but that the terms agreed previously will suffice and no lengthy negotiation will be required. Gradually, HERON will accumulate a collection of such agreements making it more efficient for HERON than for any individual institution to seek to clear rights in material to be included in an ER system. Furthermore, HERON aims to become a repository for digital copy.

HEIs seeking permission to digitise material from the CLA, either through HERON or directly, will be asked by the CLA to place a digital copy in a repository such as HERON so that it may be accessed by other users thereafter, thus avoiding duplication of effort.

Clearly, any future use of the digital copy would also have to be licensed. The model described later in this report is informed by the eLib supporting study of ODP/ER services, by cost and charge developments such as those published by the CLA and the PLS, and by HERON. The economic impact of rationalisation of licence negotiation and of digitisation will be explored using the model as will the ramifications for libraries of the CLA White Paper and the PLS mandate.

For example, the textbook substitution model (referred to by the PLS as the Bookshop Materials model) reflects the fact that libraries increasingly provide access to core reading materials that, previously, students would have bought from booksellers. Libraries cannot afford to pay to provide all students with core texts and further reading.

The crisis that libraries now face has been precipitated to some degree by student demands that they do so. However, librarians are uncomfortable with the prospect of charging for student reading materials. To do so would be to qualitatively change the role of academic libraries which would then be open to competition from other organisations which charge to supply information. Booksellers also would be affected by a move to supply core texts directly through the library.

INFORMATION GATEWAYS

Very little work has been done on the economics of information (or subject) gateways, also known as portals and hubs. Cataloguing the Internet is an activity undertaken by various types of organisation to attract users to their sites with a view to promoting their primary products/services or enhancing their reputations. Examples of this type of activity include:

- BioMedNet which, offering pointers to useful sites among many other discipline-based services, is effectively a discipline-based Internet community owned by Elsevier Science and funded, in part, by advertising (http://www.biomednet.com/gateways/bac);
- The Wiley student resource centre which includes subject-specific sub-sites each of which revolves around specific high-volume Wiley

texts (http://www.wiley.co.uk/products/worldwide/canada/src/index.htm#links);

- Oppedahl & Larson LLP Patent Law Web Server, a site created and maintained by a professional law firm, which includes links to sources about all aspects of intellectual property (http://www.patents.com/index.sht);
- Various HE sites which having created pointers for their own users make them universally available (http://www.stir.ac.uk/infoserv/).

The perceived quality of these types of pointers is related to the site on which they are located. For example, links from an HEI may be considered more credible or impartial than those from a commercial organisation. Information gateways whose primary purpose is to provide pointers to other networked resources without promoting a different primary product would appear to be unique to the UK.

The eLib subject-based gateways (SBGs) have co-ordinated identification and evaluation of Internet resources and provide links to Internet resources within specific subject areas. Every resource which is linked from an SBG has been assessed by an expert in the relevant subject area and deemed to be of high-quality. None of the SBG projects developed an economic model for maintenance and development of a service beyond the grant-funded period. However, an eLib supporting study conducted by Haynes *et al.* evaluated three different models for the transition of the SBGs from project to service status.

These models varied depending on the proposed funding sources. The first was a JISC-funded service, i.e. one which would continue to rely on 100% grant funding. The structure of SBG organisation would remain unchanged.

The second model would increase JISC funding in the first two years with a view to migrating to a service funded 50:50 between JISC and other sponsors. This model includes a considerable degree of rationalisation in the organisation of SBG activities. The third model would end JISC funding and require services to find alternative sources to fund their activities.

The Haynes report recommended that the JISC pursue the second of these models. This required additional JISC funding for two years to employ a managing director who would seek complementary funding for an ongoing service. Many of the functions undertaken individually by eLib SBG projects would be rationalised and centralised to reduce duplication of effort and to allow for greater

PRESERVATION AND ARCHIVING

Acceptable archiving and preservation strategies are essential preconditions to the widespread acceptance of electronic journals by authors and librarians. Many questions relating to archiving and preservation require answers before economic factors can be explored. For example, there is the question of who should archive. Publishers are reluctant to accept what, traditionally, has been a library responsibility.

They are waiting to find out what the role of national libraries will be in a digital environment before they commit themselves in this regard. Furthermore, the long-term commitment of publishers and other stakeholder groups is questionable. It has been suggested that the only way to ensure 'systematic archiving of electronic publishing would be to assign that role to national institutions funded to do so and backed up by legislation'.

The UK research community generally agrees that preservation should be the responsibility of a publicly funded national agency. Preservation issues are of great concern to the UK HE community. They have been the subject of several eLib supporting studies, of a British Library Research Study and issues continue to be explored by the CEDARS project. Economic modelling however, has not yet been undertaken.

JSTOR

Successful attempt to develop a model for archiving and preservation in electronic form of scholarly journals is JSTOR. One of the aims of JSTOR is to help libraries with space problems. JSTOR is also designed to be a trusted archive. Development of the archive has depended on the cooperation of publishers holding copyright in the journals included therein. It is important to those publishers that JSTOR should not cannibalise subscription income.

Thus, current issues of journals are not included in the JSTOR archive. JSTOR operates a 'moving wall' whereby entire backruns of journal issues are included in the archive except those published during the previous X years. Every year the contents from X-1 years ago are added to the archive.

The duration of X varies from publisher to publisher but generally is between 3 and 5 years. The JSTOR archive is funded by fees from institutions accessing the contents. The JSTOR team has calculated and compared the costs associated with:

- A centrally managed electronic text archive (including the cost of migrating content to keep pace with technological development);
- Storage, processing, reshelving and maintenance of a hard-copy collection.

A key factor in making JSTOR financially viable is that it is available widely and thus, costs are spread across a large number of institutions both in the US, and now also in the UK. JSTOR aims to be as equitable as possible in pricing access to the archive. Price discrimination is applied with a view to setting prices according to the value derived by each institution.

Thus, institutions are banded according to size and annual access fees are varied on that basis. Pay-per-use was dismissed as a possible pricing mechanism because it 'usually yields prices higher than the marginal cost of providing the product' and JSTOR 'did not want to force students and scholars to have to decide whether it would really be 'worth it' to download and print an article'.

This contrasts with the view that it is prudent to charge a print fee as this discourages indiscriminate use of printing resources, i.e. a fee would encourage users to filter information before rather than after they have printed. JSTOR received start-up funding from the Andrew Mellon Foundation but is expected to be self-sustaining over the longer term.

JSTOR appears to be a pragmatic and useful model for archiving and providing electronic access to backruns of journals. The capacity of JSTOR, however, is limited; currently the project aims to include backruns of a minimum of 100 journals before the year 2000.

To preserve in electronic form and make available worldwide all developments in scholarly communication is a monumental task requiring co-operation on an international scale. It is notoriously difficult to secure international agreement for any type of activity and it is beyond the scope of this project to explore the ramifications of such an initiative.

PRE-PRINT ARCHIVES

The most famous example of an electronic pre-print archive is the Physics archive developed by Paul Ginsparg at the Los Alamos National Laboratory (LANL) (http://xxx.lanl.gov). The archive is very successful and is used by authors and readers throughout the world.

Development of the archive was funded by a grant from the US National Science Foundation. The full cost of developing and running the archive is not clear. Odlyzko estimated the cost per paper at $5. Then, to pre-empt disagreement on this figure he recalculated using wildly extravagant estimates of the costs of personnel and storage space.

He estimated that the upper limit would be $75, i.e. that it could not possibly cost more than $75 per paper to run such an archive. In the absence of grant funding, a cost-recovery model would be required.

Given Odlyzko's figures, if the international physics community were to subscribe to this service either on an individual or institutional basis, the subscription charge would be small. Nevertheless, the administration of subscriptions would increase the total cost. An alternative model might charge authors to place pre-prints in the archive.

This would be unlikely to succeed however as authors are reluctant to pay page charges even to submit papers tojournals where the benefits of publication are clear. Harnad is trying to establish a similar pre-print archive in the cognitive sciences. This project (CogPrints) is funded by eLib.

Other than grant funding, no economic model for a pre-print archive has been published and so no model will be explored here. It should be noted however, that increasing use of preprints effectively transfers the information filtering function either to libraries or to end users. Publication in a specific journal confers on a paper a mark of quality that is recognised by the readers. When all papers are freely available and unrefereed, the user must seek to identify high quality papers for herself. The time taken to do so is a cost; thus, in economic terms, preprints are not free. Physicists reading material from the Ginsparg archive tend to read only articles written by colleagues with whose work they are familiar This suggests that they are unwilling to filter the material for themselves. It also makes it difficult for newcomers to establish themselves in the field.

Issues Related to Digital Library Service and Resource delivery

Licensing

The application of national copyright law to the electronic environment is not straightforward; legislation tends to predate the digital era. Furthermore, the business of providing access to copyright materials in electronic form tends to be international.

Combined with the Internet 'gift culture' whereby users expect electronic content to be available free of charge, copyright on its own is inadequate for regulating use of copyright materials. Rather than relying on copyright law, content suppliers tend to use licences to detail precisely the terms on which their copyright material is made available to end users.

In the words of Karen Hunter of Elsevier Science, 'publishers view licences 48 and contracts as a more robust, clearer method of resolving what might otherwise be ambiguities as to permitted use and limitations'. Licence terms have important implications for libraries.

As the availability of an increasing proportion of library material depends on relationships beyond the organisational boundary, library managers must consider the impact that this has, among other things, on their ability to control budgets and guarantee access beyond the current licence term.

Clearly, the pricing model detailed in a licence and the level of prices are important in determining the costs and benefits to licensor and licensee. At present, prices tend to be very high for a variety of reasons including:

- That publishers often tie the price of electronic copy to the print price and offer both formats as a bundle;
- That by becoming the source site, the publisher takes on some of the library roles and costs.

Although pricing is an important element of a licence agreement it is only one of many issues that determine the costs and benefits conferred on the licensor and licensee. At present, pricing models offered by individual publishers vary considerably and are complex. Negotiation on a licence terms requires expertise, and takes a great deal of time. As licensing becomes increasingly important and common so do legal advice and staff with the knowledge and experience required to negotiate favourable and consistent licence terms. Guidelines published by the US Association of Research Libraries (ARL) in 1997 recommend that institutions 'create a contract team' consisting of 'appropriate staff from the library, legal office, purchasing department and information technology division to provide information and develop contract expertise'. This type of recommendation suggests that licensing electronic resources is very much more expensive in terms of personnel than acquisition of print resources by library staff. Furthermore, it illustrates the importance to all stakeholders that licences be kept simple and terms be standardised wherever possible. This is the rationale behind CHEST and behind initiatives like the UK National Electronic Site Licence Initiative (NESLI).

NESLI has based its model licence on one developed by a collaborative working party of representatives from the JISC and from the Publishers Association (PA) (http://www.nesli.ac.uk/nesli-licence.html). This model has been revised by NESLI in an iterative process involving all stakeholder groups.

When electronic resources were first offered to libraries by publishers, licences tended to be extremely restrictive with regard, for example, to use and users. This can be understood with reference to the size and importance of the market to academic publishers and the apparent naivety about copyright among users accustomed to the internet 'gift culture'. A great deal of progress has been made towards increased trust, goodwill and understanding between different stakeholder groups.

Librarians have identified licensing issues of importance to them and initiated dialogue with publishers. In the US an informal organisation calling itself the International Coalition of Library Consortia (ICOLC) and representing initially US library consortia, but later also consortia from Australia, the UK and the Netherlands, published a Statement on Current Perspectives and Preferred Practices for the Selection and Purchase of Electronic Infrastructure (http://www.library.yale.edu/consortia/statement.html).

This is essentially a wish list which elicited responses from several publishers thus initiating dialogue which continues at annual meetings of the ICOLC. The most recent (7th) draft of the NESLI model contract, published in September 1998 (http://www.nelsi.ac.uk/nesli7.html) addresses many of the issues raised by the ICOLC 50 and by writers on licensing such as Okerson.

For example, terms dictate that access to licensed material will not be withdrawn when subscriptions are cancelled and that licensees will be given the opportunity to subscribe to electronic copy only. NESLI is also considering the type of usage data that it can feasibly provide and is working towards seamless access from OPAC entry to abstracts, Tables of Contents, and full text. By offering standardised terms, NESLI aims to minimise negotiation costs for both parties but acknowledges that the terms in this contract will not be acceptable to all publishers. There are often stark differences between the commercial interests of publishers and the library mission and negotiation is not often straightforward. The US experience to date is that negotiation of terms of use of electronic journals is often adversarial and protracted, and the resulting licences are lengthy and complex but clearly there is a willingness to simplify the licensing process and thus reduce costs for all parties.

User Behaviour in the Online Environment

User acceptance is key to the success of digital library resources and services. A resource can be technically impressive but unless it is acceptable to the target audience it will not be used. Research on user needs should be practical rather than hypothetical as potential users' reported needs differ from those of experienced users.

Thus, studies which provide access over a sufficient period to allow users to learn and repeatedly use a system are likely to be most useful. Research on user behaviour tends to focus on electronic journals but user needs and behaviour with reference to electronic texts and monographs have also been explored. There is a remarkable degree of consensus among researchers of user behaviour in the online 51 environment. It would appear that researchers consistently identify the same essential pre-requisites for a successful online resource and the same deterrents to use.

Core Functionality

Identification of core functionality is important as journal readers use only those functions that meet their needs. As additional functionality increases production costs and may impact on price, superfluous functions should be avoided. Users consider the core functions to be the facility to browse, search and print from an electronic journals service. Research repeatedly emphasises the fact that users do not read on screen but prefer to use print copy.

There are various reasons for this, including portability, the facility to annotate and guaranteed future access. Some users claim that a virtual filebox may reduce the need to print.

This would reduce anxiety about accessing materials in the future but does nothing to address the requirement for annotation and portability. Although Butterworth reports that scientists' interest in electronic journals relates primarily to improved functionality and lists linking to references as one of the required functions, the SuperJournal project found that users consider linking to be 'nice to have' rather than essential. Creating links to references can be expensive especially for journals that are published in PDF format so it is essential that the importance of this feature to users be established.

Critical Mass and Currency

Users consider it essential that any service should offer a critical mass of resources both in terms of breadth and depth. Access to a limited selection of journal titles, whether they be published by a single publisher or by a range of publishers, is not considered sufficient incentive to learn to use a new system. Users also expect an electronic journal service to offer a backfile of a minimum duration. The SuperJournal Project found that users consider the minimum requirement for a journal service to be a backfile of 5–10 years. Others consider the minimum useful backfile to be 25 years.

Furthermore, many users expect an electronic journals service to offer a wider range of titles than is currently available in print from the library.

System Performance

System performance is a necessary prerequisite if users are expected to use digital resources and services. Both academics and students are subject to time constraints and users are reluctant to learn to use new systems unless there are clear benefits. Lowlevel problems demoralise users and it is difficult to entice them back if they have been disappointed. Time taken to download and print materials from a system is also important.

At present many users consider the delay to be excessive and consequently, would not print. Staff from the library at the University of Columbia have found that the online books system is used as a sophisticated catalogue. Users search for items of interest in the digital environment but when they have identified an item and wish to read more than a few lines, they seek a print copy from the library shelf. This finding echoes that, noted earlier, of the ELINOR project at De Montfort University. It is no surprise that users consider the online books system to be an adjunct rather than a replacement for print.

Convenient, Fast Desktop Access to a one-stop Shop

Desktop access is considered to be important as is speed and ease of use. Users prefer not to have to login at all and complicated login procedures invariably deter use. The SuperJournal project found that when users experienced difficulty with the login procedures they did not attempt to use the system again. Furthermore, 90% of requests for user support from the SuperJournal helpdesk were from users who had forgotten their personal ID for logging in.

Having accessed the system, the time taken to identify and retrieve material is important; users are not prepared to follow long chains of links to access relevant content. A single commopn interface is also an important feature and the interface should be familiar so frequent upgrading and redesign is unacceptable. Furthermore, users expect an electronic journals service to offer seamless discovery and access. The user should have the facility first to identify material that she wishes to read by searching or browsing tables of contents, second to link to the abstract of any items that interests her, and third to link to the full-text of any article that she wishes to read in full.

Format

A significant proportion of electronic journals are delivered as portable document format (PDF) documents especially when the electronic format is produced as a parallel of the print format. It is claimed that PDF is cheap to produce in these circumstances but is inappropriate for electronic delivery especially when pages have two or more columns.

Nevertheless, PDF currently has advantages over HTML. Users of Super Journal service claimed to prefer reading HTML on screen but when offered a document in either HTML or PDF format, the majority selected the latter.

This may be related to the fact that users prefer not to read on screen and print material if they intend to read more than a few lines. Super Journal users claim to prefer prints from PDF because they look like printed journal pages and, unlike HTML documents, they have page numbers.

Benefits of an Electronic Service

Access to digital library resources tends not to be restricted to library opening hours and generally, two or more users may access an item simultaneously. Improved access is considered to be a benefit of digital library services. However, although Super Journal users claimed that access outside library opening hours is important, most use occurred during office hours.

Users also believe that the digital medium should facilitate faster publication; where items are published in both print and digital formats, users expect the latter to be published before or at the same time as the former.

Benefits of Print and Photocopies

Generally, studies of user needs and behaviour in the digital library have revealed a range of different functions associated with print and photocopies that users consider to be 55 important. Until equivalent or improved features are available in an electronic environment many users will remain attached to print. These features include ease of browsing and reading; most current users have been familiar with print since childhood and are skilled in its use. A ubiquitous equivalent level of familiarity and skill is likely to be available to future users who are currently in the primary education system. Studies also report an emotional attachment to print.

Whether or not this attachment will remain among future lifelong users of electronic media remains to be seen. Another feature of print that currently give it an edge is its portability. Users tend not to read at their computers and often read journal papers at home or when travelling.

The facility to annotate a print copy is also important as is the fact that they can legally cache materials for future use. Finally, some users consider presentation in print resources to be superior to that in digital resources. For example, high-quality graphics cannot be satisfactorily reproduced on prints from electronic resources. This is particularly important with regard to colour images.

Disciplines

Although many research findings apply to all users, differences between disciplines should be recognised. The Los-Alamos pre-print archive is commonly cited as an example of discipline-specific behaviour which has contributed to the success of a digital library resource.

There has long been a culture among physicists of distributing preprints. Physicists differ from other sciences in this respect and it is argued that the success of the Los Alamos archive derives in part from 56 this culture.

It is reported also that electronic journals are embraced more readily by those in disciplines that have not been adequately catered for in a print environment, for example musicology and other disciples to which non-printable elements are important.

Future research on user behaviour in the online environment should differentiate between users from different disciplines. Unfortunately, initiatives such as ATHENS which are designed to streamline delivery of digital resources can subvert attempts to gather data on different types of user.

NEW PUBLISHING OPPORTUNITIES

It is perfectly possible for an online journal to work in all respects exactly like a print journal. However, the online medium does make possible new ways of doing things—new ways of publishing, new ways of covering costs, and new processes—which may help to address the problems of a struggling journal.

New Ways of Publishing

Publish Often, Print Infrequently

This approach may be particularly attractive if you have difficulty publishing issues on time, whether this is due to lack of funds to pay for printing and distribution, or to a shortage of articles. Online issues would be published regularly and frequently, but you might only produce one, archival, print issue per year. This can help to improve regularity of publication, whilst at the same time saving some of the print and distribution costs.

Article-by-article Publication

This approach may be even more attractive if rapid publication is important to authors in your subject area. Articles would be published online individually, as soon as they are ready. In addition to offering fast publication for authors, this will bring readers back to the online journal frequently, thus increasing usage.

Separate Online and Print Content

Some journals have separated their print and online publications so that they are almost different journals—an example of this is 'electronic long, paper short' used in the British Medical Journal. This model publishes the full article online, but only publishes a shorter version of the article within its print journal. Some journals include additional sections within their online journal, and some exclude some materials from online version that appear in the print journal. However, if you decide to publish different content in the print and the online publication, this brings extra complexity into the way of dealing with your content, which is likely to increase your editorial costs overall.

New Publishing Processes

Open Peer Review

The Internet makes it easy for readers to comment on papers after they are published by the journal. This may be done once papers have gone through the normal peer review process, or it may precede or even replace it. Some journals then allow authors to modify their articles in the light of feedback. However, this makes for considerable extra complexity, and makes it essential that readers know which version of the article they are actually reading; this approach may not be welcomed in all disciplines, as scholars differ in their willingness to expose their unfinished work to their colleagues, so it is important that you know your reader/author community before making a decision.

Index

You may be able to do without an index if the web site allows searching of the full text of articles, particularly if it also allows searching by specific fields. However, human indexers add considerable value-electronic searching will only find the exact word you are looking for, whereas an indexer can think of synonyms, and will not index irrelevant occurrences of the word. If you can afford it, many publishers believe that a human-compiled index is still worth having.

CHALLENGES

Although publishing online presents many opportunities for journals, it can also present some challenges. Two of the most important challenges are presented here.

PERPETUAL ACCESS AND ARCHIVING

This is an issue which is worrying publishers and libraries the world over. In the print environment, a library which has subscribed to a journal in the past will always have the copies to which it subscribed, even if one day it has to cancel its subscription. However the same may not be true in the electronic environment, where the library does not 'purchase' the online journal, but merely 'rents access' for a specified period of time. Thus the library never holds the content locally, but relies on third-party servers to deliver the content.

Many publishers have now changed their agreements with libraries so that the library has perpetual access to any journal issues to which it subscribed; however, this means that the publisher needs to ensure good records and administration of online access to make sure that this works smoothly over time. Print journals are relatively easy to archive but there is no easy way of archiving an electronic-only online journal. Even if the archiving library makes backup files of the journals, these may need to be updated over time as technology changes.

Links to other sites—one of the most attractive features of online journals—may become inactive due to the impermanence of World Wide Web addresses. Some publishers have signed an agreement with archiving organisations to preserve their journals permanently; this has the advantage that they can also provide ongoing access to customers after they have ceased to subscribe, or even in the event of the publisher's own service failing, or of the journal or publisher going out of business.

Much work is going on in various countries to extend their legislation to provide for legal deposit of electronic materials in the same way as is currently required for print. For example, the UK law was updated in 2003, and in 2004 the British Library started a pilot project to test deposit of online journals. Another related consideration is the digitisation and online publishing of your historical print content. Although it is costly, there are benefits to placing all issues of your journal online so that they can be searched; there is evidence that usage of older issues increases. Some organisations will fund the digitisation on the condition that subsequent access is free.

CITATION AND DEFINITIVE VERSION

Electronic publication gives rise to a whole range of new questions, such as: How do you cite a reference in an electronic-only journal? Or to an article pre-published online? What do you give as the publication date for an article which is published online before the print issue is available? What is the definitive version of the journal—the online or the print? There are more fundamental issues, too, about what counts as 'publication' in an environment of potentially continually updated documents; these are all difficult and, so far, largely unanswered questions.

One issue that has been problematic for journals wishing to move to online-only publication has been the way that these journals are perceived by the research and academic community. In the past they have not always been recognised as credible publications by the relevant authorities when considering tenure and promotion based on publication. Fortunately this attitude is changing, and it has been assisted by the acceptance of online-only publications within indexing services, giving them recognition within the journal publishing community.

Citations can be made far more useful, in online journals, by linking directly to the cited item. This is facilitated by the Digital Object Identifier which provides a much more permanent link than a URL. The DOI/CrossRef system is now being used extensively; it does not in fact require sophisticated publishing although there are charges, these are relatively small.

An illustration of how DOIs may be used in citations can be found on the BMJ web site, in the area called 'Online First' which contains articles that have been accepted, but are not yet published, or assigned an issue. On this web page, the readers are instructed to cite the articles using their DOIs and the date of publication online. In some communities this has become an accepted method of citation, but it is early days and it is still to gain acceptance in many areas of academic publishing and research.

HOSTING ISSUES

Where a journal is published online can affect its success or failure as the online site can help or hinder the journal by the technical facilities and visibility that it offers. The price of online hosting is another important consideration. There are various options open to the journal publisher.

OWN/ORGANISATION WEB SITE

The benefit of publishing your journal on your own web site is that you have complete control over the web site—the design and the 'look and feel' of the site. Although there are, of course, costs associated with this option, no external supplier is involved. However, there are also disadvantages to publishing online this way. These may include a lack of technical skills and support for the journal, and a lack of current awareness of online publishing standards and compliance with new protocols.

In addition maintenance and updating of the web site may not receive enough attention if it competes with the other requirement of the institution's own web site. In addition, the journal may suffer from low visibility, since, it may be difficult to locate within the institution's web site, and visitors will not be attracted to discover it.

COMMERCIAL HOST

Several commercial companies are now hosting scholarly journals on behalf of their publishers. They also frequently provide value-added benefits, for example file conversion, and supply of metadata to abstracting and indexing services, as well as all the benefits of a sophisticated system which is continually being developed. They are also experienced in dealing with subscribers and access-controlled environments, and ensuring security of the online journal from hackers and unauthorised access.

Against this, there are some disadvantages. The prime one, for a journal with little access to funding, is that they charge for their services, and although most of them offer a price which is reasonable within the budgets of western journals, they may be too costly for journals from the developing world. It should also be remembered that commercial hosts may only provide a hosting service; although they can offer advice on matters relating to online publishing, they are unable to take on the role of a publisher. However, some do offer marketing services—for additional payment—to help increase subscriptions and visibility through promotion.

SUBSCRIPTION AGENTS

Some subscription agents also now offer to host online journals on behalf of publishers. Again, they offer a high level of technical competence and value-added benefits. However they are unlikely to take your online journal unless they feel able to earn sufficient revenue from sales. They will deduct the fee for their hosting from revenues that they obtain, in which case you would not have to find the money up-front.

Another potential disadvantage is that they may not be effective at increasing the journal's visibility outside their own customer base.

AGGREGATORS

A number of companies will put your journal content online as part of a large package which they sell in its entirety to libraries.

OTHER ONLINE HOSTS

There are a number of organisations set up specifically to support the online hosting of journals from developing and transitional countries. Further information about online hosts can be found on the web site of the Association of Learned and Professional Society Publishers, and the International Network for the Availability of Scientific Publications:

- African Journals OnLine (AJOL) is an initiative originally established by INASP, and now managed within South Africa, to host African-published journals. The web site contains abstracts only for most journals, but in addition it has been developed to host full-text journals where required. Currently there is no provision for charging for access but this is likely to be offered in future for journals which require it.
- Bioline is an initiative set up by the Electronic Publishing Trust to host online versions of journals from developing countries around the world. They will convert print journals into electronic format; however, Bioline also supports training to help publishers prepare their own e-files. Bioline

only supports journals that are willing to publish under the Open Access model.

- CLACSO provides support for a digital library of social science journals from member institutions within Latin America. Its digital library site hosts the full text of journals and other publications from the member organisations; the site currently operates under the Open Access model.
- Hrcak is a project of the National and University Library in Zagreb, Croatia, to host Croatian journals online.
- Sabinet is a South African company which hosts and sells African-published journals as a single package–access is thus restricted to subscribers, but this model does provide some revenue to the journals.
- SciElo is another Latin American initiative which hosts full-text, Open Access journals within the biomedical and applied sciences. This platform only accepts journals which are judged to be of high enough quality—so it provides both support for publishers and also quality assurance for users.

MULTIPLE HOSTING

You can–of course–host your journal on multiple web sites, using different hosting services. Although full-text hosting on more than one web site is unusual and probably unnecessary, a common model is for your own web site to host a homepage for the journal, with detailed information about the journal, the editorial board, guides for authors, etc., but to use a commercial host for the full text content. You may, however, wish to consider also including your content in the collection of one aggregators as well.

CHOOSING AN ONLINE HOST

Choosing an online host is an important decision for all journals, and although it is quite possible to change hosts, the decision of which to go with should not be undertaken lightly. There are many considerations to be taken into account, which are described more fully in a recent publishing Guide Sheet from ALPSP but the first two questions to be asked are:

- What technology and resources do you have within your organisation, and what do you need to buy in from external companies/suppliers.
- How much can you afford to pay for online hosting.

WHAT CHANGES DO YOU HAVE TO MAKE TO YOUR PROCEDURES

Whether you decide to do it all yourself or not, electronic publication will require you to change the way you do things. It is important not to overlook this aspect. You may need to re-examine all your processes—from receipt of submitted manuscripts to final publication—in order to make sure they are as streamlined, and in as logical an order, as possible. In fact, this exercise is often highly beneficial in improving both cost and time-efficiency!

EDITORIAL

The peer review, revision, and editing of articles, as already pointed out, does not become any less important if they are to be published electronically. In addition, editors may need to add electronic links within the article, within the journal, to other publications and to additional material. The majority of authors may be able to submit their articles in electronic form, and should be encouraged to do so, as this will facilitate the editorial processes. Electronic editorial processing software is available to manage the entire editorial process from online author submission to article acceptance. These software packages can help to streamline the editorial process, but are not essential to online publishing.

They have several advantages:

- There are no postal delays for authors submitting articles, or for the editorial office, editors and reviewers during the editorial processes, since, everything is managed and held online.
- The systems automate much of the correspondence, which can assist the editorial office.
- Most systems maintain and generate records of article progress, which may be accessible to authors as well as the editorial office. In addition, systems generally provide for a database of reviewers; this assists the editorial team in choosing the most appropriate reviewers for each manuscript.
- Since, the packages operate online, the editors, reviewers, and authors can all access the database and upload or download articles from any Internet connection worldwide, thus facilitating work when they are not in the office.

However these systems also have some disadvantages:

- They require everyone involved in the journal to have online access.
- They only save the time spent in postal delays—they do not reduce the time required to review, correct or finalise the articles.
- They require the authors, reviewers and—especially—the editorial team to be competent in using online systems, since, they are not always very user-friendly.
- They require reviewers and the editorial team to have adequate computer equipment, and either to work entirely online, or to be able to print out articles locally for reviewing, etc.
- Unless the majority of authors, reviewers and editors do make use of the software, such systems can actually increase the workload of the editorial office, who will need to load articles online themselves.

- And of course, most of them also cost money—usually in the form of a software licence fee.

Copyright

It is essential that, when acquiring copyright or the right to publish from your journal contributors—which you should always do—you make sure that you have also secured the electronic rights. It is also important to double-check that you or the author have obtained electronic rights for any other material you wish to include, such as illustrations or quotations from other publications. Examples of appropriate agreements have been produced by ALPSP and INASP.

PRODUCTION

Your methods of production are unlikely to be entirely suitable for publishing in the online environment, and this area of your activities is the one to be most affected by the introduction of online publication. It is sensible to get the articles into electronic form as early as possible; all the subsequent processing should then be done on the electronic version, and both print and electronic version should be output from the same file at the very end of the process. It is highly inefficient to work on a paper version, and then convert it to electronic at the very end.

The first change is that the final articles will need to be in suitable format for online as well as print publication. The most efficient approach is to process all articles in a 'neutral' format from which both print and electronic outputs can be produced. PDF files are adequate for straightforward journals, and of course this does preserve the appearance of the printed page; some systems may require the header information in other formats to enable searching and indexing. For more sophisticated electronic publication, PDF files are not sufficient—HTML or XML will be needed.

To produce appropriate files, you will need either to train staff and purchase appropriate software and computer equipment, or to identify and recruit suitable external suppliers to undertake this work; if it is done in-house, you will need to adapt the existing journal production system to ensure that the correct files are produced. If you decide to introduce additional functionality within the online version, you will also need to introduce production systems to implement this. Illustrations may cause problems if authors cannot supply them electronically, since,—at some point–they need to be converted into digital files for electronic publication. If the authors cannot supply e-files for all artwork, either you or the printer/typesetter/designer need to be able to scan the artwork so that the appropriate e-files can be created for online publication.

The electronic files must be carefully checked for accuracy, as it is surprisingly easy for errors to creep in when they are converted. You will need to devise—and stick rigourously to–a system for naming the electronic files for each article, and for every table or illustration associated with that article;

it is sensible to include a version numbering/dating system so that you do not use an earlier version by mistake. When deciding to publish online you need to consider carefully whether your existing staff have the necessary level of skills to undertake the work required, and whether you have the hardware and software needed. To produce the files required you may need to outsource the work that was previously done by departmental/journal staff, or you may need to change your existing suppliers if they do not have the skills, experience and equipment to provide what you need. Alternatively, the online host may undertake some or all of the file conversion work. If you decide to have different content in the print and online versions you need to ensure that the production set-up takes this into account, and that you are able to manage the administration of different versions.

MARKETING AND PROMOTION

Marketing, in the true sense of discovering what your market wants and then providing it, is every bit as necessary for electronic journals as it is for print journals. Many journals are not sufficiently visible—*i.e.*, not enough people know about them, or are able to discover them—and although publishing online may help, it is vital that some promotional activity is undertaken if online publication is to achieve the goal of making the journal more visible, and thus more used. For any journal—in print or online—conducting market research to identify what readers and authors want is essential.

In addition to talking to as many potential authors and readers and possible, try to carry out systematic surveys by questionnaire. If you see electronic publication as being a way to make your journal more international, your market research should be international too. This may cost money, but not as much as you could lose if your journal fails. An electronic journal will not sell itself, any more than a print journal. You will need to make sure that those who should be interested in reading it, and writing for it, are aware of its existence. This is not simply a matter of mailing a leaflet.

If you can obtain suitable lists of e-mail addresses, this is much cheaper than a postal mailing; be careful, however, about sending 'promotional' messages to e-mail discussion lists, as this is considered unprofessional, and may generate a strong negative reaction, although straightforward information about journals is welcomed on many lists. You should always check the 'rules' for posting to a listserv with the listserv manager.

In addition, you could involve the editorial team in promoting the journal by, for example:

- Referring to the journal within their e-mail signature;
- Handing out leaflets at relevant meetings, and
- Ensuring that their institutional library is not only aware of the existence of the journal, but also makes it visible to users.

Online publication relies on readers coming to the web site, rather than sending the print journal to their library or their desks. Bringing people back to a web site is particularly important if the journal is published infrequently or irregularly. E-mail alerts are a good way to tell people about the latest issue when it becomes available online, and can be set up manually or you could offer the facility to sign up to an automated alert on the journal's web site.

Linking to and from abstracting and indexing databases, and citation linking using DOI and CrossRef are also important ways to bring readers to your content. To ensure visibility to researchers and librarians you must make sure your journal is covered by the major Internet search engines. Another very important way of ensuring visibility to your community is to make sure your journal is included in secondary databases. The major services used to be resistant to including electronic-only journals, but this is no longer the case.

The one often considered most influential is ISI although their acceptance procedures are quite stringent and the number of journals they include is restricted. However, you cannot include your journal in too many such databases; identify as many as you can which are relevant to the subject matter. You may be asked to provide a free subscription, but this is a very small price to pay. If you can supply 'headers'—bibliographic details and, ideally, abstracts—in electronic form, so much the better; unfortunately, however, there is as yet no standardisation about the format in which they require them.

You should also make sure that your journal is listed in Ulrich's International Periodicals Directory, which is the major reference source for librarians. Some abstracting and indexing databases—such as Medline—require the journal's header information in XML format. If you are unable to obtain these files from your supplier, INASP have a template available for use which simplifies generation of these XML documents. Once a journal is made available online, the process of gathering feedback from readers and authors can be much easier than for a printed title, as the Internet facilitates two-way communications. Online feedback forms, direct links to e-mail addresses, and discussion forums all permit much more effective exchange of information.

SALES

Printed journals need little or nothing in the way of salesmen. Libraries decide which journals they want, and then choose their preferred channel for buying them. However, site licensing of electronic journals does require detailed discussion and negotiation with each customer; this is time-consuming, and if you decide to do it yourself you are likely to need extra staff with the appropriate skills. The alternative is to have someone else, such as a subscription agent, do it for you—but you need to be willing for someone else to negotiate prices on your behalf. Bear in mind that the price for a single library may represent several subscriptions; if libraries join together to form consortia, this is even more likely to be the case. Selling to library consortia is a particularly difficult and time-consuming process, and the publisher with only a small number of journals can easily get squeezed out. Initiatives are, however, being developed to help smaller publishers work together to sell a single, larger collection of journals in these circumstances. It may be beneficial to try to work with other publishers, whether internationally or in your own country or region, to overcome these problems. In some countries, the tax situation will be made more complicated if you are selling electronic journals; they may attract tax where printed journals do not. You will need expert local advice on this.

SUBSCRIPTIONS ADMINISTRATION/CUSTOMER SERVICE

If you decide to restrict access in any way you will need to administer this process, providing passwords or other access controls to new users, disabling those which have come to an end, and ensuring that your system can identify authorised users when they try to access the system. All of this will entail even more complicated administration than is required for a printed journal, and will require considerable technical expertise. Customers do not need any help to use print journals; however, the situation is different with electronic journals. Some customers will forget their passwords and you will need to reissue them.

Others will be unable to get access even though apparently using the correct password. Even if you make your journal available free of charge, you will find that some of your customers have technical problems in accessing or using it.

Thus you will need to provide some kind of helpline for customer support, whether on the telephone, on e-mail or both; customers will become very frustrated if help is not available at the exact moment when they need it, so the helpline should ideally be manned full-time during working hours, even if not for 24 hours a day. Of course, if you decide to use an intermediary to provide access to your electronic journal, all of these problems will be taken care of, although naturally at a cost.

WHAT MIGHT IT COST

It is impossible to put precise figures on the cost of publishing a journal electronically; however, it is vitally important to work out your own probable costs in full detail, and not to underestimate either the time or the money that will be required. A summary of the cost differences between print-only, online-only and online-plus-print is given in the table. However, indirect costs should never be ignored!

Item	Print Only	Online Only	Online Plus Print
Editorial costs	Yes	Yes (no change)	Yes (no change)
Copy-preparation	Yes	Yes–plus	Yes–plus

costs (*e.g.*, copyediting, typesetting, design and proofing)		additional costs for e-file preparation	additional costs for e-file preparation
Printing and binding	Yes	No	Yes
Distribution	Yes	No	Yes
Marketing and promotion	Yes	Yes	Yes
Sales	Minimal	Yes–sales and negotiation of licences	Yes–sales and negotiation of licences
Customer support	Minimal	Yes	Yes
Long-term archiving and maintenance costs	Yes (warehousing and some file archiving)	Yes (e-file and online maintenance)	Yes (including print and e-file archiving)
Financial management of subscription/licence payments subscriptions are	Yes (if charge for subscription)	Yes (if still have subscribers to online content) costs if online	Yes (if still charge subscription for print– possible additional sold separately)
Financial management charges	Yes (if charge author fees)	Yes (if charge author fees)	Yes (if charge author fees) of author

TIME

Someone will need to be responsible for thinking through all the questions raised in this document, and making the necessary decisions. This is not a one-time process; your electronic journal will need to be continuously monitored and managed to an even greater extent than a print journal. There will be additional complications to your production processes and new skills and procedures to be learned. If you do it yourself, your subscriptions administration and customer support will also be more labour intensive.

MONEY/PEOPLE

While, taking the 'electronic only' route will save costs on paper, printing, warehousing and despatch, these savings can very easily be offset by new costs.

The areas in which you will incur costs are as follows:

- *Hosting:* Whether you undertake to build and host your own journal web site, or to pay an external provider, you will have start-up and then ongoing costs.
- *Equipment:* You may need to purchase new equip-ment to manage the electronic processes.

- *Online Costs:* You may need to increase your access to the Internet.
- *Staff and Training:* You may need to devote some funds to building skills within existing journal staff, and perhaps to also recruit additional staff.
- *Production Costs:* If you reduce or eliminate print you may make savings on costs such as postage, printing, warehousing and distribution. Further postage savings may be made in the editorial office if you introduce an electronic submission and peer review system. However, you may incur additional costs if you need to outsource more work or to pay for additional services from your existing providers.

It is impossible to give definite guideline costs, as there are so many variables—the number of articles received and published, the number of subscribers, the number of other journals handled by the same system, not to mention local variations in equipment, service and labour costs.

Depending on the accounting principles followed by your organisation in dealing with overheads, your journal's finances may appear to benefit from a reduction in direct third-party costs; some organisations may not allocate a share of internal overhead costs to the journal.

However, it is misleading to ignore these overhead costs altogether in arriving at a realistic appraisal of the journal's financial health. Of course, if you decide to charge for access, some of the additional costs could be offset by increased revenues; however, you need to be realistic in your expectations.

SELL IT YOURSELF, AND/OR GO THROUGH INTERMEDIARIES

Making the journal available electronically is only half the story. If you rely on subscription revenue, you then need to sell the journal, which includes not only making the sale, but also arranging electronic access and managing whatever access control mechanisms you have selected. In addition, you would be wise to consider the licences which you want your customers to have; unlike print journals, electronic journals provide users with a wide range of possible uses, some of which you may not want to allow.

It is possible to have one or more intermediaries handle online sales for you; many subscription agents are now offering this service, for a fee, for electronic journals. This can make very good sense, as most libraries already deal with sub-scription agents for their printed journals. Furthermore, most subscription agents' systems offer the user the ability to obtain access to all their electronic journals through a single access mechanism; this is obviously preferable for the user, as the alternative is having to use different web sites, with different passwords, for each journal.

It is obviously easiest if the agent is also acting as host for your journal; if they are not hosting your journal, you will need to provide them with basic 'header' information for each issue in electronic form so that their users can search these on the subscription agent's site, and from there gain access your journal web site. Taking this route will increase your overall costs, since, you will need to pay the intermediary, but it is very likely also to increase the accessibility, and thus the use, of your journals.

DIFFERENT SUBSCRIPTION SALES MODELS

Singly or 'Bundled'

If you are fortunate enough to publish a number of journals, there may be benefits in selling them as a single package. The evidence shows that usage of titles to which customers did not previously subscribe can be unexpectedly high. If you also publish books or other content related to the journal's subject, an even richer package could be created; you could also include links to material on other sites. Another possibility would be to collaborate with one or more other publishers to create a larger package.

Electronic Version Free to Print Subscribers

You may want to do this either permanently, or for an initial period as a form of promotion. It will require an access control system, and you will need to assign a password or other form of identification to every subscriber. Be careful not to increase the print subscription price too steeply, or subscribers will feel—with some justification—that they are being asked to cover the cost of the electronic version, whether they want it or not; this could lose you print subscribers.

Electronic Version Sales

You may decide to set a separate subscription price for the electronic journal. If there is a parallel print version, it is sensible to consider the relationship of this price to the print subscription. Should it be the same? Or more? Or less? You might want to offer a discount for combined print-plus-electronic subscriptions.

Electronic Version Sold to Print Subscribers for an Extra Charge

A number of publishers are making an additional charge to include the electronic subscription; the supplements range enormously, from 10 per cent to 50 per cent or more. An alternative is to consider the print subscription to be the 'add-on', charging a substantially reduced rate to those who subscribe to the electronic version only.

Individual Subscriptions

The majority of print journal subscription income usually comes from libraries and institutions, but many publishers also sell at a lower price to individuals. You might want to consider offering individual subscriptions to your electronic journals, on one or more of the models. It is indeed arguable that the real benefits of electronic journals are more attractive to the individual reader than they are to the library.

However, you should also bear in mind that if you offer library subscriptions, particularly on the basis of site licences, individuals may already have good access to the electronic journal through their place of work. On the other hand, low-priced individual subscriptions may be the most practical way of permitting users to access the journal when they are not at their place of work. If you offer more than one kind of electronic subscription, and if the privileges or permitted uses differ, remember that your system will need to be able to distinguish the different kinds of subscriber at the point when they access the system.

Member Subscriptions

For those societies and associations which get much of their income from membership subscriptions, and who provide members with their journal free or at a very low cost, electronic journals can present something of a problem. If members see access to their own personal copy of the journal as one of the main benefits of membership, but have access at their own desk through a library subscription at their place of work, there is a risk that they will be inclined to discontinue their membership. Society and association publishers will need to think carefully about this, perhaps offering additional electronic benefits or services only to members.

Annual Subscription or Any-time Start

It is possible to sell a subscription based on either an annual basis or any-time start. With an annual basis, regardless of when the subscriber pays, they will be provided with the journal issues published within the calendar year; this is generally preferred by libraries as it is easiest for them to manage. With an any-time start, customers will receive 12 months' subscription starting from the date of payment. This may be attractive for users, but may also cause complications and additional work for the person who has to manage the subscribers. You may also find it more difficult to work out how much journal revenue to allocate if your organisation's financial year does not coincide with the subscription year.

Site Licences

Universities, companies and other institutional journal subscribers are always very interested in obtaining site-wide access to electronic materials. Access which is only possible from one or more specified computer terminals in the library is very much less attractive than being able to provide it to each faculty or departmental library and office. It is therefore a good idea to work out a licensing policy, and an access system, which permits this. Defining the 'site' may be quite difficult, particularly for a multi-site organisation such as a large company.

Pricing is a particular problem, since, organisations vary greatly in size and in the potential or actual number of users. If you simply have a price based on the print subscription price, then large and small organisations will pay exactly the same, while at the same time none of them will need multiple subscriptions—so you may end up losing revenue. Some method of pricing based on number of users might be more equitable, although it will be more complicated to work out the appropriate price for any given customer.

Although pricing for a set number of 'simultaneous users' has worked well for computer software and databases, it has not proved a popular model for e-journals. Different publishers have looked at the funding of the institution, the total number of faculty and students, or just the numbers in the most relevant department. In most cases, publishers have found it simplest to establish a relatively small number of 'price bands' based on these measures.

Consortium Licences

It is becoming increasingly common for institutions, particularly universities, to band together in order to make better use of their limited budgets, and to share the availability of the materials to which they subscribe. This can be a very effective way of getting your journal content to a much larger community, while still only necessitating a single negotiation. Combined institutions, however, make very powerful negotiators and you need to be careful to make the right pricing decisions and not to allow yourself unintentionally to do business at a loss. It is also difficult for a publisher with only one or a small number of journals to sell to large customers and consortia—and equally difficult for the customer.

The process is no less time-consuming for one journal than for a hundred, and it requires specialist skills and knowledge. Some organisations are trying to act on behalf of many small publishers to overcome this problem. For example the Association of Learned and Professional Society Publishers, in partnership with subscription agent Swets, has established the ALPSP Learned Journals Collection which acts on behalf its smaller member publishers to sell their journals to libraries and consortia throughout the world—it does not, however, offer hosting for online journals. Similarly Project Muse in America, and SABINET in South Africa offer publishers a service both to host their journals and to sell them to libraries.

SINGLE ARTICLE SALES

It is often argued that, since, a reader will only be inter-ested in some articles, it would be better if he or she could buy those articles separately. While the costs of administering such a system might be prohibitive in the print environment, it is in principle much easier electronically, although the publisher does need a suitable journal system which can provide access to individual articles and collect payment, whether by invoice or by credit card.

One of the problems of this system is that individual readers are often unwilling to pay for articles that they think the library should obtain on their behalf. Publishers have feared that single article sales could reduce the demand for subscriptions, but in fact studies so far do not bear this out—if anything, this seems to tap an additional source of revenue sold in excess of 2000 articles to non-subscribers during 2005, and a survey by ALPSP in 2005 showed approximately 25 per cent of the publishers that offered this service found it was becoming a significant source of revenue). Most commercial hosts and numerous other intermediaries and specialist document suppliers are set up to manage such transactions; the reader needs to be able to pay by credit card online, and the intermediary will retain an amount of the payment to cover its costs.

OPEN ACCESS

The traditional publishing model restricts access to the publication by requiring payment by or on behalf of the reader. However, some argue that in the online environment scholarly information should be free to the reader. It is also possible that Open Access journals will achieve higher visibility and use, since, anyone can read the journal content.

Open Access publishing does remove the cost and complexity of access controls, although it may introduce the requirement for a system to handle author-side payments, and, of course, as with any other electronic publishing model, if the publisher wishes to maintain some form of print version then the costs associated with print will be retained. In general, Open Access simply means 'free access to online research information'. However, there are a number of formal statements which associate various other conditions with this basic idea. It is important to stress that Open Access does not require any specific commercial model—the key point is that the user does not pay to view the material.

There are also various models of Open Access that are designed to minimise any impact on subscription revenue:

- *Delayed Open Access:* Offering free access after a specified period. The length of time after publication which is necessary to avoid loss of subscriptions is likely to vary depending both on the subject area and the frequency of publication of the journal.
- *Short-term Open Access:* Providing free access to articles for a short period after publication, after which they are only available to subscribers. The argument for this is that this provides immediate impact and raises citation of the articles and visibility, but does not affect subscription revenue, as people are still willing to pay for ongoing access. This may not give sufficient protection, however, for all journals.

- *Selected Open Access:* Some journals make selected articles freely available whilst the rest remain behind an access control system.
- *Hybrid Open Access:* Increasing number of journals are experimenting with Hybrid Open Access. This means that the author can choose to pay the publication charge to make his or her article Open Access immediately on publication. Articles by authors who choose not to pay remain behind the access barrier. Depending on the proportion of articles paid for, the publisher can gradually reduce the subscription/licence price for the remaining content. This model enables a publisher to test the author demand for OA without putting existing subscriptions/licence income at risk; many publishers are currently experimenting along these lines.
- *Partial Open Access:* It is possible to make the journal's primary research content available under an Open Access model, but to make a charge for other value-added content such as editorials and review articles, and/or for additional services. For example, several of BioMedCentral's journals charge subscriptions to cover non-primary material—so does the British Medical Journal.

It is important to remember that the Open Access model only works for online publications. Many Open Access journals still sell a print version on subscription; in addition to covering the costs of printing and distribution, this may also help to defray the journal's other costs.

WHO PAYS FOR OPEN ACCESS

If the user does not pay, any money required to produce the journal needs to come from somewhere else.

Common sources for OA journals include:

- *Funders:* Many journals in developing countries already rely on funders, whose aims may be best satisfied by making the content freely available.
- *Organisations:* Many parent organisations already support their journals 'in kind' by not recharging the cost of accommodation, support services, staff, equipment, etc. Some also provide direct financial support by paying for third-party costs.
- *Government Funding:* Some countries provide support for journals out of government funds, and govern-ments may prefer the funding to be used to ensure greatest access to their content.
- *Author-side Payments:* Some subscription journals, particularly in the USA, already charge authors, although this is becoming less common; some journals in Western Africa, particularly in Nigeria, also charge authors. A number of Western OA journals rely on author-side charges: the authors pay a publication charge on acceptance. A recent

study shows that this is in fact a less common funding model for OA journals than it is for subscription journals.

These fees are unlikely to come from the author's own pocket. More likely sources are:

- *Research Funds:* Some research grants already include publication fees, and this may become more common in future.
- *Libraries:* Some publishers encourage institutions to make a single annual payment, in return for which they waive or reduce publication charges for authors based at that institution.

SELF-ARCHIVING

Another way of achieving widespread free access to journal content is for the author to post a freely accessible version of his or her article online. This may be a pre-print or a post-print. It may be deposited on the author's or his or her institution's home page, or in a subject-based or institutional repository. In the last decade the number of online repositories of articles—both subject-based and institution-based—has grown.

Subject-based Repositories

These are most common in disciplines where researchers are accustomed to distributing their work to each other informally before publication, or see a need to make their research available quickly. The longest-established is arXiv, which was established in 1991 and covers some disciplines of physics and related subjects. Initially, publishers in other disciplines often refused to consider for publication articles which had already been posted in such repositories; however, these days most publishers accept this.

Institutional Repositories

A relatively recent development has been the introduction of institutional repositories. These are similar to the subject-based repositories, but are being developed to preserve the intellectual output of an institution, which often includes theses, working papers., lecture notes and teaching materials. The number of institutional repositories is growing, but the majority contain little content so far and even less in the way of journal articles. The cost to the institution of establishing, maintaining and archiving the repository also has to be taken into account.

Support for Repositories

Some research funders, such as the National Institutes of Health (USA), the Wellcome Trust (UK) and the Research Councils UK, are introducing new rules for the researchers whom they fund, requesting or requiring them to deposit copies of their published articles within subject or institutional repositories either on or at a specified time after publication. In the absence of a specific mandate, few authors have so far complied—it remains to be seen whether making this compulsory will have the desired effect.

Impact on Journals

It is sometimes argued that pre-prints are not a threat to publishers, since, the publisher has added value to the published version. The threat to the business of the journal is even more obvious when the final published articles are posted in repositories; this enables readers to bypass the journal entirely. It seems possible that, if all or most of a journal's content became freely available in this way, subscriptions to that journal might be adversely affected.

If that happens, what will happen to the peer review and quality filtering mechanism currently provided by journals? However, at present many publishers' policies do allow authors to deposit a version in such repositories; there is, though, growing concern about the dangers of this and some publishers are changing their policies, for example to specify a period of time from publication before which the author may not deposit his or her article. Ideally, a research funder's policy should respect these embargoes. publishers only institute them in order to ensure the continuing survival of their journals.

LICENSING CONSIDERATIONS

When you sell a printed journal, it is fairly clear and well understood what your customers are and are not permitted to do with the material. However, in the electronic environ-ment there is much less agreement about what is allowed; abuse is also far more risky for the publisher, since, it is far easier to make a perfect copy of an original item in the electronic environment and distribute it widely. It is therefore sensible to draw up a statement of what customers may and may not do, which they will be asked to accept formally. This should be done whether access is paid for or not. There are different ways of bringing the licence to the attention of the user.

The individual user may be presented with a short summary on screen of what is permitted and forbidden, and you might even want to configure your system so that they have to click on a button marked 'I agree' before they go any further. When a sale is made to an institution, the customer might be asked to sign a more detailed printed licence as part of the sale. The latter approach does allow for a certain amount of negotiation if necessary, although obviously you would wish to design your licence so that it was acceptable to most of your customers without involving both them and you in the time and cost of individual negotiation.

Some of your terms and conditions of use would depend on whether or not the electronic version is free or not, but others would be applicable in any case. You would undoub-tedly want to permit users to search, retrieve, and print articles from the journal; you might or might not also allow them to save individual articles electronically on their own computers. You should think about the best policy on allowing users to re-send articles, particularly electronically, to other people outside the subscribing institution—a number of publishers do allow this on a small-scale, personal basis.

It is unlikely that you would want users to sell articles or redistribute them systematically on a large scale, or to mount all or possibly any of the content on other web sites. While you will probably want a signature or other indication of acceptance of the terms and conditions when a sale is made to an institution or consortium, it is not always easy to enforce these. Within the academic and scientific communities, a culture of trust and honesty generally prevails and evidence of misuse is infrequent.

Some very useful work has been done to produce 'model' licences, or licensing frameworks, which will help you to devise a suitable licence for your own journals. All have been produced in discussion between publishers and customers, and thus try to address the concerns of both. While you may not wish to use any of them as they stand, without considering carefully the implications of the various alternatives they present, they may save you a great deal of time in working out appropriate wording, and they will also help you to make sure that you don't leave anything out of your licence.

One such example was devised in the UK by a group of university librarians and publishers. The LibLicense site also provides much useful information about licensing and licences. Some publishers have stopped requiring their customers to sign a licence at all—instead, they have a clear statement on the journal site of what is and is not permitted. So far, no problems have been reported with this approach, and of course it saves everyone a great deal of time and expense.

CREATIVE COMMONS

The Creative Commons provides a simple guide to drawing up licences for the Open Access environment. These licences grant the user wide-ranging rights to re-use the content, whilst still protecting the copyright in that content. The copyright owner can select the most appropriate version of the licence. For example, all INASP materials are published under one of the range of Creative Commons licences, which allows re-use for non-commercial purposes, but requires that the re-user must always credit the author.

ELECTRONIC JOURNALS METHODOLOGY

For this research, the authors used Ithink modelling software. Ithink uses a mapping language designed to facilitate visualisation of the 'interrelationships which constitute a process, a strategy or an issue'. The key elements in an Ithink model are described below.

It is thaught to represent graphically the interrelationships that characterise each system modelled. The elements in the models then had numbers or ranges of numbers added and simulations were run. The models were deliberately made simple and aim to capture the essential features of the systems modelled.

They are intended as generic rather than specific examples. Many of the model elements are defined by equations which describe the relationship of that element with one or other elements in the same model. The relationships represented by the equations are generally informed by the literature. However, some assumptions are inherent in these relationships. The bases of the equations and the assumptions in each model are described in 'documents'. These documents may be viewed by double-clicking the element and selecting from the dialogue box a button labelled 'document*'.

The asterisk indicates that a document exists. Some elements are self-explanatory and so are not documented within the model. As these assumptions inform the results of the 'what if' scenarios and sensitivity analyses, they are most appropriately presented alongside those results.

Thus, the assumptions are documented in the Results and Discussion section of this report. Copies of the models described here are available from the authors and can be examined by using the free runtime version of the Ithink software package. This is available at the following URL: http://www.cognitus.co.uk/IS/IS.htm.

The runtime version of the software can be used to view and manipulate our models, but any changes that the user 64 makes cannot be saved. A brief guide for users of this modelling software is appended to this report.

The models were designed to facilitate greater understanding of the economic factors and the economic relationships between different stakeholders in each of the processes modelled. Model variables can be manipulated using so-called 'sliders', and the effects can then be monitored.

For example, in a model of electronic journal production and delivery any of the following elements could be varied using sliders: the number of subscriptions; the number of manuscripts submitted; the overhead rate applied to staff costs; the journal acceptance/rejection rate; or the profit margin applied by the publisher.

Holding all other variables equal, a user might, for example, vary the number of subscriptions and observe the effect on subscription price or individual article price. Similarly, in the model of an ER system, the user could vary the number and size of classes to establish how this would affect, for example, total cost, the institution fee, and the fee per student.

MODEL ELEMENTS

Stock

A stock represents an accumulation. For example, in the model of an electronic reserve system the repository of digitised materials is represented by a stock. The items accumulate by flowing into and/or out of the stock. The total content amounts to the inflow minus the outflow at each time period in a model simulation. In many of the stocks represented in the models described here the inflow and outflow are equal.

For example, a journal editor receives a number of manuscripts Stock 65 every year. Of those, she rejects a very small percentage and the remainder are sent for peer review. However, the repository in the ER system has no outflow as items must be stored for possible future use. Thus, its content increases annually.

Flow

A flow is like a pipe. It either fills or drains a stock in the direction of the flow arrow. A cloud at either end of a flow indicates an infinite source or destination of the 'stuff' flowing to or from a stock.

If the flow source were a stock and that stock were empty, the value of the flow equation would not flow into the destination stock. Thus, a cloud is a device which indicates that the source of 'stuff' passing through the flow is beyond the scope of the model.

For example, where the flow 'journal acquisitions receipts' flowing into the stock 'journal acquisitions budget' originates with a cloud, this means that the entire library or institutional budget is not represented. It is assumed that the library or institution provides funding to acquire journals.

Converter

A converter informs other elements in the model. It may contain a constant value, for example, VAT which is 17.5%, or a variable value which may be manipulated by the model user by means of a slider.

Alternatively, it may represent an algebraic relationship between other elements in the model or it may represent an external input such as the rate at which items selected for digitisation in the ER model are duplicates of items already held in the repository. The latter may be a ramp, i.e. the initial value is X% and it rises annually by Y%.

A converter may also be the repository for a graphical function which sketches the relationship between an input and an output. For example, the output may be the price of a subscription and the input the number of items in a database. A graphical functions can also be used to sketch non-linear relationships.

EVALUATION OF ITHINK MODELLING SOFTWARE

Ithink was an effective tool for the research described here. It allowed the authors to map the interrelationships in a system before numbers were introduced.

The documentation supplied with the software is clear and comprehensive. Two versions of the software are available: Ithink Strategy and Ithink Analyst. The latter includes additional modelling features. These features were not required to build the models described in this report. Ithink software is available for educational use at half of the full price.

The educational RDN budget Emplmnt cos ts No employees RDN staff rate for Ithink Strategy is available for $299 and Ithink Analyst for £479. The price includes documentation. There were a few drawbacks. Among them were the fact that the software prohibits circular relationships. For example, in the model of a non-commercial journal, we wished to define the overhead applied when calculating total publication costs as a percentage of sales income.

However, as total publication cost is one factor determining price and price is one factor determining sales income, this relationship would have been circular and was prohibited. Another drawback for this project is the difficulty of printing the models. The software is designed as a learning tool. To be most effective models should be manipulated by users. Thus, prints of the models are considered to be of limited value. Nevertheless, the output of this research project had to be documented and published. Although the authors expect interested parties to request copies of the models, they also believe that illustrations would contribute to understanding of written reports and papers.

Unfortunately, several of the models would be illegible on anything smaller than an A2 sheet of paper. It is for this reason that we recommend that interested readers should download the runtime version of Ithink software and request copies of our models. Requests for discs with the models should be addressed to either of the authors of this report (l.l.halliday@lboro.ac.uk or c.oppenheim@lboro.ac.uk).

The authors built six Ithink models based on economic models of different aspects of the digital library. These include four economic models of electronic journal production and delivery. Development of electronic journals is more advanced than most other areas of the digital library. The selection of models evaluated here reflects this.

The other two models evaluated are a resource discovery network and a National Electronic Reserve Service (NERS). The former is based on a recent eLib supporting study of subject-based gateways and is informed by the JISC call for proposals to develop a Resource Discovery Network Centre (JISC circular 10/98). The latter model is based on the eLib-funded national electronic resource service, HERON and is informed by relevant eLib publications and by publications of other stakeholders such as the CLA and the PLS.

ELECTRONIC JOURNALS MODELS

There are four Ithink models of electronic journal production and delivery. The first is a model of a non-commercial electronic journal with traditional economic characteristics. In this model, costs are recovered from sales of subscriptions and individual articles.

A "Traditional model" is presented first to facilitate easy comparison with journal production and delivery in a print environment. The second model is based on the economic model proposed by Harnad and Hemus and is hereinafter described as the "Harnad model". The third is a 'market' model based on Fishwick *et al.*'s eLib supporting study on the economic implications of different models of publishing scholarly electronic journals and is hereinafter referred to as the "Fishwick model".

The fourth model is an alternative model, proposed by the authors, which is informed by the other three models. The Traditional model is presented first and assumptions informing different elements in the model are explained.

The Harnad model, the Fishwick model, and the authors' alternative model are then described. Where elements and assumptions in these models differ from those in the Traditional model these are documented.

The values of several elements in each of these models were varied and the models run to monitor the effects. The costs and benefits for different stakeholders of manipulating model elements was established and model sensitivities were identified. The results are described.

Non-commercial Electronic Journal with Traditional Economic Characteristics

The characteristics of this model are very similar to those of the scholarly print information delivery chain. Editors and referees are unpaid other than a contribution from the publisher towards editorial office costs.

A traditional pricing mechanism is applied, i.e. costs are recovered through sales of subscriptions and of individual articles. The model differs from the print system in that the entire editorial process is conducted electronically and the product is delivered in electronic form to libraries.

Libraries are free to obtain subscriptions/individual articles directly from publishers or to obtain them from an information broker. It is assumed, if a library chooses the former, that terms will be negotiated between the library and the publisher. The model consists of four interconnected sectors: content origination, publication, information brokerage, and the library function.

Content Origination

In this sector, manuscripts are first submitted to the editorial office for review. The number of incoming manuscripts is specified so that the number of papers published was limited to a realistic level. The model simulates production of a single journal. We assumed that the journal publishes approximately 120 papers per annum.

Theoretically, an electronic journal need not be constrained by a predetermined limit on the number of papers that it can publish annually because distribution and storage costs are low. However, other resources required for production are related to journal size and these are likely to restricts growth in the short to medium term.

For the purpose of the modelling exercise, the authors assumed that the number of papers published per annum in an electronic journal is similar to the number published in a print journal. The rate at which manuscripts are submitted to any journal fluctuates. However, if an excess of manuscripts is accepted and, in turn, the publication delay is unacceptable, it is reasonable to assume that potential authors will be discouraged from submitting to that journal.

The editors also would regulate the number of papers accepted by increasing the rejection rate to maintain an acceptable publication delay. In the model, the number of papers submitted was specified with reference to the rejection rate to ensure that 120 papers were produced per annum. Most manuscripts submitted for publication are refereed but a small percentage is rejected immediately usually because the subject matter is unsuitable for publication in that journal.

The immediate rejection rate wan this model is 2% and is based on an established print peer reviewed journal. The total rejection rate in the model is varied to monitor the effect. Rejection rates vary between journals, and vary significantly between disciplines (i.e. in the humanities 90% is not uncommon whilst in the pure sciences 10% is common). It is assumed that the editor spends a total of 30 minutes per paper.

This represents time spent scanning the manuscript content, deciding whether or not to have the paper refereed, selecting referees, and considering revisions and whether or not to return the paper to the referees. We assumed that all but 2% of manuscripts are refereed, each of them by two peers. The average paper is revised once.

It was assumed that each referee spends two hours reviewing the manuscript in the first instance and that revision takes one hour. Thus, each referee spends three hours per paper and therefore, each paper takes six referee hours to process. It was assumed that one hour of an average editor or referee costs £50 including full employment costs and overhead.

This is a conservative estimate which does not vary with overhead rate. The total cost to HE is calculated as the cost of editorial and refereeing work minus the contribution from the publisher towards the costs of the editorial office. This cost to HE is an opportunity cost as it is not accounted for in the financial transactions between different stakeholders.

It was assumed that the publisher contributes £160 per accepted manuscript towards the costs of the editorial office. This assumption is based on figures given. The model includes no clerical administration cost, as most of the clerical administrative tasks are automated and journal production staff undertake what remains. Thus, the editorial and production functions are interlinked. This organisational model is based on that of the *Conservation Ecology* Project.

Publication

Production costs in the model vary with the overhead rate applied. It was assumed that overheads cost 120% of production costs, but a rate of 60% was also tested. The authors would have preferred to calculate overhead as a percentage of sales income because distribution incurs additional administration costs and thus costs vary with the size of the subscription base.

However, calculation of the overhead in this way would have required a circular connection between elements in the model which is prohibited by the software package. As the model is non-commercial, it was assumed that the publisher does not seek to make substantial profits. However, some profit margin is required to develop the journal. We applied margins in the model at a rate varying from 0% to 20%. The journal is produced by a half-time production editor and a half-time systems administrator.

The cost per paper was estimated at £275. This is based on a part-time journal production editor and a part-time systems administrator each earning, pro rata, £25 000 who also cost an additional 20% of that figure in National Insurance Contributions (NIC) and pension contributions.

This gives a total employment cost of £30 000. An overhead was not applied to staff costs in this instance. Assuming that these staff members can produce a journal consisting of 120 papers per volume (per year), the cost per paper is £250. An additional £25 was added to this figure to cover any other expenses. Subscription fees in the model vary with the level of use.

The price increases as the user base decreases because there are fewer subscribers or purchasers of individual documents to share the costs.

The price of an individual paper is double that of a paper sold as part of a subscription to reflect the increased risk to the publisher when she sells papers individually rather than in volume sized bundles. This price may be calculated by dividing the subscription price by 120 to generate a per-paper price and multiplying the resulting figure by two. All subscription and article prices include VAT at 17.5%.

HEIs in the UK are currently required to pay VAT on purchases of electronic information, but not on print information. The authors acknowledge that it can take several years for journal start-up costs to be amortized and the duration varies considerably. In the interests of simplicity, the journal modeled here is assumed to be an on-going concern, i.e. start-up costs are not included.

The flow element 'other publisher income' represents sources of income derived from the journal publication other than sales of subscriptions and individual articles. Other source of income may include, for example, advertising or sponsored supplements.

This figure is calculated at 4% of subscription and individual article income. This figure was derived from the journal costing form referred to above.

COST OF STORING DIGITAL JOURNALS

The cost of storing digital journals is currently very low and is falling. It is assumed that this cost is incurred by the publisher and that the work related to storage would be undertaken by the Systems administrator in the normal course of her duties. The cost of storage space itself is based on a rough estimate that it costs £100 per gigabyte per annum to store digital content. It is estimated that an HTML journal volume occupies approximately 30 Mb. This is a liberal estimate based on figures supplied by Stuart Peters with reference to the electronic journal *Sociology Online*. Thus, a volume costs £2.93 per annum to store. After 13 years the cost of storing that journal is £26 per annum. Storage costs are likely to decrease significantly over the period but no attempt is made to predict the degree of this decrease.

Information Broker Function

The information broker (subscription agent) undertakes administrative work that saves time and money for both the library and the publisher.

The various tasks involved are not represented. The information broker also generates management information which she supplies to both the publisher and the library as appropriate. As the type of information and thus its value and the cost of processing it are unknown as yet, this function is not represented. It is assumed that the information broker negotiates favorable licence terms for libraries. Libraries pay an annual fee to the information broker. In the model, this is based on the fee charged by NESLI. NESLI charges institutions a fee to use SwetsNet which amounts to £1 per title subscription up to a maximum of £560 (A. Prior, personal communication, 17 March 1999).

In the model, the fee paid by an institution is determined by the amount of service delivered to the institution as determined by number of subscriptions and number of individual articles delivered; the latter is divided by 120 as a proxy for a single journal title.

It is assumed in the model that when an individual at an HEI has received a document electronically, the document will then be available to other researchers at the institution free of charge. This assumption is based on the practice of Elsevier Science with regard to institutions participating in the PEAK project. Publishers pay for the services of information broker by supplying publications at a discounted rate. Generally, discounts from publishers to subscription agents are in the region of 7%. This figure is used in the model.

It was beyond the scope of this study to explore the costs to information brokers of the variety of services that they provide. It was assumed that the discount from the publisher and the fee from the library is sufficient remuneration.

HE Library Function

The cost to the library of negotiating the licence terms on which journals and/or individual electronic articles are supplied is represented by a negotiation fraction for each of these resources. This fraction is based on the cost of an individual, professional negotiator working at full capacity plus the cost of 1 hour per week to five other senior staff members in HE.

This is a modest estimate of the cost based on current practice in the US where licence negotiation often involves a team of senior staff who sometimes meet as frequently as every week.

The hourly rate for employing a senior staff member (including employment costs and overhead) is £50. Electronic Individual Article Supply (EIAS) directly from the publisher is likely to be negotiated based on access to a bundle of titles, perhaps within a single subject area or perhaps the publisher's entire list. The negotiation process itself is likely to take longer than negotiation for a single title as both parties have more at stake. However, the cost of the negotiation may be spread across all EIAS acquisitions for, at least, a single year. In the model, the cost of negotiation for EIAS directly from the publisher is based on 33 senior staff hours at £50 an hour (representing three 1-hour meetings attended by the negotiator and five other participants and 15 hours of negotiation and related tasks by the negotiator).

It is assumed that negotiation reduces the subscription cost and the EIAS cost to the library to 10% less than the standard price. It was assumed also that the library acquisitions budget is £505 per active researcher.

This figure is based on SCONUL figures for an average academic library acquisitions budget and on the number of active researchers. It was assumed that an average institution has 1174 active researchers. This is a rough estimate based on SCONUL figures. It includes the total mean number of teaching and research staff which is (arbitrarily) divided in half, the mean number of research only staff, and the mean number of postgraduate research students. In the model, the cost of licence negotiation is deducted from the library acquisitions budget.

This does not reflect reality. However, the cost of licence negotiation is directly related to the acquisition of journals and it is deducted from the acquisitions budget in the model so that the total cost of acquiring journals directly from the publisher may be compared with the cost of acquiring them from via an information broker.

It was assumed that the publisher commits as much time and effort to negotiating licences as the library. Thus, the negotiation fraction deducted from the library journals acquisitions budget is also deducted from the publisher gross income to indicate publisher spend.

COSTS OF PROCESSING, STORING AND ISSUING PRINT JOURNALS

The cost of processing, storing, issuing and other tasks related to print journals is included in the model for comparison. Odlyzko claims that these costs are the cause of the serials crisis and suggests that for every $1 that a library spends on journal acquisitions, it spends another $2 on these related activities. He based this assertion on the fact that Association of Research Libraries (ARL) statistics consistently show that acquisitions represent approximately 30% of the budgets of research libraries in the US and Canada.

The assumption is that if this material is acquired in digital form, these additional library costs can be eliminated. This assumption is, it must said, contentious. The cost of storing digital journals is likely to be much lower than the cost of storing print but the cost of maintaining that store and of technical migration to ensure that the content is available in the future will be significant. Furthermore, it is likely that in a digital library, the tasks currently undertaken by librarians will be as important as they are now.

These tasks may be undertaken by other stakeholders and the nature of the tasks will change to some degree. Nevertheless, the costs of undertaking them will be incurred and will be included in the price of scholarly literature. Figures used for calculating these costs are based on those calculated for use in planning the JSTOR project.

The cost of storing a single volume of the journal *Ecology* for 1 year is $3.07. This figure is used here as a basis for calculating storage costs for journals.

It has been inflated and converted at the current rate to give £2 per volume. Bowen estimated that circulation costs for current issues of journals amount to a total of $45 (currently £29) and that circulation costs for past issues also cost $45. In the model, the term 'current issue' refers to the current year and two previous years.

After that period has elapsed, the cost of circulating back issues will be added to library costs at the same rate as circulation of current issues. Bowen estimated that binding of current issues costs $20 (currently £13) and processing and check in a further $20 (currently £13). Finally, he estimated that the cost of conserving and preserving backruns is $5 (£3).

The total cost per title per annum ranges from £60 in year 1 to £113 in year 13. As a percentage of the current mean journal subscription fee in the UK this represents 58–109%. These figures are lower than Odlyzko suggested, but are still significant when scaled up for a whole journal collection. For example, the cost of processing, storing and issuing a collection of only 1000 titles ranges from £60 000 in Year 1 to £11 3000 in Year 13. The mean number of titles held by a library is 4880.

The cost to the library of processing, storing and issuing a print collection of this size ranges from £292 800 in Year 1 to £551 440 in Year 13. As a percentage of total gross library expenditure, this represents 9–18

COST TO THE LIBRARY OF USERS PRINTING FROM JOURNALS

At present, researchers use the library to browse but photocopy papers that they intend to read. In an electronic environment, they will print from a laser printer. A photocopy costs about 2.5p/page. A laser print costs approximately double. However, printing from a laser printer does not require the researcher to stand at the machine and photocopy each page of the journal in turn. When this opportunity cost is taken into account the difference in price between photocopying and laser printing is likely to be negligible.

However, were researchers to begin to read on screen rather from than from printed copy, this cost would be saved. For this reason, the model calculates a very approximate print cost as follows. It is estimated that each active researcher prints 2160 pages per annum. This figure is based on a rough calculation of the number of pages per paper multiplied by the number of papers read by an active researcher per annum.

A selection of 36 papers printed from a variety of electronic journals was sampled and the average number of pages was found to be 10. The number of papers read by each active researcher is based on figures derived from a citation analysis conducted for the FIDDO project. On average, each of 1500 authors cited 18 papers. It has been estimated that one third of all influences is cited so it is assumed that each author reads 54 papers when preparing a paper for publication. As many academic departments in the UK currently require research-active staff to publish four papers per year, this is taken as a standard and it is assumed that researchers read a total of 216 papers per year. If each paper consists of 10 printed pages, in an electronic environment, each researcher will print 2160 pages. Thus, an institution with only 200 research-active staff will incur print costs of £21 600.

It is assumed that an average institution has 1174 active researchers as calculated above. Based on this figure, the cost to an institution for printing is £126 792. The size of the fund supplied to the library for acquisitions is based on the number of active researchers multiplied by a financial sum per active researcher. The sum per active researcher is based on SCONUL 1996/97 figures and reflects mean subscription costs plus mean binding costs plus mean ILL transaction costs divided by mean number of active researchers.

Model Simulations

The overhead rate, the profit margin applied by the publisher, and the number of subscriptions were varied and the effect on subscription fees monitored. The results are recorded below.

At an overhead rate of 120% and a profit margin of 20%, subscription fees for 200, 500, 1000, 2000, and 20 000 subscriptions are £809.62, £323.84 £161.92, £80.96, and £8.10 respectively. If the overhead is maintained at 120% and the profit margin is reduced to 10%, the subscription fees for 200, 500, 1000, 2000, and 20 000 subscriptions are £742.15, £296.86, £148.43, £74.22, and £7.42 respectively.

If the overhead is maintained at 120% and the profit margin is reduced to zero, the subscription fees for 200,500, 1000, 2000, and 20 000 subscriptions are £674.69, £269.88, £134.94, £67.47, and £6.75 respectively. If the overhead is reduced to 60%, at a profit margin of 20%, the subscription fees for 200, 500, 1000, 2000, and 20 000 subscriptions are £588.82, £235.52, £117.76, £58.88, and £5.89 respectively.

If the overhead is maintained at 60% and the profit margin reduced to 10%, the subscription fees for 200, 500, 1000, 2000, and 20 000 subscriptions are £539.75, £215.90, £107.95, £53.97, and £5.40 respectively. If the overhead is maintained at 60% and the profit margin reduced to zero, the subscription fees for 200, 500, 1000, 2000, and 20 000 subscriptions are £490.68, £196.28, £98.14, £49.07, and £4.91 respectively. It is clear from these figures that a non-commercial journal making a modest profit and recovering full costs (120% overhead) can be supplied to users for a modest fee as long as the subscription base consists of at least 500 subscribers.

HARNAD MODEL

The Harnad model differs from the traditional model in that all costs are recovered through author submission fees. Again the entire editorial process is conducted electronically. Journals are available on the Internet free of charge to any user. However, as delivery through a common, familiar interface is important to users and one function of the information broker is to deliver material through a common interface it is assumed that the library pays to use an information broker to deliver Harnad-modelled journals.

Even if all journals were produced on a Harnad-type model, the library would seek to obtain such a service. It is beyond the scope of this project to determine the feasibility of the latter scenario for the information broker.

Content Origination and Publication

Manuscripts are submitted to the editorial office for review. The model simulates production of a single journal consisting of 120 papers per annum. Only authors of papers which are refereed are charged a submission fee. Thus, the 2% of authors whose papers are rejected immediately do not contribute to publication costs. The contribution of editors and referees is the same in this model as in the traditional model and again, the cost of this contribution is an opportunity cost as this work is unpaid. The total publication cost is calculated based on journal production staff costs which are the same as those in the traditional model, overhead and storage of the back list as it accumulates. Overhead is applied at a rate of 120% and of 60%. Clearly, the alternative method of calculating overhead referred to above could not have been used in this model as there is no sales income. The submission fee is calculated as the total production cost divided by the number of papers refereed. No profit margin is applied. Harnad's is a model in which publication is conducted by, and for the benefit of, HE. It is assumed that future development would be funded by HE grant or other HE sources of income. The cost of storing the journal back list is calculated as above.

Information Brokerage and HE Library Function

In the model, the cost to the library of obtaining information brokerage services is based on the charges levied by NESLI. There is no requirement for the information broker to negotiate with a publisher on behalf of the library.

This would represent a significant proportion of the cost of NESLI services. However, it is assumed that the information broker in this model provides the other services offered by NESLI such as management information and catalogue records as well as the common interface for delivering journals. The fee charged by NESLI for using SwetsNet is £1 per title subscription up to a maximum of £560. The NESLI pricing mechanism would appear to be based on a traditional model, i.e. one in which publishers charge subscription fees, as NESLI also plans to seek fees in the form of a discount on subscriptions from publishers.

This is likely to be at a rate of approximately 7%. Where subscriptions are free of charge, the library would be expected to pay for that part of the NESLI fee that, otherwise, would be recovered from publishers.

The rate applied in the model is based on the average cost of a journal subscription and the fee per institution is based on the amount of service delivered, i.e. the number of subscriptions. The average subscription fee used is the mean subscription fee paid by UK libraries for journal subscriptions in 1997 as indicated by the LISU Library and Information Statistics Tables 1998. NESLI would seek 7% of the subscription price from the publisher (£7.26). In this model, the library pays 20% of that figure, £1.45, up to a maximum of £812.

Thus, the total figure paid by the library is £2.45 per title up to a maximum of £1372. In this model, the library incurs no costs from negotiating journal licences with publishers. It is assumed that the library acquisitions budget consists of £505 per active researcher. The costs of processing, storing and issuing print journals calculated above are unaffected by differences in the journal models as is the cost of printing from electronic journals.

Model Simulations

The overhead rate applied to production costs and the journal rejection rate are varied and the effect on submission fees is monitored. The results are recorded below. If the overhead on production costs is 120%, at a 10% rejection rate the submission fee is £878.90. This figure falls to £97.66 for a 90% rejection rate. If the overhead on production costs is reduced from 120% to 60% the submission fee is reduced and ranges from £639.21 for a rejection rate of 10% to £71.02 for a rejection rate of 90%. For a 10-page article, a fee of £639.21 represents a page charge of £63.92.

If the submission fee were £639.21 the page charge for a 20-page article would be £31.96 but for each of those 20-page papers the model requires two corresponding 5-page articles, submitted at a cost of £127.84 per page.

If the overhead on production costs is reduced to 30%, the submission fee is further reduced and ranges from £519.36 at a rejection rate of 10% to £57.71 for a rejection rate of 90%. Clearly, submission fees are reduced in line with reductions in the overhead rate applied to production costs. We argue that an overhead rate of 120% is realistic.

Thus, if the overhead rate is reduced, the remaining overhead must be covered by the host institution as a subsidy. Presumably, this could be justified with reference to the kudos gained from producing a reputable peer reviewed journal and only if journal production responsibilities were spread across the HE sector. However, even at an overhead rate of just 30%, fees are not reduced to within the range that Harnad would expect. He suggests that fees of tens of dollars a page rather than hundreds of dollars a page would be acceptable and estimates that it would cost approximately $400 to produce a 20-page article. This converts as approximately £250 for 20 pages, i.e. a page charge of £12.50.

In the model, a page charge of £12.50 would not cover the production costs of any journal with a rejection rate below 80%. If an overhead of 120% were applied, a page charge of £12.50 would cover publication only if the rejection rate were 88% or more.

If an overhead of 60% were applied, a page charge of £12.50 would cover publication only if the rejection rate were 84% or more. If an overhead rate of 30% were applied, a page charge of £12.50 would cover publication costs only if the rejection rate were 80% or more.

Nevertheless, fees are reduced to a level close to that charged for submission to many US journals. The latter also charge subscription fees which the Harnad model avoids. Thus, although costs are not reduced to the level anticipated by Harnad, cost recovery by author submission fees is a viable model.

Clearly, in this model, rejection rate is a key factor determining viability as submission fees are much higher for papers submitted to journals with high rejection rates. This effect would make submission fees in the natural sciences much more expensive than those in the humanities. In the former, rejection rates tend to be around 10–20% and in the latter, they tend to be around 80–90%. This may appear to be reasonable as research in the natural sciences is more likely to be funded by substantial grants, so it may be argued that natural scientists can better afford to pay high submission fees. However, the difference between disciplines of the cost of submitting a paper for publication is misleading. Most academic papers are published even if they are rejected by the first or second choice of journal. In disciplines where the rejection rate is high, presumably authors often have to submit the same paper to several journals before it is eventually accepted for publication and thus, they would be required to pay several submission fees.

Ultimately, the total cost to scientists and humanities scholars would be similar. It may, however, be argued that in these circumstances cost would regulate quality. In other words, authors would not go to the expense of constantly submitting (and paying submission fees) a paper they knew to be inferior. This argument, whilst valid, is countered by the argument that rejection rates in the humanities do not simply reflect an abundance of poor-quality material. Humanities subjects are characterised by debate rather than the scientific method. Quality assessment in these subjects is more subjective than in the sciences. Thus, material that is rejected by referees selected by the editor of one journal may be commended by referees selected by the editor of another journal. It is likely, therefore, that the majority of authors will persist with their articles. As expected, in this model the cost to users of journals is very low.

Thus, any HE subsidy for journal production and development could be offset by savings in acquisitions costs. A library providing 4880 Harnad-modelled titles to its users could expect to pay only £11 956 in fees to an information broker. Compared with subscribing to an average journals collection at the average price (£103.71) for a total cost of £506 104 this represents a huge saving for the library.

New Journal of Physics

Working examples of the journals modelled by those who seek to change the economic characteristics of the scholarly information delivery chain are rare. Many journals available in electronic form are published in parallel with print and the price mechanism is traditional. Many other journals that are produced only in electronic form are grant funded and recover costs neither from authors nor from users.

A new electronic journal, *The New Journal of Physics (NJP)* is published by an established publisher of peerreviewed scholarly journals, the Institute of Physics Publishing (IoPP). The *NJP* is published only in electronic form and is no doubt intended to cover its costs; this it does from its authors.

Thus, to a degree, it exemplifies the Harnad model. However, whereas Harnad suggests that costs be recovered through submission fees, the IoPP seeks to recover the cost of publishing the *NJP* through acceptance fees. Presumably, fees paid by authors of papers that are accepted for publication must cover the cost of all papers submitted. The IoPP charges $500 for production of an accepted paper in the *NJP* and the journal is available to access free of charge over the Internet. This suggests that the *NJP* can be published for $60 000 per volume (based on a volume of 120 accepted papers).

The IoPP encourages authors to submit only papers that are of the highest quality and of wide appeal which suggests that they wish to keep the rejection rate as low as possible. It is common for physics journals to have rejection rates of approximately 10%. The Ithink model produced to test Harnad's theory was revised to simulate the characteristics of the *NJP*. This revised model was run and the results show that if the overhead rate on production costs is 120%, the total production cost for a volume of the *NJP* consisting of 120 10-page papers ranges from £114 000 at 2% rejection rate to £115 000 at 10% rejection rate. If overhead is applied at a rate of 60%, the cost is approximately £84 000. If the journal were to recover these costs through a submission fee then, at an overhead rate of 120% the fee would range from £958 to £882 for rejection rates of 2% and 10% respectively. If an overhead of 60% were applied, the fee would range from £697 to £641 for rejection rates of 2% and 10% respectively.

The submission fee decreases as the rejection rate increases. However, if costs are recovered through an acceptance fee, as proposed by the IoPP, then at an overhead of 120%, fees range from £958 to £960 for rejection rates of 2% and 10% respectively. If an overhead rate of 60% is applied, fees range from £697 to £698 for rejection rates of 2% and 10% respectively. The fee increases with the rejection rate. Hence the desire of the IoPP to keep the rejection rate of the *NJP* low. These figures suggest that production of an electronic journal costs a great deal more than a sum that can be recovered from acceptance fees of about $500 (£311). Presumably, over the longer term, the IoPP expects to recover costs from some other sources. It will be interesting to monitor the success of this new journal.

Fishwick Model

The Fishwick model is significantly different from either of the other models in that it introduces 'normal' market feedback mechanisms into the academic information delivery chain. Both submission fees and subscription fees are used to recover costs as Fishwick argues that both users' requirement for reading material and authors' requirement for publication create demand.

The financial cost of producing a Fishwick journal is much higher than the cost of the other journals modelled because the editor and referees are paid for their contributions. Again, the entire editorial process is conducted electronically and journals are delivered in electronic form.

Libraries are free to obtain subscriptions/individual articles directly from publishers or to obtain them from an information broker. It is assumed, if the library chooses the former, that terms will be negotiated between the library and the publisher.

Content Origination

In this sector manuscripts are submitted to the editorial office for publication and authors are required to pay a submission fee. Only authors of papers which are refereed are charged a submission fee. Thus, the 2% of authors whose papers are rejected immediately do not contribute to publication costs.

Fishwick *et al.* propose that a submission fee should contribute to refereeing, editorial and production costs. Thus, all authors submitting a paper for publication contribute to production costs regardless of whether or not the paper is accepted. The alternative would be to charge a submission fee which covers only editorial and refereeing costs and, on acceptance, charge an additional publication cost. However, this would incur an additional administration cost. The contribution of editors and referees is the same in this model as in the traditional model. However, both referees and editors are paid for their work at an hourly rate of £50 including overhead and any other related employment costs. The submission fee consists of the total cost of editorial, refereeing and editorial office work on the manuscript plus a contribution to publisher costs. Fishwick *et al.* do not suggest an appropriate rate at which authors should contribute to publication costs nor do they suggest a suitable rate at which authors should be paid royalties on sales of their papers. In the model, authors contribute 10% of the production cost and receive royalties at a rate of 5% of usage fees. Generally, authors, their employers, or their funding sources will pay the fee but a small number of papers will be submitted by authors who cannot pay the fee. In these cases, the editorial office will apply, on behalf of the author, for publication assistance from public/charitable bodies. Any royalties accumulated from publication of these papers will be paid to the body which funded publication.

Publication

Production costs in the model vary with the overhead rate applied. It is assumed that overheads cost 120% but a rate of 60% is also tested. As in the traditional model, a profit margin varying from zero to 20% is applied. Fishwick *et al.* suggests that the basic product be simple unedited text and that a more sophisticated product be available at a higher price.

Research suggests that users and librarians expect electronic journals to have additional functionality and would not consider it worthwhile learning how to use a system simply to access text which they would then print.

It is assumed in this model that users would subscribe only to a more sophisticated product, i.e. that the minimum requirement would be hotlinks to cited papers. Production costs are based on this assumption and consist of the two part-time staff members described above with reference to the Traditional model. Authors contribute 10% towards production costs and the remaining 90% is recovered through subscription/individual article fees. This journal would be more expensive than the others to administer because of the additional tasks associated with unfunded papers. As well as manuscript management administration, the cost of the following tasks would be incurred:

- Receiving applications for assisted publication;
- Applying to funding bodies on behalf of those applying for assistance;
- Administering receipt of submission fees;
- Administering royalty payments.

It would cost £19 500 to employ a part-time secretary on a pro-rata salary of £15 000 if the overhead applied were 120%. If the overhead were 60%, it would cost £14 400. A cost per-paper is required for the model. It is assumed that the cost of applying for assistance with publication costs would be spread across all papers and that the secretary could administer 600 papers per annum. This would be the number received by a journal with an 80% rejection rate. Thus, the cost per paper is £32.50 (£19 500/600) if the overhead rate is 120% and £24 (£14 400/600) if the overhead rate is 60%. Fishwick *et al.* suggest that published papers be sold to users either by subscription to the publisher's whole list, by subscription to specific parts (e.g. within a specific subject areas), by a two-part tariff which consists of a reduced subscription price combined with reduced transaction costs relating to individual articles, or simply on a pay-per-use basis. These different pricing mechanisms are different risk-sharing schemes. When the publisher shoulders most of the risk in a pay-per-document model the price is higher but when the library shoulders most of the risk by subscribing to a whole database from which users may select only a small proportion of the content, the price per paper is lower.

These different pricing mechanisms were not modelled. To include them in the model would be to introduce too many variables and thus, simulations would reveal economic factors that apply only in very specific circumstances.

Only subscription and individual article fees are included in the model. Subscription fees vary with level of use as in the Traditional model. It is assumed that the journal is an ongoing concern, i.e. that journal start-up costs need not be amortised

Information Brokerage

Assumptions informing the role of the information broker were the same in this model as in the Traditional model.

HE Library Function

Assumptions informing the HE library function were the same in this model as in the Traditional model.

SUBMISSION FEES

The submission fee covers the cost of the editorial process and contributes to publisher income for use in the production process. However, it is not informed by subscription price or any of the elements affecting price and thus, it is not affected by the profit margin applied by the publisher.

It varies only with rejection rate and the rate at which overhead is applied. The latter alters the submission fee because the fee includes the cost of administering the manuscript which is not insignificant in this model. If the overhead is applied at a rate of 120%, submission fees will range between £446.56 for a journal with a 10% rejection rate to £368.44 for a journal with a 90% rejection rate. If the overhead is applied at a rate of 60%, submission fees will range between £413.92 for a journal with a 10% rejection rate to £357.10 for a journal with a 90% rejection rate.

These fees fall within the range charged by many US journals and thus, are not entirely unacceptable. Unlike the Harnad model however, they contribute little to a reduction in costs for the user.

SUBSCRIPTION PRICE

The subscription price does not vary with rejection rate because it is determined by the cost of producing the 120 papers published in the journal. It does not include the editorial process which is covered by the submission fee.

If the overhead is applied at a rate of 120% and the profit margin is 20%, the subscription price if 200 subscriptions are sold is £728.66. The subscription price if 500 subscriptions are sold is £291.46.

The subscription price if 1000 subscriptions are sold is £145.73. The subscription price if 2000 subscriptions are sold is £72.87 and the subscription price if 20 000 subscriptions are sold is £7.29.

If the overhead is applied at a rate of 60% and the profit margin is 20%, the subscription price if 200 subscriptions are sold is£529.93. The subscription price if 500 subscriptions are sold is £211.98. The subscription price if 1000 subscriptions are sold is £105.99.

The subscription price if 2000 subscriptions are sold is £52.99 and the subscription price if 20 000 subscriptions are sold is £5.30. If the overhead is applied at a rate of 120% and the profit margin is 10%, the subscription price if 200 subscriptions are sold is £667.94. The subscription price if 500 subscriptions are sold is £267.18. The subscription price if 1000 subscriptions are sold is £133.59. The subscription price if 2000 subscriptions are sold is £66.79 and the subscription if 20 000 subscriptions are sold is £6.68. If the overhead is applied at a rate of 60% and the profit margin is 10%, the subscription price if 200 subscriptions are sold is £485.77. The subscription price if 500 subscriptions are sold is ££194.30. The subscription price if 1000 subscriptions are sold is £97.15. The subscription price if 2000 subscriptions are sold is £48.58 and the subscription if 20 000 subscriptions are sold is £4.86. If the overhead is applied at a rate of 120% and the profit margin is zero, the subscription price if 200 subscriptions are sold is £607.22.

The subscription price if 500 subscriptions are sold is ££242.88. The subscription price if 1000 subscriptions are sold is £121.44. The subscription price if 2000 subscriptions are sold is ££60.72 and the subscription price if 20 000 subscriptions are sold is £6.07. If the overhead is applied at a rate of 60% and the profit margin is zero, the subscription price if 200 subscriptions are sold is £441.61. The subscription price if 500 subscriptions are sold is ££176.64. The subscription if 1000 subscriptions are sold is £88.32. The subscription if 2000 subscriptions are sold is £44.16 and the subscription price if 20 000 subscriptions are sold is £4.42.

AUTHOR ROYALTIES

Author royalty is based on income from subscriptions and sales of individual articles, i.e. it is based on the price of subscriptions and individual articles. It is not affected by the rejection rate because editorial and associated administrative costs are covered separately by submission fees. Nor is author royalty affected by the number of subscriptions sold.

Subscription price varies with the number of subscriptions sold so that journals/individual articles may be delivered to users at the cheapest rate possible; this a non-profit initiative.

The royalty is affected, however, by the overhead applied to production costs and by the profit margin applied by the publisher as both of these things vary the price of the product. If overhead is applied at a rate of 120%, a profit margin of 20% is applied, the mean royalty received is £24.03.

If overhead is applied at a rate of 60%, a profit margin of 20% is applied, the mean royalty received is £17.48. If overhead is applied at a rate of 120%, a profit margin of 10% is applied, the mean royalty received is £22.03. If overhead is applied at a rate of 60%, a profit margin of 10% is applied, the mean royalty received is £16.02. If overhead is applied at a rate of 120%, a profit margin of zero is applied, the mean royalty received is £20.03.

If overhead is applied at a rate of 60%, a profit margin of zero is applied, the mean royalty received is £14.56. Individual articles are priced at double the rate of a paper sold as part of a subscription. However, prices of papers and subscriptions vary with the number of subscriptions and individual articles sold, i.e. with income from sales. Thus, although a single paper may sell well on an individual article basis, the mean author royalty will be static.

The royalty is included in Fishwick's model as an incentive to publish only high-quality material. A very successful paper could recover the submission fee through royalties such as these.

For example, the royalty for a journal produced when an overhead of 120% and a profit margin of 10% are applied is £16.02. In this case the submission fee is £413.92. To recover the submission fee, the author would be required to attract 22% of the royalty funds available for that title in a single year. The

Fishwick model is expensive. Submission fees are not insignificant and, primarily, they pay for work that is unpaid in other models.

Furthermore, although authors contribute 10% to production costs, the effect on subscription fees is small. Thus, in financial terms the model does not compare well with the others. Nevertheless, like the other models, subscription fees generated for this model are modest compared with fees of commercial publishers.

Alternative Model Proposed by Authors

Like the Fishwick model, the alternative model proposed here recovers costs through a submission fee and a subscription fee in recognition that both authors and users create demand for publication of scholarly articles.

However, this is not a market model and does not introduce payment for editors and referees. The model differs from the standard non-commercial model only in that a proportion of the production cost is recovered from submission fees.

6

Promotion and Evaluation in Library Science

INSTITUTIONAL REPOSITORIES

FACILITATING STRUCTURE, COLLABORATIONS, SCHOLARLY COMMUNICATIONS, AND INSTITUTIONAL VISIBILITY

The advancement of information and communication technology (ICT)—Internet in particular—has caused enormous changes in the world we are living today. Many things are not what they used to be decades, or even years ago. Imagine how we communicated and shared information in the fifties, when computers were still 'archaic' and the Internet was still in its inception stage. Compare that to the numerous communication gadgets and the information overload that we have today. All those changes happened in only a little over fifty years. Libraries as information providers have also undergone massive changes due to their close association to the way people communicate, collect, manage, use, and share information.

Any advancement in ICT will have direct and indirect impacts on the ways libraries provide their collections and services to their user communities and society in general. Some advancements might be welcome by libraries. Others might be perceived as threats to the existence of libraries since, they are perceived as 'things' that would cause libraries to become obsolete, or at least redundant, amidst the new emerging technologies.

Some have also caused mixed reactions among librarians, who might 'love' and 'hate' them at the same time. Librarians usually love advancements in ICT since, they can help tremendously in the librarians' efforts to fulfill the information needs of their users. However librarians might also notice that many (or most?) of their traditional roles as librarians have been, or will be, taken away from them by those advancements. Digital libraries (DLs), which include all of its variants such as institutional repositories (IRs), is one of the most important changes in libraries triggered by advancements in ICT. DLs have caused fundamental changes in the way libraries operate. It has also challenged the traditional roles of libraries and compelled them to redefine their roles in this new environment. Discussions in this stage are the results of the expansions and 'conversations' from several of my previous journal articles on IRs. However they will take into account as much as possible and where appropriate, recent developments and discussions about IRs. The discussions will also use Desa Informasi (Information Village)—an institutional repositories project at Petra Christian University (PCU) Library in Surabaya, Indonesia—as a study case. The project is not intended to serve as an example of a success in IRs implementation. In fact, it is still far from an ideal implementation of IRs. It is being used solely for the purpose of sharing experiences gained from its execution. Naturally, perspectives raised in the discussion will be of an academic librarian in a developing country. The environment, where the project is being carried out—a medium-sized private university with mostly undergraduate students—will certainly offers certain influences into the discussions as well.

ICT ADVANCEMENTS AND THE FUTURE OF LIBRARIES

The rapid developments of ICT since, the birth of computers and the Internet has contributed so much in changing the way we live our daily life. They affect the way we do things, which includes the way we do our jobs. They even affect the way we relate to one another in terms of personal relationships, as well as professional ones. Almost everything we do in daily basis has something to do with ICT. It ranges from simple stand-alone applications to collaborative and networked systems. Nowadays it's almost unimaginable to write an article without the help of a word processor application, online dictionary or thesaurus, reference management application, and online journal databases.

All these advancements have offered invaluable help for people from any professions in terms of working more effectively and productively. Some ICT advancements however can cause fundamental changes in the traditional roles and functions of certain professions. They fundamentally alter the ways in which people or institutions provide products and services. Libraries—especially academic libraries—and their librarians have been living through these inevitable, yet often subtle, transformations. Nowadays most librarians are familiar with—or at least aware of—approval plans, selector services, new acquisitions of library materials with embedded electronic bibliographic records, copy cataloging, self-check-in/out, Internet search engines, virtual reference services, etc.

All these roles and/or functions (acquisition, cataloging, reference, etc.) were traditionally the domains of (local) librarians. Local librarians used to have the authority over or in charge of performing these roles and/or functions. However the new environment affected or created by ICT advancements has created new 'arrangements', where these basic roles and/or functions are gradually being taken over by ICT, or at least transferred to other institutions outside the libraries. In short, traditional roles and/or functions of librarians are being challenged by the rapid technological changes, which usually also leads to social changes. Librarians need to 'redefine' their roles and/or functions in the new landscape of the future information society. Davenport stated something that I believe is a good response to the challenge.

She suggested that librarians should have "expanded, more collaborative roles in the creation and dissemination of knowledge," which will empower (academic) libraries to assume new role and/or function as learning space instead of information storehouse. It is now up to librarians on how to assume this 'new' role and/or function in the new landscape. Digital libraries (DLs) and/or institutional repositories (IRs) offer opportunities for librarians and libraries to re-assert their influence in the creation and dissemination of knowledge. DLs/IRs is a strategic move for libraries to maintain their relevance in the new landscape of ICT-savvy society. However before going into any further discussions, we need to be on the same page on what we call digital libraries (DLs) and/or institutional repositories (IRs).

INSTITUTIONAL REPOSITORIES

IRs is one of the relatively new terms generated by advancements in ICT, one that needs to be defined to enable us to proceed with our discussion.

One of the pioneers in IRs—Clifford Lynch—gave one of the most fundamental definitions of IRs:

- "A university-based institutional repository is a set of services that a university offers to the members of its community for the management and dissemination of digital materials created by the institution and its community members. It is most essentially an organisational commitment to the stewardship of these digital materials, including long-term preservation where appropriate, as well as organisation and access or distribution."

It is worth to mention specifically that Lynch defined IRs as 'a set of services' instead of merely digital contents. Lynch also sees "institutional repositories as a species of digital library than a publishing platform," which is a sufficient ground for me to conclude that 'the terms IRs and DLs ... interchangeable'. Lynch's definition—'a set of services'—suggests his far reaching look into the future. However for the sake of flow of discussion, let's talk first about (digital) contents of IRs. There are several different views on what IRs should contain. These different views don't necessarily contradict one another. They rather define IRs contents from different scopes and perspectives, which in my opinion can complement one another.

McDowell gave a more technical classification of IRs contents by stating:

- "IR contents were classified into the following types: ETDs; e-prints (pre-or post-print articles); working papers and technical reports;

conference proceedings and presentations; ejournals and e-books; learning objects; multimedia files (digital audio/video); datasets; pictures (images); digitized archival documents and university records (historical texts and primary sources); non-scholarly institutional publications; undergraduate student work; graduate student work (non-ETD); and course content (syllabi, assignments, lectures)."

Crow defined IRs contents more concisely as "scholarly; produced, submitted, or sponsored by an institution's faculty (and, optionally, students), or other authorised agents; non-ephemeral; and licensable in perpetuity".

In terms of contents of IRs, Lynch suggested that:

- "A mature and fully realised institutional repository will contain the intellectual works of faculty and students—both research and teaching materials—and also documentation of the activities of the institution itself in the form of records of events and performance and of the ongoing intellectual life of the institution."

It is interesting to notice that Lynch's definition doesn't limit IRs contents to "the intellectual works of faculty and students—both research and teaching materials" only. Instead it also encompasses "documentation of the activities of the institution itself in the form of records of events and performance and of the ongoing intellectual life of the institution". Desa Informasi (DI) adopts Lynch's definition for IRs contents and assumes that Crow's and McDowell's definitions as 'subsets of Lynch's' and summarises them into the characteristic of 'locally-produced' contents.

Desa Informasi then expands the definition to also include contents that have 'features of local entities'. Using parallel terminologies from the traditional (hardcopy) collections, the 'locallyproduced' contents are the equivalence of 'grey literature', while contents with 'features of local entities' are the equivalence of 'local collections'. The term 'local content' is a familiar term among Indonesian librarians in defining both characteristics, and it will be used in this stage to refer to contents with both characteristics. DI started off as a limited-in-scope of theses digitisation project to address the physical space limitation of PCU Library, which then evolved into an institutional repositories project. DI utilises a custom-made web-based application called iSPEKTRA to manage digital objects using modified Dublin Core metadata set.

Although "interoperability on a metadata level has clearly been the most active area in digital repositories ... spurred by the Open Access movement, numerous repositories exposed their metadata through standard protocols," iSPEKTRA has not yet addressed the interoperability issues in terms of compliance to Open Archives Initiatives—Protocol for Metadata Harvesting (OAI-PMH). It is a crucial issue that is being addressed along with the development of the new version of iSPEKTRA. DI divides its collections into Themes instead of one big collection in order to create 'added value' to the collections. The main consideration is that "having several smaller thematic collections of interest to the communities is far better than having one big collection consisting of just about anything people can throw into the collection without any defining 'character' that binds them together".

The current DI collections are as follows:

- *Digital Theses:* Petra Christian University students' theses collection in digital format; mostly PDF documents. There are also an increasing number of multimedia resources generated by the students of Faculty of Art and Design.
- *eDIMENSI:* Digital version of articles from DIMENSI, scientific journals published by various academic departments of Petra Christian University.
- *Petra@rt Gallery:* Works of art by campus communities or works of art that are exhibited/displayed at Petra Christian University campus; mostly photographs and digitised-images. The collection contains wonderful visual resources, capturing and immortalising the intrinsic knowledge and values of art in the works documented. Some of the wonderful themes are the Visual Poetry, Café Décor, Chairs of Indonesia, Destination Branded, Nusantara Bersatu, etc.
- *Petra iPoster:* Posters of events or issues related to Petra Christian niversity.
- *Petra Chronicle:* Historical documents related to Petra Christian University.

The collection themes clearly represent the 'locally-produced' definition of DI contents. One other collection that represents the definition of 'features of local entities' is the Surabaya Memory collection. It contains digital heritage resources on Surabaya city. Another newly-planned collection will be the 'Chinese in Indonesia' digital collection, which is intended to supplement the special collection of the same name.

This latest collection (still in planning stage as of the time of this book's publication) is created as support system for the newly-established Center for Chinese Indonesian Studies at Petra Christian Universities.

FACILITATING STRUCTURE AMIDST INFORMATION OVERLOAD AND CHAOS

As with most IRs, 'student work accounts for the largest percentage of items' in DI. Digital Theses is the largest collection in DI so far. This phenomenon happens in many institutions implementing IRs since, "ETDs are simply the lowest hanging fruit, and new submission batches can generally be counted on each semester". ETDs are also the 'preferred' contents since, they "raise the profiles of the students who author them, the faculty and departments who foster them, and the institutions that provide them to the world". The following tables will give readers a glimpse of DI collections.

Table. Brealdown of Desa Informasi's Digital Collections by Themes

Collection Name/Theme	# of Records Objects	# of Digital (bytes)	Total Size
Digital Theses	12,618	134,268	170,284,316,475
eDIMENSI	809	809	282,689,311
Petra iPoster	120	244	365.416.831
Petra@rt Gallery	261	854	4,132,526,401
Surabaya Memory	258	657	402,415,694
Petra Chronicle	180	559	2,489,567,862
TOTAL	**14,246**	**137,391**	**177,956,932,574**

In their article titled "Size isn't everything: Sustainable repositories as evidenced by sustainable deposit profiles," Carr and Brody stipulated that 'sustained deposits' is a more accurate measurement than merely the size of IRs, since, it reflects 'community engagement.' They stated that "one of the measures of repository success should therefore be the university community's take-up of these services".

Table. 7.2 Breakdown of Desa Informasi's Digital Collections by Types of Document

Collection Name	# of Digital Objects				
	Text	Image	Moving Image/Video	Animation	Audio, etc.
Digital Theses	115,830	18,228	119	24	67
eDIMENSI	809	0	0	0	0
Petra iPoster	0	244	0	0	0
Petra@rt Gallery	57	797	0	0	0
Surabaya Memory	25	632	0	0	0
Petra Chronicle	160	399	0	0	0
TOTAL	116,881	20,300	119	24	67

They warned against using the size of IRs as the only indication of 'healthy' IRs. Referring to Davis and Connolly's 2007 article titled Institutional repositories: Evaluating the reasons for non-use of Cornell University's installation of DSpace, they noticed that "a repository can exhibit respectable overall growth that is attributable mainly to special-case batch imports". Along this line of thinking, we should then analyse the deposit profile of DI to see any indication of its 'health.'

Table shows the growth of digital resources in DI from 2005 up to 2010. Carr and Brody used daily deposit profile in their survey of IRs by utilising ROAR registry of Institutional Repositories. However since, such data is not available for DI, Table uses annual deposit profile instead.

Table. Growth of Desa Informasi's Digital Collections

	2005/2006	2006/2007	2007/2008	2008/2009	2009/2010
# of Records	3,178	5,025	7,697	10,857	14,246

Growth from Previous Year	N/A	1,847	2,672	3,160	3,389
# of Digital Objects	N/A	39,438	68,510	98,092	137,391
Growth from PreviousYear	N/A	N/A	29,072	29,582	39,299

We can conclude from table that DI has a 'healthy' deposit profile since, the growth of its contents is sustainable. Table shows a steady growth in # of Records and Digital Objects every year. It is an indication of community engagement in supplying resources for DI. We can also conclude from our discussion so far that higher education institutions produced intellectual works in numerous subjects and formats besides the obvious scholarly works (theses and dissertations, journal articles, and research reports). Student works usually comprise the bulk of the works. Unfortunately most lecturers and academic departments don't have the 'sensitivity' or the expertise needed to identify these student works as intellectual outputs that can be re-used as learning resources.

They don't know how to collect, organise, manage, and re-use/serve these digital objects as learning resources. Davenport observed that "lack the organisation and structures that would allow campus departments to easily share such information". Based on my observations, most faculties only keep the digital version of the resources on CD Roms and stack them in cabinets. This practice will consequently make the resources hard to be found and re-used. It's as if faculties are lost amidst the chaotic and unstructured information overload. Academic libraries could and should jump into the scene to introduce some sense of structure into the seemingly chaotic information resources produced by students. IRs can be introduced as an elegant solution for the academic departments' need for organising these works and re-use them as learning resources.

JISC (Joint Information Systems Committee) suggested this approach when it reported that IRs "are increasingly expected to act as corporate information management tools (records management and content management systems) and data sharing platforms (*e.g.*, for the re-use of research data and learning objects)". This is one of the variations of IRs implementations and a common approach in Indonesian higher education libraries.

However libraries should not just offer the IRs platform as a solution and then leave the academic departments, faculties, and students on their own to figure out how to self-archive (uploading their works into the IRs) and help them organise those resources. Based on an article by Erickson, Rutherford, and Elliott, Salo warned against this approach when she reminded the readers that "the term 'self-archiving' has been taken too literal, abandoning faculty to their uncertainties and incapacities". Librarians should actively assume their 'new' role as IRs managers to increase the probability of a successful implementation of IRs by providing needed assistance to students and (especially) faculties in populating IRs. Libraries should do extra efforts to assist the academic departments, faculties, and students to get their works into IRs.

However in their efforts to populate IRs, it is of a strategic importance for libraries to always present the issue as the academic departments and lecturers' interests, not merely the libraries'. Mediated-deposit services was the method of choice for content acquisition for DI since, it was formally launched in 2005. Local conditions required it and the fact that librarians would be the ones in charge of managing the contents–including the metadata—sounded more promising in the long run.

The approach also asserts the role of librarians in providing some sense of structure into the whole collections. This choice turns out to be the right one since, it works so far, while the alternative doesn't look too promising. In her article Salo stated that "the notion that faculty members will actually push buttons and type metadata in order to deposit materials into IRs is an article of faith among repository-software developers. In practice, however, most deposits are third-party mediated, many by librarians, some by support staff or IT personnel". Salo's assertions and experience in DI prove that although mediated-deposit services might sound more 'expensive' and labour-intensive, it does offer more sustainability for IRs and more visibility to the role of librarians in the overall landscape of universitywide information management/ organisation. Content acquisition strategy is different from one collection to the others, based on the nature of the contents.

For example, the content acquisition for Digital Theses is pretty straight forward since, it 'piggybacks' on the university-wide theses deposit policy, which mandates all graduating students to deposit their theses to the Library in hardcopy and softcopy format. Contents for Petrart Gallery on the other hand are much harder to acquire since, they are produced sporadically without any fixed-patterns. However it is crucial that content acquisition process establishes some kind of connections to the 'administrative systems of the university or the local communities it serves' as Liauw suggested, since, "otherwise the collection process will be too massive to manage sporadically and the sustainability of the flow of resources from the communities into the IRs will depend largely on fluctuating individual interests". Contents for eDIMENSI are acquired through formal cooperation with the university's research center, which acts as the publisher for DIMENSI journals. This approach ensures 100 per cent incorporation of all articles published by the center into DI. Petra iPoster provides valuable lessons in its content acquisition effort and deserves a longer description.

It is a common practice in Indonesian universities for the Public Relations office to be in charge for approving posters that will be posted on campus premises. We would have thought that a formal cooperation with the Public Relations office would guarantee 100 per cent acquisition of posters at PCU by requiring poster-issuing units to provide the digital version of the submitted posters. However experience showed that it isn't as simple as that initial assumption. User behaviours play critical roles in this matter. Poster-issuing units usually don't have the digital version since, they outsource the design and printing process to outside vendors. It requires extra time and effort to get them from the vendors. Other reasons might simply be the reluctance of the poster-issuing unit to spend more time preparing the digital copy to be submitted to the Public Relations office, especially when people are usually under a tight deadline to put the posters up.

A request to provide an extra hardcopy poster as an alternative, instead of the digital version, was not successful either. We then noticed that another unit—the Campus Facility Management unit—is in charge for taking down 'expired' posters all across campus based on the expiry date stamped on each poster by the Public Relations office. We saw it as an opportunity to collect the posters for inclusion into Petra iPoster. So, instead of discarding the posters we merely ask the Campus Facility Management unit to send the posters to the Library.

This never-thought-of-before approach proves to work well since, it does not require any—or at least too much–disruption in the unit's daily operations. Aschenbrenner *et al.,* suggested this approach by saying that 'repositories become a natural part of the user's daily work environment'. The authors were referring to the overall aspects of IRs but the principal can be applied in a narrower scope to content acquisitions in IRs. We don't encounter too many difficulties in acquiring contents for Petra Chronicle since, most historical materials related to PCU will be deposited to the Library. The Library has had supports from various parties in developing Petra Chronicle and Petra iPoster since, the personal nature of the resources, which have certain appeals to the nostalgic aspects of various stakeholders.

The support only increases with the upcoming 50th Anniversary of PCU in 2011. In acquiring contents for IRs, librarians should actively come to the academic departments, lecturers, and students as someone who is offering an information/resources management system to address their needs for organising faculty and student works. IRs can be offered as the solution that will help in introducing and facilitating structure amidst the bulk and numerous different types of faculty and student works. Librarians will then be able to re-assert their role as information managers for their campus communities. Surabaya Memory (SM) presents another challenge in its content acquisition due to the nature of its contents that features 'local entities,' which translates into public participation in the content development. Unlike contents for other collections in DI that are locally produced, contents for SM is developed by involving the campus communities as well as general public. There has been some level of public participation from individuals and organisations that lent their personal or institutional collections relating to the heritage and history of Surabaya city. However the current level of public participation is still not as well as expected. Liauw observed that the two main reasons for this lack of participation are "the lack of information-sharing culture and the sentimental/personal values of heritage-related resources to their owners or copyright holders." Bluntly put, "some people have been making money out of selling duplicates of old photographs and manuscripts".

On the other side, some individuals have been spending a lot of money to acquire old photographs and manuscripts into their personal collections. The money spent in acquiring those resources has become a big obstacle to share the resources—not even their digitised version—with the society. It's also a common knowledge that 'big collectors tend to collect for their own enjoyment". Facing such challenges, Liauw suggested two strategies to help alleviate the problem.

The first strategy is to collaborate with big collectors to hold exhibitions. When we have gained their trust it usually (but not always) is easier to solicit their participations by contributing some of their collections to SM. The second strategy is to "network with other heritage-based organisations to identify individuals with possession of cultural heritage materials". I would like to also add that it is very important to show to stakeholders (especially those big collectors) that the shared resources will benefit the society. Although content acquisition itself has posed many challenges, it is essential that we do not view any IRs projects only as a matter of populating it with the desired contents. McDowell offered another perspective on IRs.

He offered a definition from functional point of view, which defines IRs as:

- An institution-wide service. Faculty members of every academic unit must be able to submit, regardless of departmental affiliation.
- Intended to collect, preserve, and provide access to, among other things, faculty scholarly output in multiple formats.
- Must be actively taking submissions.

Although DI does fulfill the definition and has managed to reach some level of sustainability in content acquisition, it still falls short in providing services and interactions/ collaborations to its users, capitalising on the acquired contents. Regarding future directions for IRs, Furlough suggested that IRs (contents) should be 'integrated into instruction, reference and collection development". Based on the IRs, such as DI, has managed to fulfill its role to "serve as tangible indicators of a university's quality and to demonstrate the scientific, societal, and economic relevance of its research activities." Let's now examine the successfulness of IRs in fulfilling its other role to "provide a critical component in reforming the system of scholarly communication...reasserts control over scholarship by the academy, increases competition and reduces the monopoly power of journals".

FACILITATING SCHOLARLY COMMUNICATIONS

Although reforming scholarly communication system has been one of the 'two strategic issues' that IRs try to address, McDowell concluded that "IR has been relatively unsuccessful in fulfilling 'original' role.' This assertion was supported by his survey, which found that "the percentage of peer-reviewed works—pre-and post-prints, e-journal articles, and e-books—is considerably around 13 per cent". It is obvious IRs has been facing serious challenges in the scholarly communication arena.

There are several reasons why IRs is not the preferred choice for disseminating researches. Aschenbrenner *et al.,* observed that "journal publication patterns are already well in place and they are often (rightly or wrongly) considered the most reliable route to scientific credit". Foster added to that observation by identifying the current established system that "rewards faculty members with tenure and promotion based on their success at getting published in respected scholarly journals" as the main reason why 'professors do not have much incentive to put their material in an experimental online archive'. There are also some faculties "who believe that self-archiving may threaten their rights over their work, their relationship with their favourite publishers, or their status in their disciplinary communities." This trend has led Salo to assert that "libraries whose support for repositories rests purely on hopes of collecting peerreviewed literature would be well-advised not to bother with them".

Another challenge in the scholarly communication arena comes from the fact that most IRs are functioning only as digital resources management system, without 'the more complex services on which users depend'. IRs might be useful and/or powerful for organising and managing digital resources, but "want something that will support the authoring process, not just the finished product". IRs also needs to strive to 'become a natural part of the user's daily work environment'. This might explain why IRs can achieve relative successes in acquiring contents from students, but not from faculties or peer-reviewed publication authors. Salo noticed that slight exceptions might apply for "younger scholars may be attracted to self-archiving as a way to game a prestige system otherwise stacked against them".

Besides all the shortcomings of IRs in the scholarly communication arena, I believe IRs has managed to reduce the total monopoly of conventional journal publishers. Many journal publishers have revised their publishing and copyright policies to allow authors to selfarchive in institutional or subject repositories. The new policies wouldn't have had materialised had it not been because of open access movement (or spirit) embodied in IRs. There are currently open access (book and journal) publishers offering alternatives to conventional publishers. More and more universities and research institutions are jumping into the open access (and IRs) bandwagon by instituting Open Access Mandates in their institutions.

Although in its current state IRs might not achieve big success in (radically) reforming scholarly communication, I believe that IRs has contributed—to certain extent—the efforts in "advancing the positive transformation of scholarly communication over the long term". The same challenge is faced by DI in acquiring journal articles from faculties. DI—as an IRs system—has not yet accommodated any authoring or collaborative process. In its current state, DI acquires contents for eDIMENSI (scientific journal articles) collections through a formal cooperation with the Research Center at PCU. The Research Center is the formal agency at PCU that manages the review, editorial, and publication processes of DIMENSI journals using the Open Journal System (OJS).

The cooperation allows the Library to batch download the newly published articles and feed them into DI. It might be the future direction to merge the two systems into a single platform, which will streamline much of the processes involved in both entities (Research Center and Library) and open up opportunities to create new collaborative features in the future.

FACILITATING COLLABORATIONS

An important aspect of IRs that is often overlooked is its potential as a collaborative platform for the campus communities. If we agree that IRs is, as Lynch stated, "a set of services that a university offers to the members of its community for the management and dissemination of digital materials created by the institution and its community members" then academic libraries have an invaluable asset in their hands.

This asset has a functions and/or roles that span traditional boundaries of campus communities, units, and academic disciplines. Due to this nature, academic libraries that implement and manage IRs will soon discover themselves introduced to a rich variety of local contents produced by different campus communities covering a wide range of academic disciplines. Cross-pollination or cross-fertilisation of knowledge is a natural consequence of exposures to such rich and diverse local contents. Contents produced by a campus community can be re-used as learning resources by other campus communities. Marketing or promotional efforts can be conducted by academic libraries to introduce these local contents to all academic departments and provide insights on possibilities of their uses for each department.

Libraries can also expand features in their IRs to be able to link to e-learning systems used on campus. The linking will enable students and faculties to access our local contents directly from the e-learning systems that they are using for teaching and learning, thus increasing exposures of the contents to various campus communities. These efforts will expose local contents from a specific campus community to a wider audience.

Thematic exhibitions will also provide rich exposures for students, who otherwise would have been 'confined' to their particular field of studies. The experience will enrich students' learning experience. Thematic exhibitions of local contents can sometimes create unique opportunities for inter-disciplinary conversations. Liauw told of an interesting story as an example of how thematic exhibitions can create such conversations.

A thematic onsite exhibition featuring photography documentary of Sedulur Sikep—an ethnic minority in Central Java, Indonesia—was held in 2006, displaying works of a student from Visual Communication Design Department. The exhibition sparked interests from other academic disciplines to conduct other researches on the ethnic minority. An English Department faculty was interested to conduct further study on the linguistic aspects of the ethnic minority. Another faculty from Interior Design Department expressed interests in doing further studies on the ornamental design on the ethnic's settlements.

This example shows that academic libraries should treat their local contents and exhibition spaces as assets to be used to facilitate collaborations and conversations across academic disciplines. Wider collaborations among different campus units and academic departments can be facilitated when academic libraries capitalise on their local contents in IRs to reach out to the society. Academic libraries can create and carry out various programmes and activities jointly with other campus communities. Surabaya Memory (SM) provided a good example on this aspect. Digital resources in SM have been used as part of the teaching and learning process by Architecture Department, Tourism and Leisure Management Department, and Hotel Management Department.

However SM has also become a collaborative platform for PCU Library and other campus units to reach out to the society in Surabaya city. Every May (anniversary of Surabaya) SM conducts thematic exhibitions in a mall in Surabaya. During the exhibition, which usually lasts four to ten days, various competitions, cultural performances, and heritage walks are held to celebrate the city's anniversary.

All these programmes and activities have been made possible by the collaborations between the Library and various academic departments. The Event Management course at Hotel Management Department has been using SM as real world projects for its students. The students are assigned to help the Library in preparing and supervising the exhibition, looking for sponsors, creating events and performances during the exhibition, etc.

The Cultural Tourism course at Tourism and Leisure Management Department has also been using SM as real world projects for its students by conducting heritage walks throughout the year for campus communities as well as the general public. IRs can also serve as collaborative platform to build networks with various parties outside the university boundaries. SM has been functioning as a networking tool for PCU. Various co-operations and collaborations have been initiated between PCU communities and outside parties through SM. Furthermore SM has served as a common platform for campus communities at PCU to reach out to the society. It is obvious from that IRs can facilitate collaborations if academic libraries are willing to go beyond merely populating their IRs with digital contents. Collaborations with various campus communities will strengthen the libraries' roles on campus and help libraries tremendously in advocating their services to the campus communities. Libraries can even increase the institutional visibility of the whole institution with their IRs projects.

FACILITATING INSTITUTIONAL VISIBILITY

Academic libraries have always contributed to the institutional visibility of their host institutions. They have unconsciously played 'silent' marketing role, promoting their host institutions in the process. Their unique nature as public spaces has allowed them to be visited by various members of the community, inside and outside of campus boundaries. Libraries are the very few institutions in the world where ordinary people would feel comfortable to visit even though they don't have any membership or institutional affiliation. Academic libraries should capitalise on this aspect to facilitate institutional visibility. Before the advent of the Internet and DLs/IRs, this would mean providing their traditional collections and services, and physical spaces to the campus communities and the society. The Internet, open access movement, and DLs/IRs have provided new opportunities for academic libraries to raise their contributions to the facilitating of institutional visibility of their host institutions. Digital contents in IRs should be provided freely to enable a wider dissemination to the global audience, which in turn will translate into a significant increase in institutional visibility. There is no longer any physical barrier that limits the scope of the dissemination of the IRs' contents as in physical library collections. This is also the experience of DI. Table shows the web access profile for 'petra.ac.id' domain.

Where Visitors Go on Petra.ac.id.

Table. 7.4 Domain Profile for 'petra.ac.id' from Alexa

Subdomain	Per Cent of Site Traffic
Digilib.petra.ac.id	59.6
Dewey.petra.ac.id	20.5
Petra.ac.id	5.1
Genesis.petra.ac.id	4.3
Careercenter.petra.ac.id	1.8
Puslit2.petra.ac.id	1.1
Fportfolio.petra.ac.id	1.1
It.petra.ac.id	0.7

Puslit.petra.ac.id	0.7
Communication.petra.ac.id	0.4
John.petra.ac.id	0.4

This is a very significant contribution that PCU Library–through DI–has made to the overall 'Internet marketing' of the university. The access statistics from Alexa is confirmed by the weblog of the DI server as shown in table. More opportunities to facilitate institutional visibility can be gained when we share metadata of our digital contents with other IRs. This can be achieved by utilising the OAIPMH or even a 'low-tech' approach by exporting the metadata and exchange them using spreadsheet application such as Microsoft Excel.

Table. 7.5 Web Access Statistics of Desa Informasi

Month	Unique Visitors	Number of Visits	Pages	Hits	Bandwidth
Sep-09	160,097	355,177	3,125,802	6,686,167	191.36 GB
Oct 2009	224,082	607,877	5,305,997	11,296,525	315.91 GB
Nov 2009	215,583	563,184	5,005,537	10,664,877	325.83 GB
Dec 2009	201,370	510,646	4,581,746	9,751,878	283.93 GB
Jan-10	212,415	538,796	4,538,643	9,769,348	295.05 GB
Feb-10	197,727	450,327	4,293,240	8,789,435	360.64 GB
Mar-10	247,483	615,001	5,058,876	10,573,688	431.89 GB
Apr-10	237,076	577,638	4,845,910	10,138,585	454.83 GB
May 2010	207,424	484,272	4,225,088	8,831,741	436.39 GB
Jun-10	199,156	454,782	3,975,456	8,281,444	496.72 GB
Jul-10	174,474	360,614	3,175,481	6,503,735	398.71 GB
Aug 2010	157,810	317,685	2,804,185	5,897,145	338.25 GB
	2,434,697	5,835,999	50,935,961	107,184,568	4,329,51GB

This approach is being utilised by DI while an upgrade to an OAI-PMH compliant system is still in progress. The Indonesian Ministry of National Education under its Directorate General of Higher Education has launched a collaborative programme to create a 'union catalog' of metadata for local contents from higher education institutions across Indonesia called Garuda. Networking opportunities like this provide increased visibility of our IRs and host institution. Rankings by independent organisations that measure web sites and online resources provide additional incentives for developing IRs.

One of them is the Ranking Web of World Universities that measures world universities' commitment to open access by looking at digital contents on their web sites. Using certain methodology it has managed to rank world universities based on several parameters. DI opens up its digital contents to be indexed by Google, which has enabled Webometrics to measure the 'Size' and 'Rich Files' stored in DI. Webometrics rankings are important for us in Indonesia since, they are being used by Directorate General of Higher Education as one of several metrics to measure performances of Indonesian higher education institutions. PCU has been ranked #5 along with big state universities in Indonesia. A good rank will surely contribute to the increased visibility of the host institutions. This fact strengthens the assertion that IRs serve as one of "meaningful indicators of an institution's academic quality ... thus increasing the institution's visibility, status, and public value".

DEVELOPING AND USING A GUIDE TO ASSESS LEARNING RESOURCE QUALITY IN EDUCATIONAL DIGITAL LIBRARIES

The democratisation of content creation via ubiquitous Internet tools and infrastructure has fueled an explosion of user-generated digital content in the commercial and educational markets. Federal agencies in the United States, such as the National Science Foundation, are actively seeking ways to integrate teachers and learners into the education cyber-infrastructure. The overall purpose of this education cyberinfrastructure is to connect people with information and with web-based tools to improve productivity, teaching, and learning. By connecting teachers and learners with tools, they become co-creators of educational content. Educational digital libraries, part of this cyberinfrastructure, have been created as places to deposit and disseminate educational content, which often takes the form of online learning resources of varying levels of granularity.

Digital library content can be created easily and deposited rapidly, placing it outside the peer review processes typically employed by publishers and professional societies, but it is unclear whether teachers are using high quality online learning resources in the classroom. To date, educational digital library developers, catalogers, teachers and school administrators have depended on one or a combination of the following proxies to establish an imprimatur of content quality: the reputation and oversight of a funding organisation, the credentials of the content creator, or the collection development policies of specific digital libraries.

However, the definition of 'quality'for organisations like those often reflects internal policies and goals, resulting in reviews or judgements that are not comparable across institutions. Further blurring the boundaries between creator-reviewer, teacher-learner and publisherconsumer, many sites employing user ratings and comment tools, such as YouTube, Flickr, iTunesU, and ccMixter provide an alternative to the evolving education cyber-infrastructure, creating a rich and diverse environment for disseminating user-generated educational content. Most educational digital libraries do not rely on even a quasi-review for assessing the quality of the content created for, or by, their users as the above sites do.

However, in the omnipresent climate of accountability within the U.S., K-12 education system at the federal, state and local levels, education digital libraries are being challenged to prove their value. For these reasons, it is useful, if not necessary, to develop a method to review the quality of online education resources. And, since, social networking tools make sharing a by-product of content creation, it is necessary to develop a standardised set of measures that can be employed across a range of education digital library environments while leveraging existing and emerging social and technical networks to enrich, facilitate, and automate the review process.

This stage describes the development of a guide to assess the quality of educational learning resources within the context of the Instructional Architect, a web-based content-authoring tool for K-12 teachers in the United States. We describe the motivation for developing this Quality Guide, the process for creating it by synthesising the rubrics of other education digital libraries, and the results of testing and using the Guide with K-12 teachers in the context of professional development workshops.

Analyses of its usability and reliability indicate that the Quality Guide influences how teachers design instructional activities using online learning resources. But, defining 'quality' remains a difficult task since, the perception of quality is dependent on a reviewer's, or user's, purpose for the learning resources and context of their use. Over the past 10-15 years, as part of the many global initiatives created to provide access to online educational resources, educational digital libraries in the United States have been developed for K-12 and higher education audiences with support from state and federal agencies: from private foundations, and from universities.

These institutions funded projects create, or provide access to, curricula that integrates online educational resources and training programmes to empower teachers to incorporate learning technologies into their daily preparation and practice and, ultimately, to design their own learning resources. Educational digital library developers have gathered online learning resources of varying levels of granularity (*e.g.*, from images to entire lessons) and of varying sources of authorship (*e.g.*, grant-funded subject matter experts; K-12 teachers; graduate students) into central online portals to enable discovery and re-use by other educators. While traditional libraries use collection development plans to guide acquisitions that are based on knowledge of their users, educational digital libraries acquire resources created as a result of projects with museums, practicing teachers, researchers and from Internet users.

The challenge is to balance collecting and providing access to many online learning resources while maintaining a level of resource quality, cataloging, and curation that distinguishes educational digital libraries from generic Internet search engines and non-educational social software. However, it is often as difficult for teachers and learners to define quality as it is for the courts to define pornography. As U.S., Supreme Court Justice Potter Steward once noted, 'I know it when I see it." The problem (or the solution?) lies in the perspective of users who are confronted with a variety of resources of indeterminate origin.

For school administrators, teachers, and learners, a high quality resource could consist of an entire lesson that meets several state standards; a web-based animation that accurately depicts a science concept. Grappling with the idea of 'quality', several education digital libraries have already created rubrics to assess their content. As we tried to apply these criteria to the content in the Instructional Architect, we observed that portions of each rubric were applicable in different settings, and other portions were specific to each digital library with little room for re-use outside of the original context. As such, our goals were:

- To synthesise the various dimensions of existing rubrics in order to identify a standardised set of criteria that could potentially be used by any digital library with online educational resources; and
- To create a guide that could be used to assess the quality of materials in the Instructional Architect projects.

This stage briefly describes our process for developing the standardised set of assessment criteria; evaluating its utility and usability with middle school science and math teachers; developing a Quality Guide for use with Instructional Architect projects; testing its reliability; and, exploring how the Guide could foster teachers' skills in designing learning resources.

PREVIOUS RESEARCH

Many education digital library builders have developed rubrics to help assess the quality of online educational resources generated by teachers, faculty and learners. However, the motivations and methods for implementing the rubrics vary as do the implied assumptions about the value of the results for each education digital library. Established publishing houses and professional societies institute peer review processes to maintain a reputation for producing quality publications thereby increasing subscriptions and membership.

For newly-funded education digital libraries, under pressure to prove their value, rubrics and a process to measure quality, were created to first establish a reputation with users. Similarly, other education digital libraries used rubrics to support access to high quality resources in a digital library or repository because use of a collection development policy for inclusion of quality resources adds value and buy-in from peer reviewers and users. Still other sites developed a rubric to guide authors in creating high quality online resources by gathering feedback from target users.

The methods by which education digital libraries collected data using rubrics and how they used that information also varied. Muramatsu and Agogino used a rubric to gather feedback from targeted users to inform collection development, while Recker, Walker, and Lawless gathered data through automated mechanisms to provide teachers with suggestions based on resources they had previously viewed and used. Establishing peer review panels and processes was not a *de facto* choice for every education digital library. Enlisting users-as-builders, or reviewers-as-builders, is a characteristic of the grass-roots environment in which many education digital libraries evolved over the last decade in the U.S.

However, many digital library developers found that gathering reviews from users was difficult, though providing incentives, in the form of awards or other methods was one way to increase acceptance and adoption of the rubric and review process and of the education digital library in general. The process of creating and testing an assessment rubric can be time consuming. Many rubric creators believe it is important to map out stakeholders and end-users, review previous work by other digital libraries and learn how to gather data. Testing a rubric with users, for formative evaluation, further refines the rubric, yielding usability information as well as real time feedback from target users which ultimately assists with the process of implementing the rubric with a larger group of users.

CONTEXT

The Instructional Architect

The Instructional Architect is a simple, web-based authoring tool designed to help K-12 teachers find, design, and use online learning resources in their classrooms. When using the Instructional Architect, teachers search for and save links to online learning resources from the Web and educational digital libraries such as the National Science Digital Library. Resources that can be linked include online content, RSS feeds and podcasts. Once resources are gathered users then create 'Instructional Architect projects' that contain instructional objectives, activities, and assessments. The resources are either embedded into the project or link out to web-based resources. In this way, teachers create Instructional Architect projects that customise resources to their local context. Figure shows an Instructional Architect project and an accompanying resource.

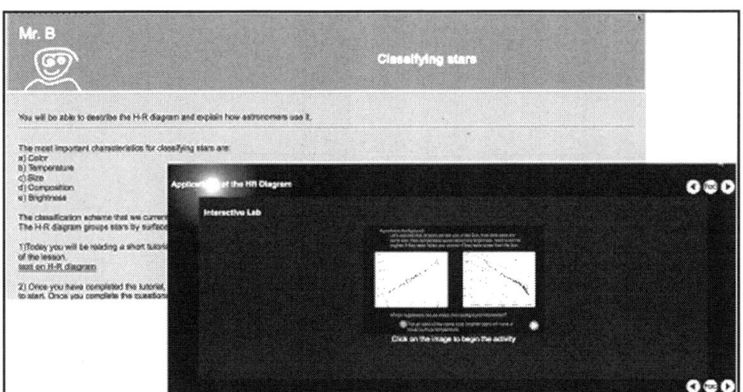

Fig. Example of an Instructional Architect Project Created by Mr. B and Related Resource

Initially the majority of users were K-12 teachers in the U.S., who participated in professional development workshops from 2005-2009. Recently, the Instructional Architect system has garnered more widespread usage and spread 'virally' to teachers not directly attending these workshops. Table 7.6 shows statistics on Instructional Architect usage and growth in the number of Instructional Architect projects and resources over the last 12 months.

Table. Instructional Architect Usage Data

Data	N	12-month growth in Per cent
Registered users	5,300	23
Instructional Architect projects created	11,500	37
Online learning resources used	52,100	67
Visits to Instructional Architect project (since, 8/2006)	1 million	64

Before any of the abundant Instructional Architect projects created by users can be ingested into educational digital libraries, like the National Science Digital Library, to become part of the education cyberinfrastructure, they need to be evaluated for quality. To support this outcome, the Instructional Architect projects must be reviewed with a rubric that is reliable across multiple sites, a process that is scalable across the thousands of IA projects, and that has useful results for end-users, reviewers, and digital library developers.

METHOD

Synthesising Existing Rubrics and Creating the Quality Guide

Following the recommendations for establishing a rubric to assess content, we began with a literature review in the disciplines of computer science, library and information science, education, and digital libraries. We selected only articles that included or referenced rubrics used to review online educational resources.

The literature review yielded articles with descriptions of 12 rubrics. In keeping with our first goal, our initial plan was to identify review criteria at the most granular level and then do a frequency analysis to identify broad topics that applied across criteria. These would then become the foundational criteria. Accordingly, we un-bundled the rubrics and identified over 200 review criteria, some of which included only one or two words and sometimes no definition.

However, when conducting our frequency analysis, we found it difficult to group similar review criteria because:

- None of the rubrics used a standard vocabulary for their review criteria;
- The definitions for criteria contained multiple concepts that defied easy categorisation; and

- Some criteria were so contextualised to their site that they became virtually meaningless when viewed out of context from the whole rubric.

These factors also made it difficult to create topic areas before and after the frequency analysis. Given the challenges of our initial approach, we revised our methods and used a card sort technique. Card sorts are typically employed as a user-centered design approach for assessing web site structure. This process has participants sort a series of cards, each labelled with a piece of content or functionality into groups that make sense to them.

This technique allows input from several experts, with the consensus between them resolving ambiguities in and across the review criteria. In preparing the initial list of over 200 review criteria for sorting, we realised that some of the most granular criteria, especially those without definitions, would prove difficult to sort, appearing as so much noise to study participants. Therefore, we culled the list to include only criteria from the literature that included a definition and that would make sense when read outside the context of its original use. Our intention was not to represent criteria as they had been used within a particular review process, but to use the criteria as presented in the literature. The result was that 104 review criteria remained for use in the card sort exercise. The card sort methodology recommends using seven to ten participants. Our sorting exercise included 10 participants who were graduate students, professors from instructional technology and education, and academic librarians. We presented the participants with a spreadsheet containing the review criteria, criteria definitions, and the source rubric or citation.

We chose the 'open sort' method and asked participants to sort the review criteria into groups of their own choosing within a spreadsheet and to provide their own titles for the groups. Participants were allowed to place criteria in more than one group as long as they indicated which criteria-group pairing represented their highest priority. Each of the ten participants created an average of nearly 13 groups into which they individually sorted the 104 review criteria. One participant sorted criteria into multiple groups but did not indicate a top priority, so rather than guessing at the intention, the results were not included. Ultimately, we analysed the nine result sets containing an average of 11 groups per participant. A detailed analysis yielded six elements from the 11 groups. These became the foundational set of criteria, which were standardised to the point where they could be used by any digital library with online education resources, thereby accomplishing our first goal.

Table. 7.7 Standardised Set of Criteria with Definitions

Standardised Criteria	Definitions and R eferences
Interface Design and Accessibility	The resource is attractive. The resource is easy to navigate. The resource contains no advertising.

	The resource contains links that work. The resource is designed to accommodate disabled and mobile learners.
Technical Reliability	The resource uses multimedia that work. The resource clearly identifies the supporting technical resources required. The resource contains help features.
Content	Resource content is accurate. Resource content is complete. Resource content is impartial. Resource content is clearly written. Resources content is maintained.
Pedagogy	The resource is engaging. The reource is motivating. The resource is interactive. The resources includes assessment(s) (Ohio Resource Center). The resource provides feedback. The resource supports learners proceeding at their own pace. The resource supports introductory, reinforcing, or summative activities.
Administrative	The resource contains direct and explicit links to state or national educational teaching standards. The resource contains information about ist author or creator, e-mail, site domain, role. The resource is described by current metadata.
Other	The resource requires a fee for access. The resources overall rating/confidence level.

Table shows the six elements, or standardised criteria, developed by study participants in the card sort exercise. Corresponding definitions and the references for them are also displayed.

☆☆☆☆☆	Interface Design Definition: Dynamic, Visually Pleasing Aesthetics, Standards, Accessibility, Navigation, Good User Interface
☆☆☆☆☆	Accessibility Definition: Technical Reliability, Reusability,Usability Design, Reliability, Adaptability ADA
☆☆☆☆☆	Content Definition: Accuracy, Organization, Quality, Completeness, Currency, Value, Interdisciplinary
☆☆☆☆☆	Pedagogy Definition: Instruction Methods, Design Methods, Learning Goals, Anticipated Outcomes, Motivation, Engagement
☆☆☆☆☆	Administrative Definition: Authority, Authorship, Metadata, Advertising, Credibility
☆☆☆☆☆	Overall Rating

Fig. Prototype of Foundational Criteria and Definitions

The definitions (*e.g.*, Resource content is accurate) are statements from the original 12 rubrics that participants associated with the standardised criteria. Using these foundational criteria, we then began to address the second goal of creating a guide that could be used to assess the quality of materials in the Instructional Architect projects.

Figure shows the prototype of the foundational criteria and definitions in beta form before it was designed to be more user-friendly and visually appealing. This subsequently became the first version of the Instructional Architect Quality Guide, and included five Likert scale star ratings for each criterion, as these are widely used by rating systems, and less-detailed definitions of criteria.

Testing the Instructional Architect Quality Guide

Twenty-eight participants were recruited to test the first version of the Instructional Architect Quality Guide. They were part of a cohort of U.S., K-12 teachers in an online graduate programme, and they completed required activities as part of an online course.

Testing the Quality Guide was directed by the following research questions:

- What is the student's view of using technology in a classroom.
- How do teachers assess an online educational resource before and after using the Quality Guide.
- Using the Quality Guide, how helpful are conducting and receiving peer reviews for the student and,
- What changes should be made to the Instructional Architect Quality Guide based on student use and feedback.

Data Sources

The participants took part in an online learning module in the context of learning how to use the Instructional Architect and the Quality Guide. They completed pre-and post-online surveys, which used a combination of open-ended and Likert-scale questions. Surveys measured the extent of participants' experience and classroom practice in using online educational resources; their attitudes about online educational resources and technology in general and their use in a classroom; and, strategies for evaluating an online educational resource.

Within the learning module, participants were placed in small groups of 4-5 participants, and they evaluated one another's Instructional Architect projects using the Quality Guide. Conversations about these evaluations were posted in a BlackBoard discussion forum and collected for analysis by the researchers. Lastly, participants wrote a reflection paper describing their experience using the Instructional Architect, how they used online educational resources in an instructional situation, difficulties and successes in designing and implementing their project, what they learned by reviewing their peers' Instructional Architect projects and by using the Quality Guide, and how they could improve their Instructional Architect project.

Reliability and Improvements

Version one of the Quality Guide was tested for reliability in order to answer research question four. Peer ratings of Instructional Architect projects using the Guide, provided by the students in the online graduate course, and were used for this analysis. The Quality Guide criteria were scored on a scale of 0-4, where zero or one star is low and four or five stars is high (*e.g.*, very clear). Means and standard deviations were run for each question.

Number	Criteria	Rating				
1	Content Accuracy	Very Inaccurarte	Somewhat Inaccurate	Not Enough Information	Somewhat Accurate	Very Accurate
		Comments:				
2	Text Clarity	Very Unclear	Somewhat Unclear	Not Enough Information	Somewhat Clear	Very Clear
		Comments:				
3	Links in Project	No Links Work	Some Links don't Work	Not Enough Information	Some Links Work	All Links Work
		Comments:				
4	Project Completeness: Includes the state Standard Learning Goal, Assesment, etc.	Very Incomplete	Somewhat Incomplete	Not Enough Information	Somewhat Complete	very Complete
		Comments:				
5	The Project:(Circle One)	a. Provides a Resorce List b. Teacher a Concept c. Reinforces a Concepts d. Provider a Summary of Content With a Learning Activity e. Don't Know f. Does Somthing else (Describe below)				
6	Overall Rating of the Project	Meets no criteria	Meets Very Little Criteria	Meets Some Criteria	Meets Criteria	Exceed Criteria
		Comments:				

Fig. First Version of the Instructional Architect Quality Guide

Criteria one through four and six of the Quality Guide were analysed using an intra-class correlation. Criteria five was not analysed as it asks for a classification on what the Instructional Architect project is doing (*e.g.*, teaching a new concept, reinforcing a concept, etc). Table shows the intraclass correlation values for each question analysed. A close look at the data shows that the teachers generally rated their peers at an average of 2 or more (3 or more stars on the Quality Guide) for any of the criteria on the Guide. This could possibly be attributed to the fact that educators as a whole tend to provide high ratings for their peer, a phenomenon observed in prior work.

Table. Means and Standard Deviations for Criteria 1-4, 6 of the Instructional Architect Quality Guide

S.No.	Criteria	Mean	Standard Deviation
1	Content accuracy	2.50	1.13
2	Text clarity	2.34	0.98
3	Links in project	3.30	0.83
4	Project completeness	2.14	1.50
6	Overall rating	3.22	1.84

As a result of the high ratings, the full range of the scale was not used, and slight departures were magnified in the intraclass correlation. The negative values indicate that there was more variation between projects than there was between raters. As is shown in the low intraclass correlation, agreement on those ratings was never high, and in most cases was non-existent.

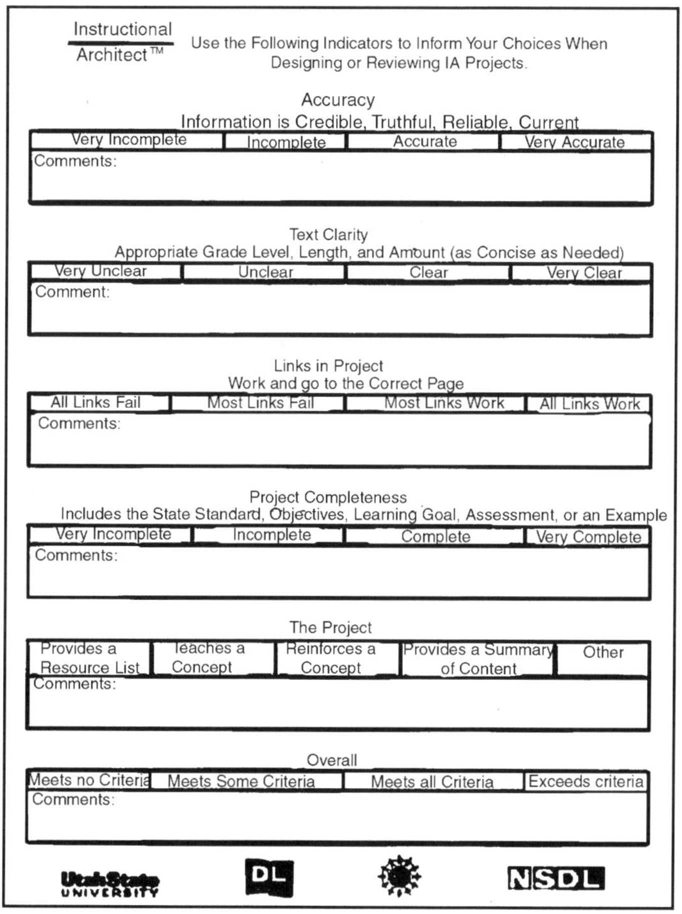

Instructional Architect™ Use the Following Indicators to Inform Your Choices When Designing or Reviewing IA Projects.

Accuracy
Information is Credible, Truthful, Reliable, Current

Very Incomplete	Incomplete	Accurate	Very Accurate

Comments:

Text Clarity
Appropriate Grade Level, Length, and Amount (as Concise as Needed)

Very Unclear	Unclear	Clear	Very Clear

Comment:

Links in Project
Work and go to the Correct Page

All Links Fail	Most Links Fail	Most Links Work	All Links Work

Comments:

Project Completeness
Includes the State Standard, Objectives, Learning Goal, Assessment, or an Example

Very Incomplete	Incomplete	Complete	Very Complete

Comments:

The Project

Provides a Resource List	Teaches a Concept	Reinforces a Concept	Provides a Summary of Content	Other

Comments:

Overall

Meets no Criteria	Meets Some Criteria	Meets all Criteria	Exceeds criteria

Comments:

Utah State University DL NSDL

Fig. Final Version of the Instructional Architect Quality Guide

Table. Intraclass Correlation (ICC) Values for Criteria 1-4, 6 of the Instructional Architect Quality Guide

S.No.	Criteria	Intraclass Correlation
1	Content accuracy	0
2	Text clarity	-0.129
3	Links in project	0.031
4	Project completeness	-0.89
6	Overall rating	-0.129

The reliability analysis suggests that the scale needs more explanation for each item and that the scale should encompass either a broader range or a dichotomous rating (yes or no). Improvements made to the Quality Guide as a result of this testing included adding more detailed definitions of the review criteria, re-arranging the order of criteria, and modifying scoring instructions. As a result of this testing, improvements were made to create the final version of the Quality Guide, which is currently used to inform and support individual teachers as they create Instructional Architect projects.

RESULTS

Research question one used data from the pre-and post-survey Likert items. Effect sizes were calculated on questions relating to participants' attitude, experience with and use of online educational resources and technology in their classrooms in order to understand changes in participants' pedagogical choices and activities in their classrooms. An effect size (dw) shows a magnitude of change and is considered small at 0.2 detectable by an expert looking closely at the phenomenon, medium at 0.5, and large at 0.8 detectable by an untrained observer. Larger effect sizes equate to larger impacts due to the intervention. Small, but positive changes, statistically significant at $p < 0.05$, were shown from the pre-test to the post-test as teachers reported that they knew how to effectively teach with technology in the classroom ($dw = 0.28$, $p < 0.05$), and they knew how to effectively use technology in their classroom ($dw = 0.42$, $p < 0.05$). From this we know that after participating in the learning module, teachers began to overcome initial barriers of using technology in the classroom and could now focus on making better pedagogical decisions about the type of learning resources they could create. We then used a qualitative analysis to address research question two with the understanding that participants had learned how to use online educational resources.

Using a constant comparative analysis, data from the reflection papers, discussion boards, and one question in the pre-and post-survey were mapped into themes and analysed. Participants reported in the pre-survey that when evaluating online educational resources they looked for fit with the curriculum, accuracy, ease of use, currency, text readability, and recommendations by others. After completing this course module, participants added in their post-survey comments that they looked for: content quality, distractions on the resource pages, credibility of the site, and engagement.

Many of the criteria they added were items listed in the Quality Guide. Thus, it appeared that use of the Quality Guide helped refine participants' approach to designing online learning resources, in the form of Instructional Architect projects. To answer research question three, the comments from the discussion boards in Blackboard where participants posted their evaluations of their peers' Instructional Architect projects were used. Some participants commented on the readability and text clarity of the Instructional Architect project, and many caught spelling errors. One participant commented after receiving some feedback, "I have learned that having a peer read through my projects can be very valuable. They catch mistakes that I do not see." Overall, 53 per cent of the participants reported that providing and receiving feedback from their peers via reviews was valuable. Two additional themes surfaced from analyses of the discussion boards during the process of peer evaluation that related to re-use of other teachers' Instructional Architect projects and ideas. *First,* participants asked if they could use an Instructional Architect project they reviewed, or said they planned to use it in their classroom. The *second* theme was that participants learned what others had done and wanted to implement the same idea in their project. A participant commented that, "Completing a peer review gives us an opportunity to see other creations and improve our programmes as we see fit."

The *final* data collection point included participants' reflection papers. Participants were asked to report on their instructional situation, successes and difficulties, what they learned from their peers and using the Quality Guide, and how they could improve their Instructional Architect project. Three areas of learning were repeatedly reported in the reflection papers: what they learned by reviewing peer work; what they learned for their own work; and, the value of re-using Instructional Architect projects. Similar ideas were also expressed throughout the discussion boards and survey answers.

PROMOTION AND DEVELOPMENT OF PUBLIC LIBRARY SYSTEM

STATE LIBRARY AGENCIES

Continuing education for professional and support staff in all the professions has been receiving increasing emphasis in recent years. The need to update current practice through new knowledge and insight of societal conditions and client needs has had its impact in the library and information science fields. The advances in automation and technology, the proliferation of knowledge, and the growing recognition of the need to provide access to the rapid delivery of information in many formats have given priority emphasis to continuing library education as a means of responding to the changes taking place in our society. State library agencies have a continuing responsibility for a planned approach to the development of library and information services in each state. This planned approach includes the need for the continuing education of library personnel to meet changing service demands.

This article reviews the background for the continuing education role of the state library agency, the development of continuing education for libraries, the implications of these developments, current programmes in progress, and trends which may indicate future change. Historically, state library agencies have had the responsibility for statewide library development, particularly public library development. The provision of advice, assistance and consultant services has been one of the primary means employed. Included in the advisory activities were the conducting of workshops and other educational and staff development programmes. State library agencies having responsibility for school library development as units of state departments of education carried on similar programmes and activities to improve school libraries. Following the enactment of the federal *Library Services Act* (LSA), state library agencies moved into a new era of growth and influence. The requirement to develop state plans and the attendant emphasis on establishing libraries, creating library systems and extending library services created the need for staff development and continuing education activities as a major component in the achievement of desired objectives. A U.S. Office of Education study of state library extension resources and services compares the data from 1955-56 prior to LSA with the re- sources and services of state library agencies in 1960-61. For the purposes of this article, the report of consultant activity and training programmes during this period is of interest. Forty-eight states reported 16,466 field visits compared to 6544 in 1955-56; 44 states held or sponsored some 1600 training programmes for over 56,000 persons from 1956 to 1961.

These pro- grams served professional (36 percent) and non-professional (22 per-cent) personnel and public library trustees (26 percent). The responsibility of state library agencies for the planning and ad- ministration of federal funds under the Library Services Act of 1956 and the *Library Services and Construction Act* (LSCA) of 1964 gave added impetus to national documents and conferences concerned with improving the capabilities of state library agencies. These reports emphasize a stronger focus on goals, purposes and long-range plans with the attendant need for highly skilled consultants and related staff development activities in the field in order to implement the statewide programme. All state library agencies view continuing education and consultant services as a major responsibility of the agency. In a recent survey, about one-half of the state library agencies considered the continuing education responsibility to be a shared responsibility and not solely the responsibility or of the state library agency. In recent years national activities of major importance have contributed to an increased awareness of continuing education responsibility and to an increase in planned activities of state library agencies. In the regional hearing conducted in 1972 by the National Commission on *Libraries and Information Science* (NCLIS),one of the identified priorities was the availability of continuing education for the development and maintenance of competencies which are needed to deliver the library and information services required by the nation. Subsequently, NCLIS funded a study in 1973 to recommend a nationwide programme of continuing education which culminated in *Continuing Library and Information Science Education.*

This report made recommendations which eventually led to the formation of the *Continuing Library Education Network Exchange* (CLENE). The NCLIS report outlines the development of library continuing education and comments on the necessity for continuing life- long learning.' Based on responses from the field, an operational definition of continuing education was developed which includes the following:

- The implication that lifelong learning is necessary to keep the individual up to date,
- Assurance that the individual carries the basic responsibility for his/ her own development,
- Diversification to new areas of interest, and
- Involvement in educational activities beyond those considered necessary for entrance into the field.

In comparison with other professions, the librarians felt that continuing education should be pro- vided for all levels of personnel, not solely professional, and that it not be limited to improved competence for the job held now or aspired to in the future. In its plan for continuing education, the report suggests roles and responsibilities of the individual agencies and organizations in order to coordinate efforts, including those of the individual employee, the employing library, the state library agency, the library schools, and state, regional and national associations. Major responsibilities outlined for the state library agencies include coordination of continuing education programmes on a statewide basis, identification of continuing education needs of the state, provision of a link between librarians in the state and national and regional plans, and the appointment of a continuing education coordinator on the state library agency staff. The other major responsibility is three- fold: the planning, implementation and evaluation of statewide continuing education programmes based on identified needs.

These initial efforts to provide a suggested outline of responsibilities continued to receive attention through CLENE as a newly formed national organization. State library agencies which joined CLENE as sustaining members, as well as the state library agency directors and continuing education staff members, influenced some of the priorities of CLENE. In 1976 CLENE received a USOE, Title II-B grant to provide an "Extended Institute to Train

State Library Agency.Personnel to Implement and/or Strengthen Statewide Systems of Continuing Education for Library/Information/Media Personnel." The workshop phase of the institute was held November 7-13, 1976, at the Illinois State Library.

Continuing education personnel from twenty-five state library agencies met to develop planning and implementation skills in continuing education. For participating states the institute spurred development of statewide coordinated planning among providers of continuing education in the state. During this period several regional consortia of states were formed with a primary concern for continuing education. CELS grew out of a survey of members of six state library associations where the need for Continuing education was strongly expressed. State library agencies are major financial contributors to this programme.

The *Western Interstate Commission on Higher Education* (WICHE) had a major continuing education component funded in large part by five state library agencies. The Western Council of State Libraries has succeeded WICHE in this regional effort. In preparation for this article, state library agencies were asked to report on activities in needs assessment, programmes in continuing education, the extent of cooperation of other agencies in planning and implementing continuing education programmes, recent changes and improvements in state library agency continuing education programmes, and trends and new developments in continuing education. Forty responses to the questionnaire were received. State library replies indicate that all state library agencies have a responsibility for continuing education. Several have stated that the agency statutes define this responsibility but most suggest that agency planning documents cover these functions.

Cooperation with other continuing education agencies is extensive; 63 percent of the respondents work closely with state library associations, and 34 percent with library schools. State universities, higher education commissions, state departments of education, and other agencies were also listed. State staff are active participants on the continuing education committees of other agencies, and either library associations or the state library agency has formed a continuing education committee for coordinated planning and programmes. The formation of continuing education planning committees representing all types of libraries is a recent development in many states. These committees are in various stages of the development of guidelines, policy statements or state plans for coordinated continuing education programmes. Examples of plans underway can be found in Illinois, Michigan, Ohio and Louisiana. Oklahoma reported the formation of a state committee in 1978, Maryland in 1977.

Pennsylvania is planning a special project in 1978 with a director and task force to develop continuing education coordination. States participating in the Western Council of State Libraries and CELS are the primary planners for the continuing *ed*ucation programme of the regional consortia. Coordinated planning appears to be one of the more significant activities now underway. Continuing education needs were identified by the majority through surveys and questionnaires at state, regional or local levels;consultations with local staffs and "perceived changes in the library climate," evaluation of current programmes and of new national library trends and programmes were also cited. The responses did not indicate the types of libraries involved in the needs assessment process. The influence of continuing education committees and recently formed task forces has not yet been felt to any great degree in the development of continuing education programmes as reported. The continuing education programmes sponsored by state library agencies are directed primarily to public library staffs, although programme offerings to reach a broader group were listed. All respondents listed public library directors and public library professional staff as participants; twenty-six listed non-professional public library staffs. However, twenty- one listed academic librarians;twelve, school librarians;twelve, multi-type participants; and two listed institutional and special library staffs.

Principal topics in continuing education programmes covered a wide range including copyright, networking, automation, planning, management, public relations and audiovisual materials. However, over one-third of the respondents offered basic or refresher courses to public library staffs in such areas as reference, children's services, storytelling, and young adult services. A few states mentioned law materials, oral history, censorship, and government documents. Workshops on community needs and development of special services to disadvantaged, senior citizens and other groups reflect the outreach programme priorities of some states. Wisconsin reported a continuing education programme for public library and staff through the University of Wisconsin using the *Education Telephone Network* (ETN). Once a month for about two hours, several topics are discussed by a group or panel. Local libraries may purchase sets of materials related to the programme. Topics covered in the last two years include:

- Networks,
- Censorship,
- School-public library cooperation,
- The independent adult learner,
- Deaf awareness, and
- Service to special groups.

Alaska and Hawaii reported the use of video cassettes to bring continuing education programmes to remote areas, and West Virginia reported that the capability now exists there to provide this form of continuing education programming. Frequently, continuing education programmes sponsored by the state library agency are executed by contract with a university or other educational organization. Some states do this extensively; others use this method for institutes in such areas as management. Recent changes and improvements in the continuing education activities of state library agencies reflected the increased emphasis and direction given a planned and coordinated programme. The establishment of a new position of continuing education coordinator was listed by five states; assignment of this responsibility to an established position was listed by many states.

Several states were engaged in "train the trainer" programmes with the shift to local library systems of responsibility for staff development and training in their own institutions, particularly for non-professional staff. State programmes will provide for more advanced and intensive training and attempt to ensure continuity in programme offerings. At least two states -North Carolina and Maryland -provide reimbursement to public library staffs for attending out-of-state institutes.

The responsibility of the continuing education coordinator for developing and disseminating information on continuing education offerings in-state and nationally; for maintaining a master calendar; for providing continuing liaison with library schools, library associations and other educational agencies; and for assuring a programme of needs identification and developing plans to meet needs were mentioned.

These activities reflect to a marked degree the influence of the CLENE report and subsequent programmes and activities of CLENE. It should be noted that state library agency personnel active in CLENE are frequently those most active in continuing education development in their respective states. Several states commented that NCLIS and CLENE had provided the impetus for renewed continuing education activity at the state level; one saw CLENE as the key to noteworthy, effective state library agency work in continuing education. The continuing education programmes of CLENE itself provide state library agency personnel the opportunity to gain knowledge, exchange information, and encourage the further coordinated development of continuing education activities of state library agencies. Changes and trends seen as important and needed for further development of continuing education include the development of more non- traditional methods for the delivery of continuing education programmes, as well as education techniques more suitable to adult learners.

States ex- pressed the need for improved needs assessment and evaluation skills and techniques. At least one-half the states were interested in a recognition system for continuing education. This seemed to be the national trend of greatest interest. Some states are currently using the *continuing education unit* (CEU) in institutions of higher education for library programmes. CEUs are directly related to certification in several states. South Dakota State Library provides voluntary certification for public libraries based on CEUs. Michigan and North Carolina have proposals for recertification of public librarians through approved programmes in continuing education and the CEU.

The "college without walls" programme in New Hampshire and Vermont has prompted library staff to indicate that continuing education programmes should provide some academic credit.

A nationally recognized CEU programme for librarians was specifically cited by several respondents. The study recently completed by CLENE, Model Continuing Education Recognition System in Library and Information Science, was first discussed in January at a CLENE meeting and is to be further examined and discussed at a national convention sponsored by NCLIS in June 1978. State library agencies will need to give the proposal and comments from the field serious study, since it has implications for an increased state library agency role.

This article has attempted to provide a summary of the development of continuing education responsibilities in state library agencies as viewed in the literature and reported from the agencies themselves. A few other points and issues need to be raised. State library agencies have a continuing responsibility for the improvement of the quality of library services in the state. In that respect they are in a unique position to assess the impact of continuing education programmes on library services in the state, and have a responsibility to do so. There is no documentation to determine whether this is being done, but the need to develop the evaluation and performance criteria for this purpose is evident. In the author's opinion this would lead to fewer programmes of longer duration, involving participants in more appropriate learning situations and plans for implementation in their libraries.

Another issue is the responsibility of the individual for his own continuing education and for the pursuit of programmes that satisfy individual needs and interests. State library agency programmes are geared primarily to the perceived needs of the institution and to the priorities of the state library plans and objectives.

To the extent that these coincide with individual needs and interests and that participation is voluntary and encouraged, the interests of both can be served. By publicizing continuing education programmes at state, regional or national levels, state library agencies are helping individuals to become aware of other opportunities.

Each state library agency needs to define its own role in continuing library education in relation to those of library schools, library associations and other providers of continuing education programmes. State library agencies should continue efforts to make possible situations in which innovators and practitioners can reach each other, invent ways to be mutually instructive and supportive, define steps by which to strengthen the drive towards improved continuing education programmes, and undertake cooperative endeavors that ultimately may matter greatly in the capacity of library personnel to deliver the library and information services needed in today's society.

EMERGING ROLE OF PUBLIC LIBRARIANS AS E-GOVERNMENT PROVIDERS

In an effort to become more efficient, governments are moving more information and services to the Internet. As part of this transition, some agencies have begun to use technology and EGovernment to justify the elimination of staff, many of whom provide face-to-face programme support. The result is fewer agency staff able to assist government programme applicants and beneficiaries. This increase in E-Government at the expense of agency staffing raises a number of issues regarding government service delivery and support. In particular, as fewer government agency staff are able to assist existing and potential beneficiaries, citizens seek a range of assistance elsewhere.

One such institution is the public library. As local agency offices close, more citizens use the public library to: use free access to computers and the Internet; receive computer and Internet skills training; search for government servicerelated information and forms; seek government programme assistance; and receive assistance in accessing government web sites, navigating programme requirements, and completing online forms. In short, the need for government agency programme and service support has not diminished, but rather, it is possible that some agencies shifted the burden of support to other entities. Although E-Government offers the potential to increase the efficiency and effectiveness of government services, E-Government as a means to reduce staff and service support may limit this potential. This is particularly the case if local agencies such as public libraries – where staff members are neither programme experts nor case workers – are expected to compensate for the reduction in government agency staff and services.

ROLE OF PUBLIC LIBRARIES IN EGOVERNMENT

The E-Government Act of 2002 states the goal of E-Government as enhancing "governmental functions and service," achieving "more efficient performance," and increasing "access to Government information, and...citizen participation in Government". Since the passage of the E-Government Act, E-Government has quickly become an increasingly popular element of service delivery at the federal, state and local levels. If E-Government services are planned and executed well, they allow government agencies to increase effectiveness and efficiency, and can increase citizen trust in government. The challenges that libraries encounter in providing E-Government vary geographically, as planning and execution of E-Government service varies between states, municipalities, and counties.

Even different agencies within county governments approach E-Government in a number of different ways, and with varying levels of success. In addition to increasing effectiveness and efficiency of services, governments have increased their use of E-Government in an effort to cut operating costs. The Florida *Department of Children and Families'* (DCF) eliminated almost ten thousand staff positions between 1999 and 2007 with the introduction of its ACCESS Florida E-Government programme, three thousand of which are attributable directly to the ACCESS Florida initiative. The DCF ACESS programme is a "modernized public assistance service delivery system... based on streamlined workflows, policy simplification, technology innovations and partnership with local community organizations".

This programme largely eliminates DCF offices, instead, funneling applicants and programme participants to a network of Community Partners for assistance with applications and administration of accounts. DCF now counts public libraries among its Community Partners – agencies and organizations willing to provide Internet access and service assistance applicants. A close examination of the DCF Community partners list reveals that, in most counties, libraries are the only partners charged with providing free Internet access to any citizen who enters requesting service.

Other partners are limited to specific constituencies. Since 1994, the Information Use Management and Policy Institute at Florida State University has conducted a national survey of public library internet connectivity. Between 1994 and 2007, Internet availability in libraries grew from approximately 21 per cent to over 99 per cent. Bertot, Jaeger, Langa and McClure write, "...by meeting user information needs through public access computing and Internet services, public libraries were able to serve a larger community need for access to e–government services and resources". The 2008 national survey found that approximately 95 per cent of public libraries provide asneeded assistance to patrons with understanding and using E-Government resources, while 69 per cent help with E-Government applications and services. Sixty three percent of respondents indicated that the public library was the only free public internet access point in the surrounding community.

Thus, public libraries provide substantial E-Government service and resource support. One can view Government to Citizen EGovernment as a three-part system comprised of the public, the government agency involved and the networks and points of access that allow citizens to participate in EGovernment with that agency. By seeking EGovernment information at the library and requesting assistance from librarians, citizens have added a fourth component to the system: the local librarian as a surrogate agency service provider. In this capacity, the librarian facilitates what ideally develops into discourse around the design of the E-Government implementation in question.

As Bertot, Jaeger and McClure write, "to develop citizen-oriented EGovernment services that achieve cost savings implies that governments...actively seek to discover what citizens want from E-Government" Dittrich, Ekelin, Elovaara, Eriksen and Hansson's 2003 article also provides a useful framework for understanding the implications of this "fourth party" service provider. The article outlines a four-part chain of interaction in E-Government development that includes developers (agencies), local designers (developers), service providers (libraries) and citizens. According to the framework proposed by the Dittrich *et al.*, it is in the best interest of all parties to collaboratively develop effective ways to collect and channel patron feedback for successful, iterative development of the E-Government system.

Citizens in need of government services do not bear sole responsibility for involving librarians in EGovernment service. Some agencies refer citizens to public libraries to access web-based forms or applications that are not available in their offices.

The DCF ACCESS web site encourages applicants to "apply for public assistance (food stamps, temporary cash assistance, and Medicaid) using the internet wherever it is available including home, a library, or a school". Because they are, in many cases, the only organizations offering free Internet access in their communities, the public library plays an instrumental role in leveling out differences in citizen access to personal computers and the Internet, moving the E-Government system away from exclusion of segments of the population, and towards "design for all". In this role, many libraries have begun to evolve into "one-stop shops" that now include assistance with government service programmes, access, and delivery. This is a substantive departure from a longstanding role of public libraries that serve as access points to government information and forms (*i.e.*, tax forms during tax season). For example, though librarians provided tax forms in the past, they did not serve as tax accountants who assisted patrons complete and file their taxes. Now, citizens come to the library seeking government programme and services assistance, not simply access to information. This shift seems to occur in direct relation to government agencies cutting back in their provision of programme support services due to the adoption of E-Government technologies.

PURPOSE AND OBJECTIVES

The purpose of this exploratory study was to identify the E-Government related needs of citizens who access government related information at the library, and to identify current library E-Government practices in order to provide practical guidance to public libraries in meeting the needs of local community members they serve. Specifically, the study addresses the following questions:

- What E-Government services and resources do public libraries typically provide?
- What types of E-Government assistance and/or resources do members of libraries' community members request?

- Why do citizens seek E-Government services and resources at the public library?
- What barriers and issues do librarians face in providing E-Government services and resources?

Answers to these questions can help ascertain EGovernment needs from a user perspective, but also foster understanding the impacts of E-Government on community-based support organizations such as public libraries.

The study was exploratory and used an iterative multi-method approach. Limited to public libraries in the state of Florida, the study used:

- Interviews with public librarians. The interviews explored and identified the E-Government services public librarians provided, and the issues encountered by public librarians in providing EGovernment services and resources.
- E-Government workshops. The study team conducted five E-Government workshops in key geographic regions to explore EGovernment service provision by libraries in the regions.
- Survey of workshop attendees. The survey asked librarians to identify the most frequently provided E-Government services, and to identify issues encountered by patrons seeking E-Government assistance in local libraries.
- Librarian-maintained reference log files. The log files captured specific E-Government service and resource transactions provided to users in libraries.
- User survey. The survey explored the reasons why users came to the public library for EGovernment services and resources, library services requested and used to engage in EGovernment services, and issues encountered while engaging in E-Government services. The survey was available in English, Spanish, and French Creole. The survey was primarily in print format, though a web-based Survey Monkey version of the survey was available in English.

The interviews and workshops informed the development of the log file and user surveys. User surveys and log files were pre-tested to ensure their usability and ability to capture valid and reliable data.

Sampling Strategy and Data Quality

The study team employed a combination of purposeful and cluster sampling for the study's data collection efforts. The study team identified and selected public librarians who provided E-Government services in their libraries, both face-to-face and through developed web sites that contained a range of information regarding federal, state, and local government services. The study team also conducted workshops in four key geographic regions throughout the state of Florida to explore library E-Government involvement and services.

Given the diversity of the state of Florida and its various communities, the regional workshops provided the study team with variations in E-Government services due to user needs in each of the regions.

The individual interviews provided more in-depth information regarding librarian efforts to develop and offer E-Government services and resources in their libraries. For the librarian logs and user surveys, the study team developed a cluster sampling approach to select libraries for participation based on:

- Library diversity — *e.g.*, urban, rural, and suburban; and geographic spread throughout the state of Florida;
- Community diversity — *e.g.*, poverty, immigrant, language, and a range of other library community factors; and
- Willingness to participate.

In all, 74 libraries agreed to participate in the study by maintaining library logs and distributing user surveys. The study team provided surveys in multiple languages based on librarian indications of the communities that the libraries served. The user surveys and log files were maintained and available for two weeks in March 2008. Overall, the study team interviewed nine public librarians individually, conducted workshops with 145 public librarians throughout the state, and received 415 librarian logs, and 210 usable user surveys. A total of 46 usable librarian surveys were collected during workshops. The data are limited due to the exploratory nature of the study and the purposeful and cluster sampling approaches. The five methodologies, however, provided detailed and overlapping findings regarding issues associated with providing E-Government services and resources in public libraries. By using an iterative and multi-method approach, the study team identified and triangulated perspectives on E Government in public libraries from both the public library and user populations.

Bibliography

Purushotham Tiwari: *Library Evaluation*, APH, 2009

K.G. Rastogi: *Reference Services in Library Science*, Alfa Publications, Delhi, 2006.

K.G. Rastogi: *The Functions of Cataloguing in Library Science*, Alfa Publications, Delhi, 2006.

Khalid K. Faruqi and Mehtab Alam: *Library Information Systems and E-Journal Archiving*, Authorspress, Delhi, 2005.

M.A. Khan: *The Principles and Practice of Library Science*, Sarup & Sons, Delhi, 1996.

Manisha Dawra: *Library Science and Theories of Management*, Rajat Publication, Delhi, 2004.

P. Balasubramaniyan: *Research Methodology in Library Science*, Deep and Deep Publication, Delhi, 2011.

P. Vidya Sagar: *Networking in Library Science*, Sonali Publication, Delhi, 2005.

R. K. Krishnan: *The Five Laws of Library Science*, Centrum Press, Delhi, 2013.

Raghunath Pandey and M.N. Velayudhan Pillai: *World Famous Public Libraries*, Jnanada Prakashan, Delhi, 2011.

Ram Shobhit Singh: *Encyclopaedia of Library Information Systems and E-Journal Archiving, Vols. I-II*, Anmol Publication, Delhi, 2008.

A.K. Gupta: *Digital Library and Education*, Pearl Books, Delhi, 2012.

Ajay K. Srivastav: *Digital Library Environment and Networking*, Sree Publications, Delhi, 2006.

Ajit Singh: *Information Technology and Library Sciences*, Ancient Publications, Delhi, 2011.

Arunima Baruah: *Library Science: Prospects in 21 Century*, Kilaso Books, 2004.

Bloom, B. S.: *Key Concepts in the Architecture of the Digital Library,* Concept Publishing Company, New Delhi, 2003.

Brook, A.: *Technology and the Changing Role of Teacher-Librarians,* Cambridge University Press, New York, 2004.

Browne, K.: *The Electronic Library: Slouching Toward the Future or Creating a New Information Environment,* Princeton University Press, Princeton, 2003.

C Praveen Singh: *Library Automation in Modern Age*, Alfa Publications, Delhi, 2008.

C. Janakiraman: *Research in Library Science*, Pacific Books International, Delhi, 2011.

G.K. Sampath Kumar: *Digital Library Automation Planning Designing and Development*, Akhand Publications, Delhi, 2012.

Gibbs, G.: *Library Management and Information Technology*, Cambridge University Press, Cambridge, 2006.

H.R. Chopra, U.C. Sharma and M.K. Srivastava: *Library Science and its Facets (2 Vols-Set)*, Ess Ess Publications, Delhi, 1998.

Harris, J. L.: *Training for Change: New Skills for the Electronic Library,* New Technology, New Librarians?, London and New York: Longman, 2005.

Hasnain Qureshi: *Principles and Practices of Library Science*, Anmol Publications, Delhi, 2006.

Jagadeesha S. and Mahesh V. Mudhol: *Library Automation Using Foxpro 2.0*, Ess Ess Publications, Delhi, 1998.

John, V.: *Putting Content onto the Internet: The Library's Role as Creator of Electronic Information,* Mizo History Association, Aisawl, 1995.

Manohar Nanda: *Library Automation*, Anmol Publications, Delhi, 2006.

Mayston, E. L.: *Cybrarians: The Information Professionals of the 21st- Century,* Oxford University Press, New Delhi, 2004.

Meadows, D. H.: *The Impact of Online Information on Traditional Library Services and the Distance User,* Cambridge Perseus Publishing, London, 2006.

Menzies, E. P.: *The Electronic Document and its Impact on the Information Chain Professions*, Kogan Page, London, 2000.

Mukherjee, N.: *Digital Libraries: Principles and Practice in a Global Environment,* Concept Publication, New Delhi, 2005.

N.R. Satyanarayana: *A Manual of Library Automation and Networking*, New Royal Book Co., Lucknow, 2003.

P. Balasubramanian: *Library Automation and Networking*, Deep and Deep Publications, Delhi, 2011.

P. Vidya Sagar: *Networking in Library Science*, Sonali Publications, Delhi, 2005.

P.P. Rawat and T. Kumar: *Encyclopedic Dictionary of Library Science and Information Technology (2 Vols-Set)*, Crest Publishing House, Delhi, 2002.

Index